THE NEW AVENGERS

CIVIL WAR

Writer: **Brian Michael Bendis**

Issue #21
Artist: **Howard Chaykin**
Colorist: **Dave Stewart**

Issue #22
Artist: **Leinil Yu**
Colorist: **Dave McCaig**

Issue #23
Penciler: **Olivier Coipel**
Inker: **Mark Morales**
Colorist: **Jose Villarrubia**

Issue #24
Artist: **Pasqual Ferry**
Artist, Page 6: **Paul Smith**
Colorist: **Dean White**
Cover: **Adi Granov**

Issue #25
Penciler: **Jim Cheung**
Inker: **Livesay**
Colorist: **Justin Ponsor**

Letters: **RS & Comicraft's Albert Deschesne**
Assistant Editors: **Molly Lazer & Aubrey Sitterson**
Editor: **Tom Brevoort**

Collection Editor: **Jennifer Grünwald**
Assistant Editor: **Michael Short**
Associate Editor: **Mark D. Beazley**
Senior Editor, Special Projects: **Jeff Youngquist**
Senior Vice President of Sales: **David Gabriel**
Production: **Jerron Quality Color**
Vice President of Creative: **Tom Marvelli**

Editor in Chief: **Joe Quesada**
Publisher: **Dan Buckley**

NEW AVENGERS VOL. 5: CIVIL WAR. Contains material originally published in magazine form as NEW AVENGERS #21-25. First printing 2007. Hardcover ISBN# 0-7851-2242-7. Softcover ISBN# 0-7851-2446-2. Published by MARVEL PUBLISHING, INC., a subsidiary of MARVEL ENTERTAINMENT, INC. OFFICE OF PUBLICATION: 417 5th Avenue, New York, NY 10016. Hardcover: $19.99 per copy in the U.S. and $32.00 in Canada (GST #R127032852). Softcover: $14.99 per copy in the U.S. and $24.00 in Canada (GST #R127032852). Canadian Agreement #40668537. **Printed in the U.S.A.** ALAN FINE, President & CEO Of Marvel Toys and Marvel Publishing, Inc.; DAVID BOGART, VP Of Publishing Operations; DAN CARR, Executive Director of Publishing Technology; JUSTIN F. GABRIE, Managing Editor; STAN LEE, Chairman Emeritus. For information regarding advertising in Marvel Comics or on Marvel.com, please contact Joe Maimone, Advertising Director, at jmaimone@marvel.com or 212-576-8534.

10 9 8 7 6 5 4 3 2 1

PREVIOUSLY:

Hoping to boost their ratings, four New Warriors, young super heroes and reality television stars, attempted to apprehend a quartet of villains holed up in Stamford, Connecticut. When confronted, the explosive Nitro employed his self-detonation ability, blowing the New Warriors and a large chunk of Stamford into oblivion. The entire incident was caught on tape. Casualties number in the hundreds.

As a reaction to this tragedy, public outcry calls for reform in the way super heroes conduct their affairs. On Capitol Hill, a Superhuman Registration Act is debated which would require all those possessing paranormal abilities to register with the government, divulging their true identities to the authorities and submitting to training and sanctioning in the manner of federal agents.

Some heroes, such as Iron Man, see this as a natural evolution of the role of super heroes in society, and a reasonable request. Others, embodied by Captain America, take umbrage at this assault on their civil liberties.

When Captain America is called upon to hunt down his fellow heroes who are in defiance of the Registration Act, he chooses to go AWOL, becoming a public enemy in the process.

NEW AVENGERS

A MARVEL COMICS EVENT

CIVIL WAR

#21

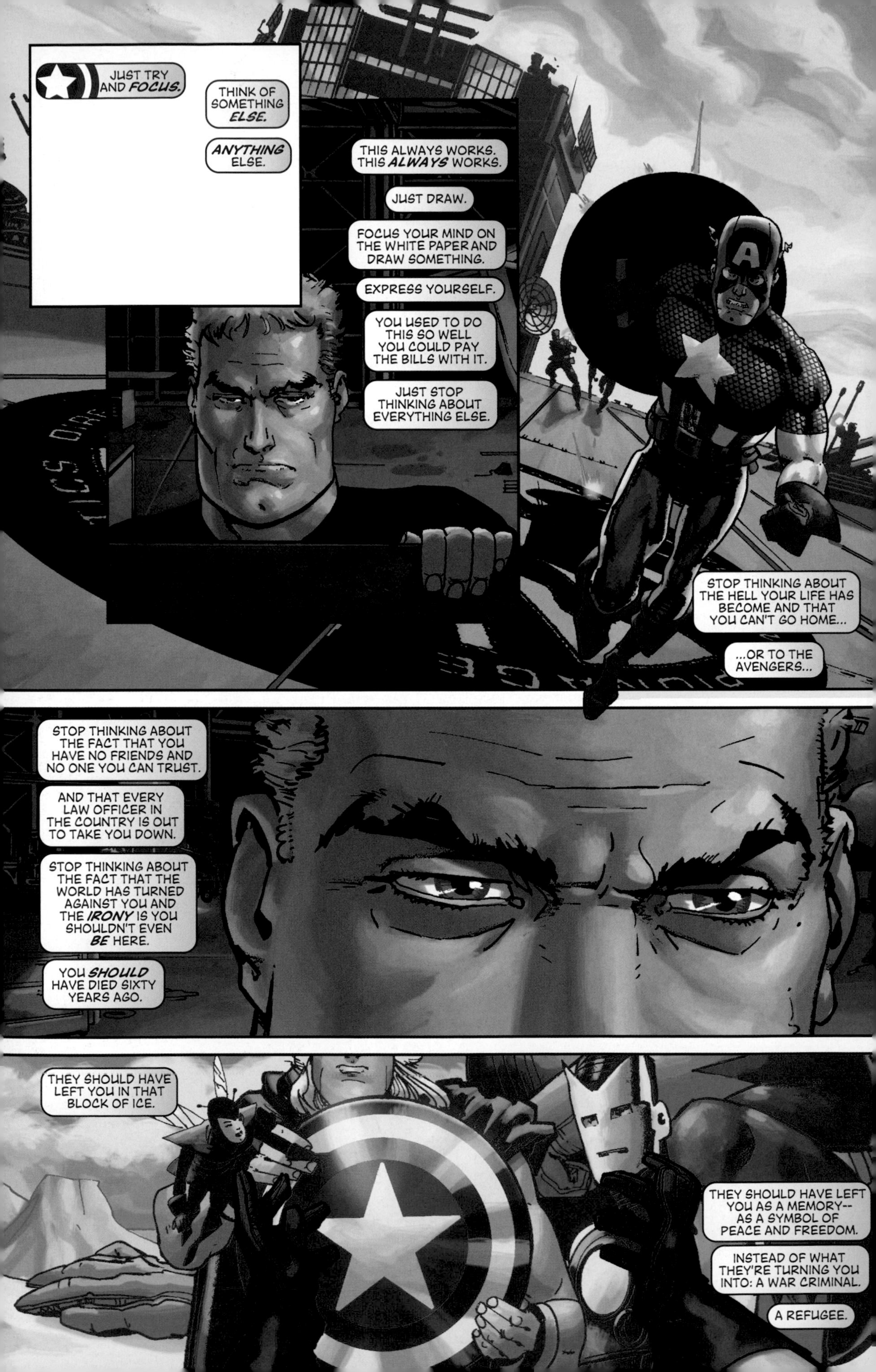
JUST TRY AND *FOCUS.*
THINK OF SOMETHING *ELSE.*
ANYTHING ELSE.
THIS ALWAYS WORKS. THIS *ALWAYS* WORKS.
JUST DRAW.
FOCUS YOUR MIND ON THE WHITE PAPER AND DRAW SOMETHING.
EXPRESS YOURSELF.
YOU USED TO DO THIS SO WELL YOU COULD PAY THE BILLS WITH IT.
JUST STOP THINKING ABOUT EVERYTHING ELSE.
STOP THINKING ABOUT THE HELL YOUR LIFE HAS BECOME AND THAT YOU CAN'T GO HOME...
...OR TO THE AVENGERS...
STOP THINKING ABOUT THE FACT THAT YOU HAVE NO FRIENDS AND NO ONE YOU CAN TRUST.
AND THAT EVERY LAW OFFICER IN THE COUNTRY IS OUT TO TAKE YOU DOWN.
STOP THINKING ABOUT THE FACT THAT THE WORLD HAS TURNED AGAINST YOU AND THE *IRONY* IS YOU SHOULDN'T EVEN *BE* HERE.
YOU *SHOULD* HAVE DIED SIXTY YEARS AGO.
THEY SHOULD HAVE LEFT YOU IN THAT BLOCK OF ICE.
THEY SHOULD HAVE LEFT YOU AS A MEMORY-- AS A SYMBOL OF PEACE AND FREEDOM.
INSTEAD OF WHAT THEY'RE TURNING YOU INTO: A WAR CRIMINAL.
A REFUGEE.

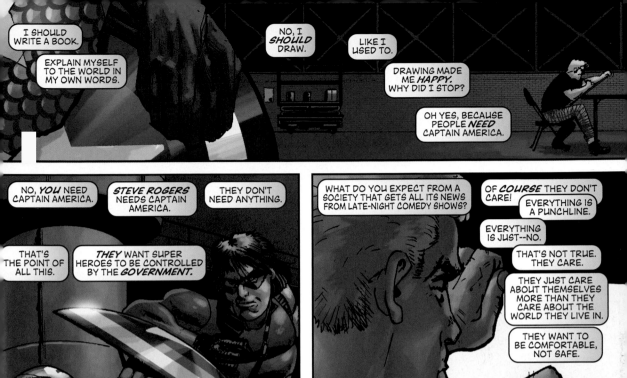

I SHOULD WRITE A BOOK.

EXPLAIN MYSELF TO THE WORLD IN MY OWN WORDS.

NO, I *SHOULD* DRAW.

LIKE I USED TO.

DRAWING MADE ME *HAPPY.* WHY DID I STOP?

OH YES, BECAUSE PEOPLE *NEED* CAPTAIN AMERICA.

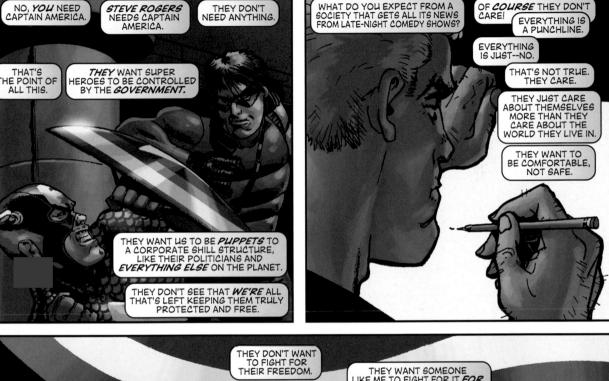

NO, *YOU* NEED CAPTAIN AMERICA.

STEVE ROGERS NEEDS CAPTAIN AMERICA.

THEY DON'T NEED ANYTHING.

THAT'S THE POINT OF ALL THIS.

THEY WANT SUPER HEROES TO BE CONTROLLED BY THE *GOVERNMENT.*

THEY WANT US TO BE *PUPPETS* TO A CORPORATE SHILL STRUCTURE, LIKE THEIR POLITICIANS AND *EVERYTHING ELSE* ON THE PLANET.

THEY DON'T SEE THAT *WE'RE* ALL THAT'S LEFT KEEPING THEM TRULY PROTECTED AND FREE.

WHAT DO YOU EXPECT FROM A SOCIETY THAT GETS ALL ITS NEWS FROM LATE-NIGHT COMEDY SHOWS?

OF *COURSE* THEY DON'T CARE!

EVERYTHING IS A PUNCHLINE.

EVERYTHING IS JUST--NO.

THAT'S NOT TRUE. THEY CARE.

THEY JUST CARE ABOUT THEMSELVES MORE THAN THEY CARE ABOUT THE WORLD THEY LIVE IN.

THEY WANT TO BE COMFORTABLE, NOT SAFE.

THEY DON'T WANT TO FIGHT FOR THEIR FREEDOM.

THEY WANT SOMEONE LIKE ME TO FIGHT FOR IT *FOR THEM,* AND NOW THEY DON'T KNOW WHAT THEY--*STOP IT!*

YOU NEED SLEEP. YOU NEED TO FOCUS.

IF YOU *COULD* FOCUS, YOU WOULD HAVE HEARD THEM COMING BEFORE IT WAS TOO LATE TO DO ANYTHING ABOUT IT...

BUT DON'T KICK YOURSELF...

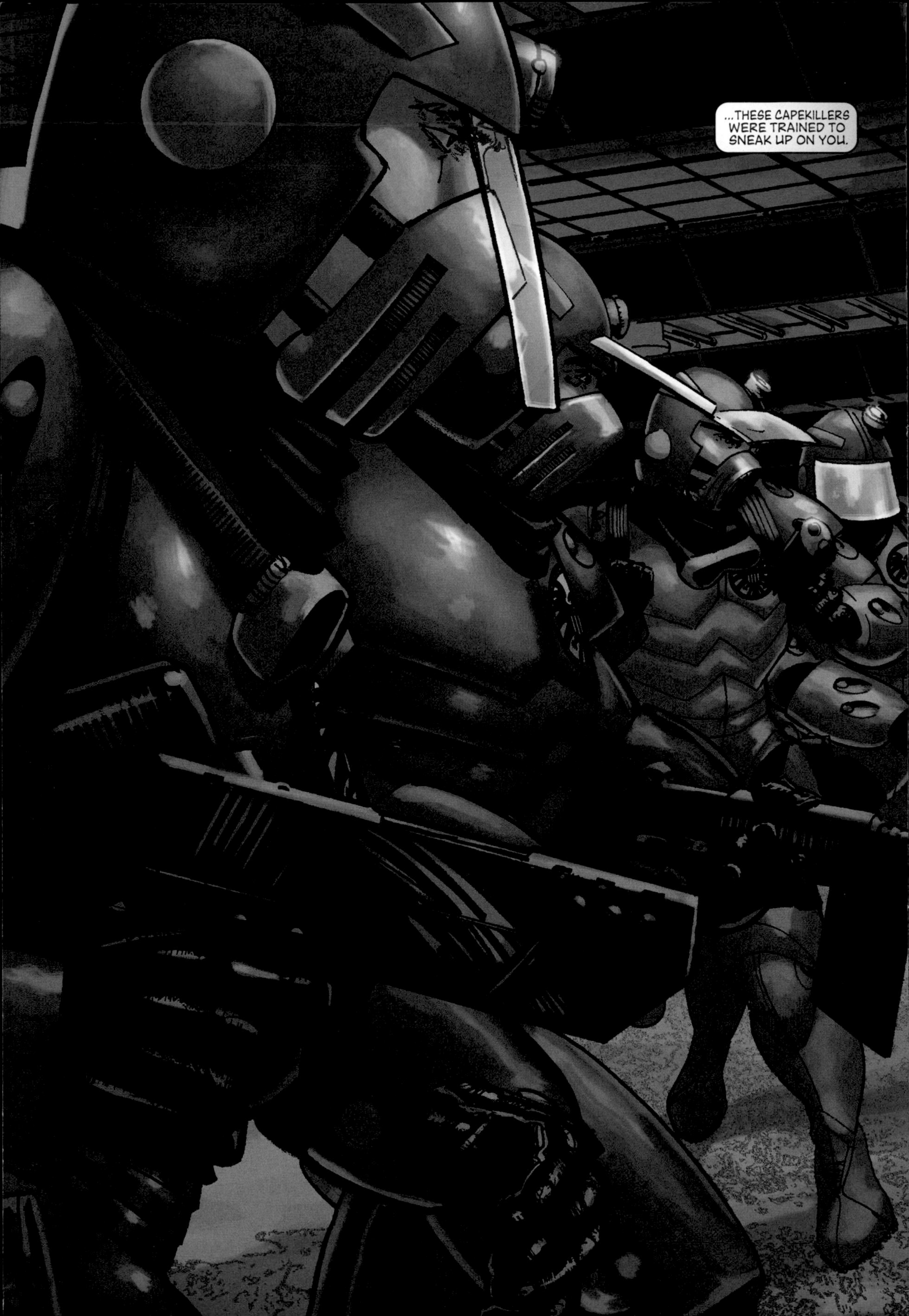
...THESE CAPEKILLERS WERE TRAINED TO SNEAK UP ON YOU.

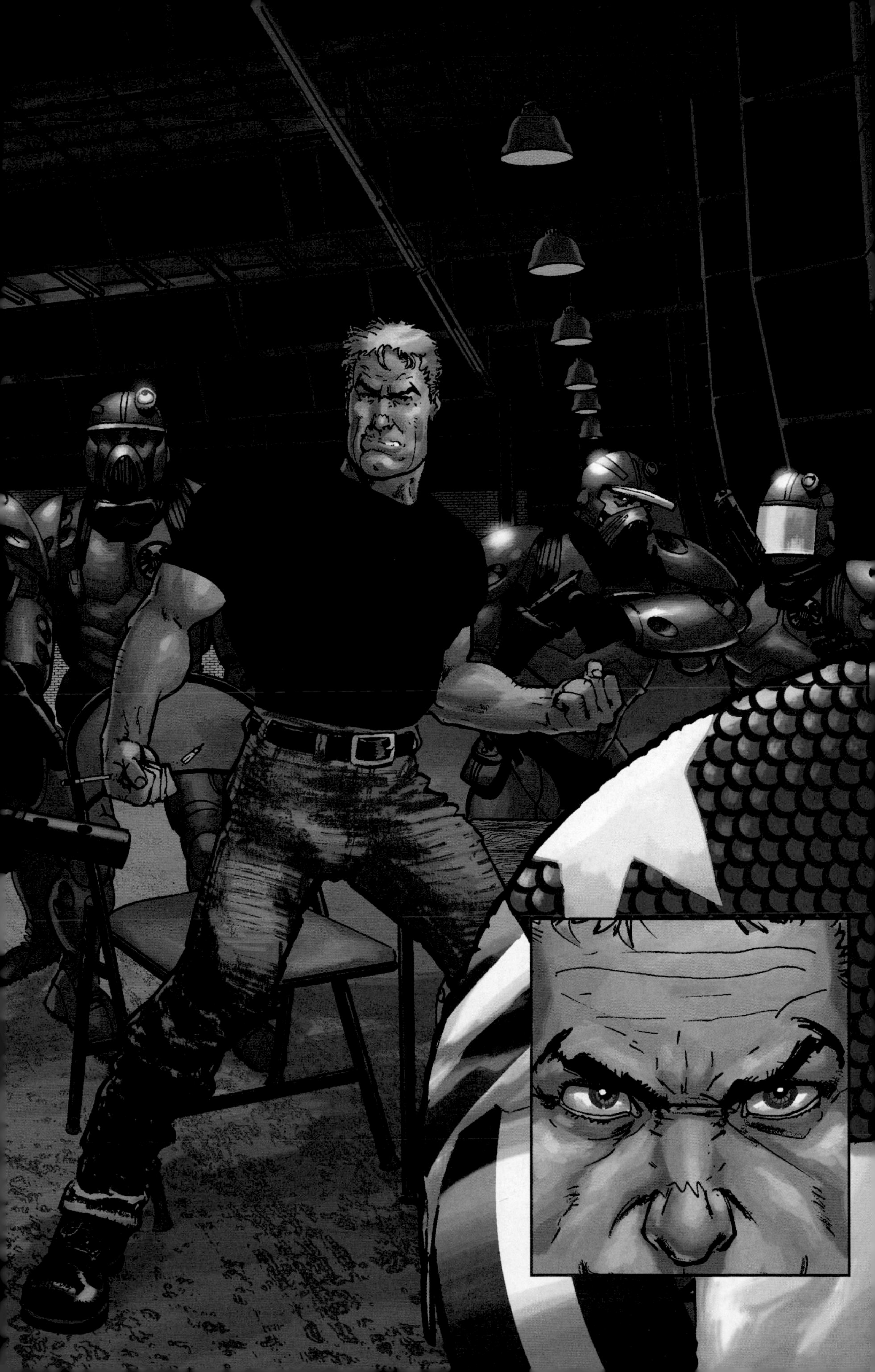

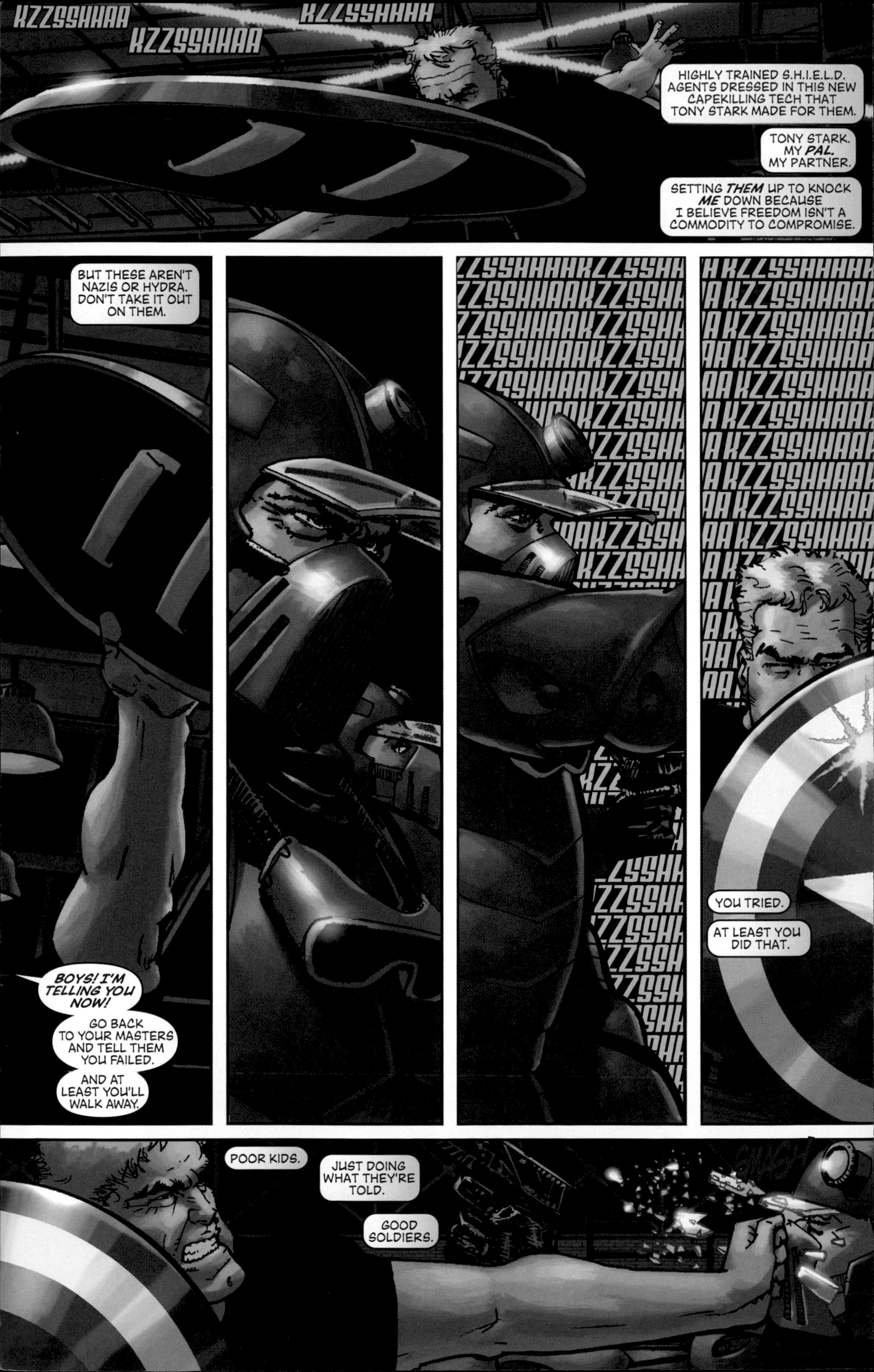
KZZSSHHAA
KZZSSHHHH
KZZSSHHAA
HIGHLY TRAINED S.H.I.E.L.D. AGENTS DRESSED IN THIS NEW CAPEKILLING TECH THAT TONY STARK MADE FOR THEM.
TONY STARK. MY PAL. MY PARTNER.
SETTING THEM UP TO KNOCK ME DOWN BECAUSE I BELIEVE FREEDOM ISN'T A COMMODITY TO COMPROMISE.
BUT THESE AREN'T NAZIS OR HYDRA. DON'T TAKE IT OUT ON THEM.
BOYS! I'M TELLING YOU NOW!
GO BACK TO YOUR MASTERS AND TELL THEM YOU FAILED.
AND AT LEAST YOU'LL WALK AWAY.
YOU TRIED.
AT LEAST YOU DID THAT.
POOR KIDS.
JUST DOING WHAT THEY'RE TOLD.
GOOD SOLDIERS.

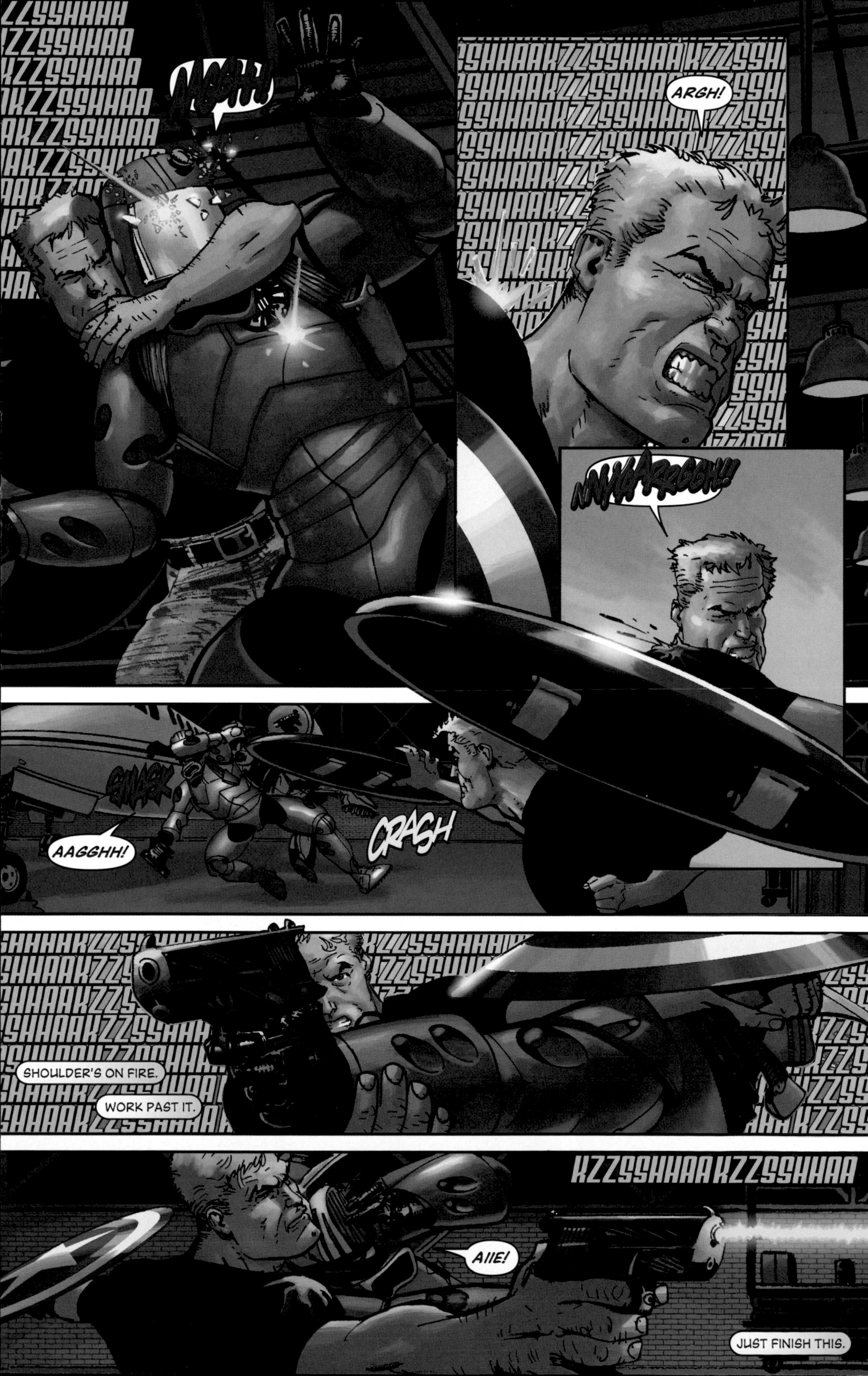
AAGGH!
ARGH!
NNNGAARRGGH!!
SMASK
AAGGHH!
CRASH
SHOULDER'S ON FIRE.
WORK PAST IT.
KZZSSHHAA KZZSSHHAA
AIIE!
JUST FINISH THIS.

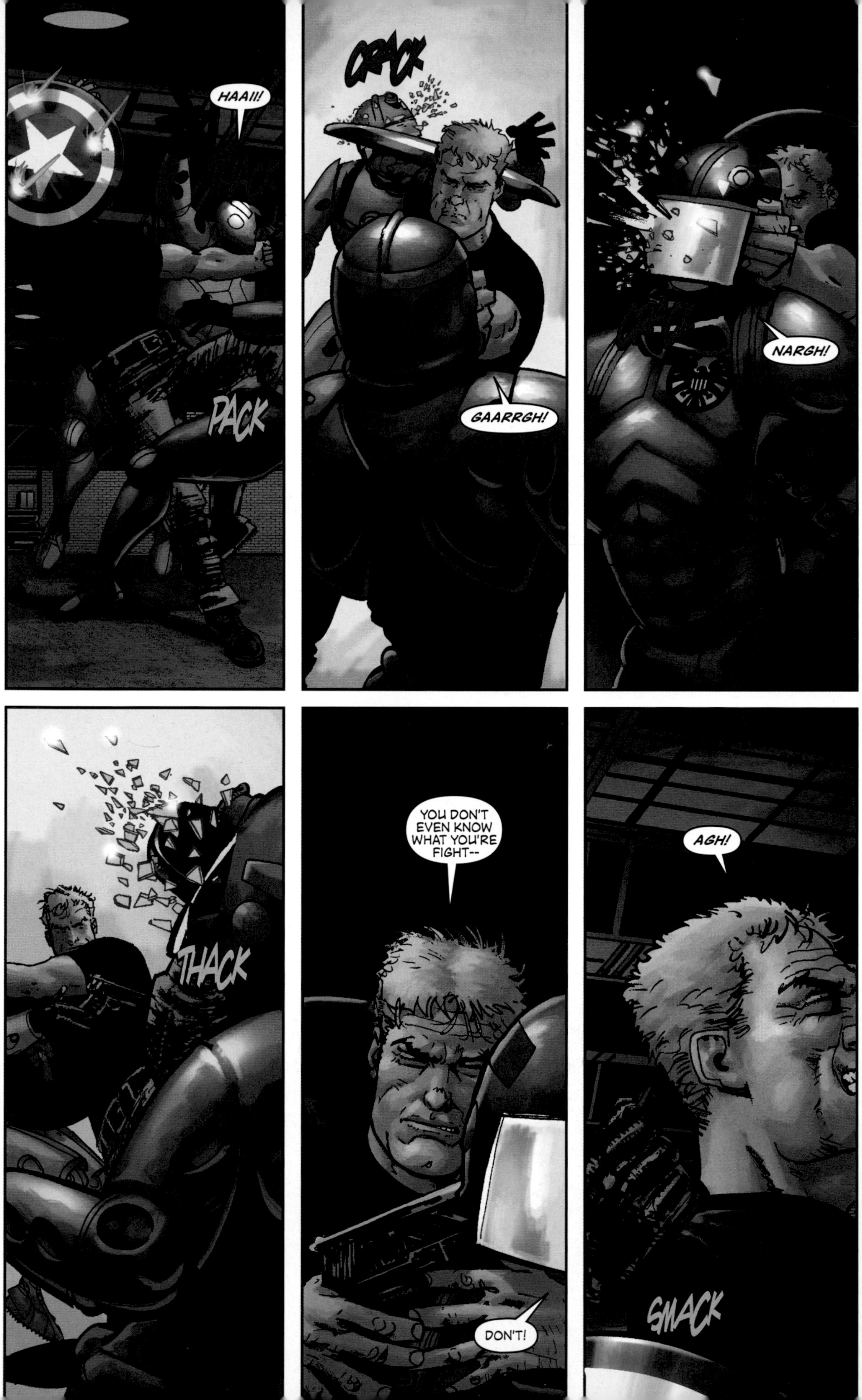
HAAII!
PACK
CRACK
GAARRGH!
NARGH!
THACK
YOU DON'T EVEN KNOW WHAT YOU'RE FIGHT--
DON'T!
AGH!
SMACK

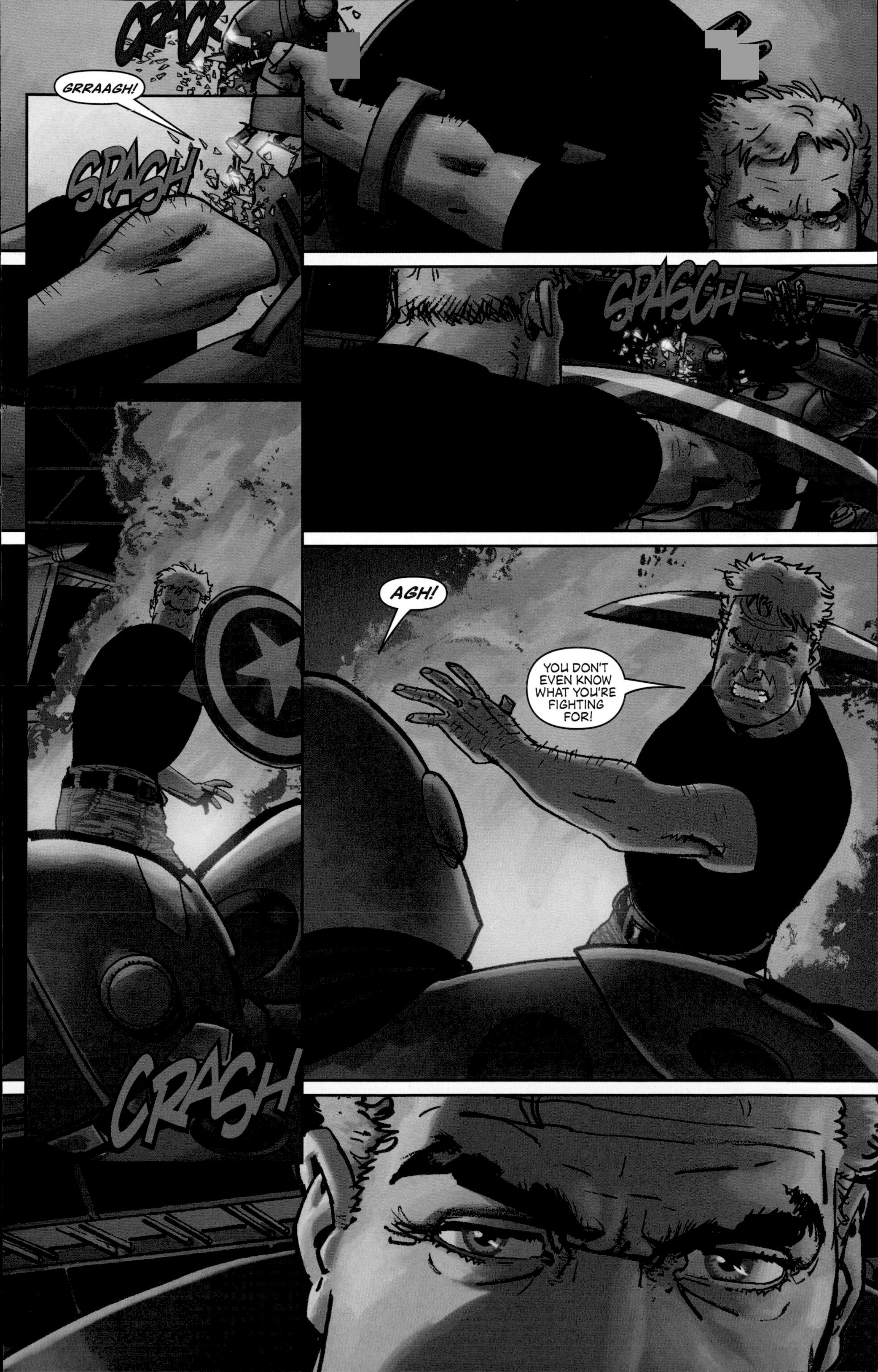
CRACK
GRRAAGH!
SPASH
SPASCH
CRASH
AGH!
YOU DON'T EVEN KNOW WHAT YOU'RE FIGHTING FOR!

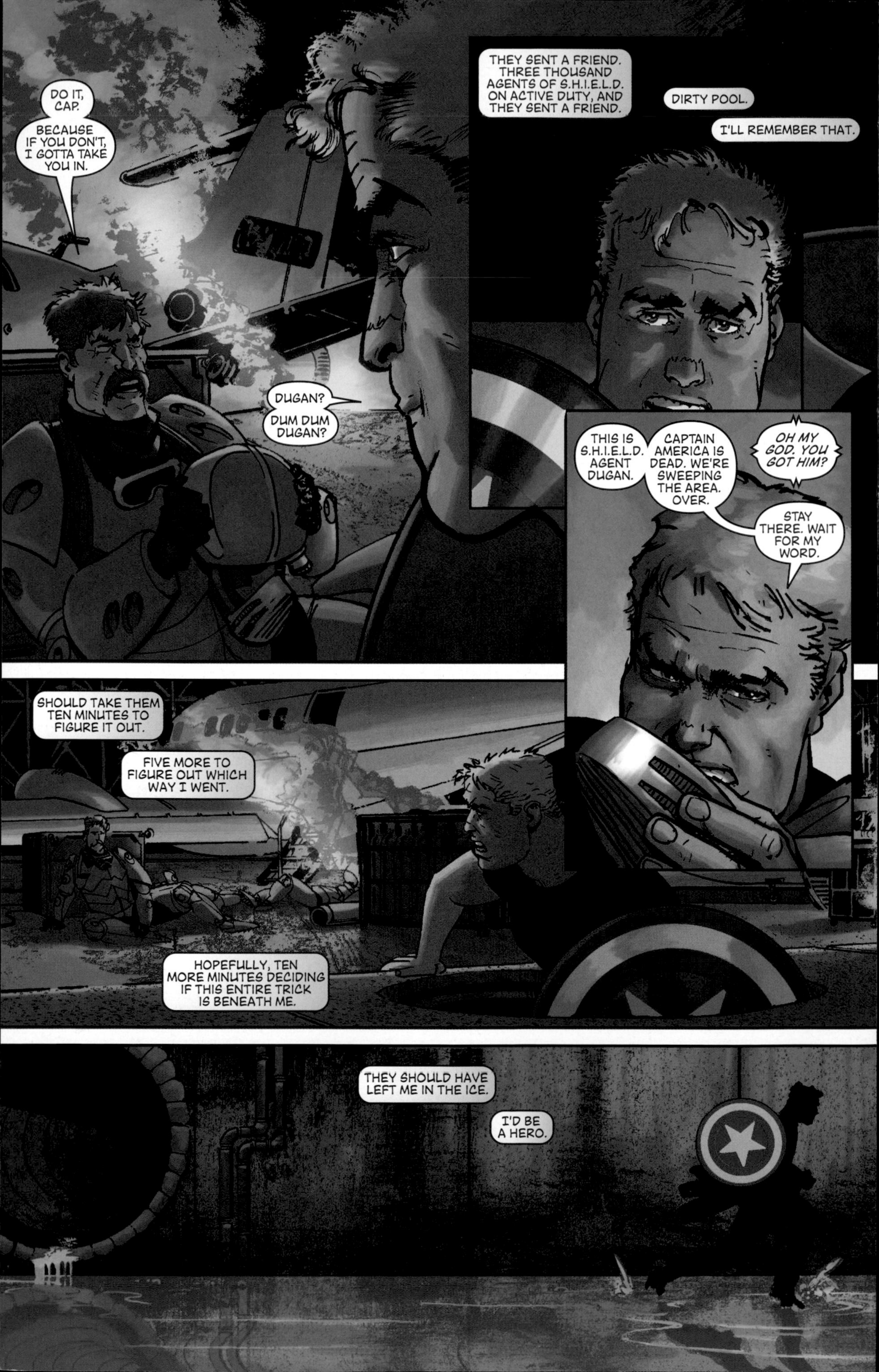
DO IT, CAP.
BECAUSE IF YOU DON'T, I GOTTA TAKE YOU IN.
DUGAN?
DUM DUM DUGAN?
THEY SENT A FRIEND. THREE THOUSAND AGENTS OF S.H.I.E.L.D. ON ACTIVE DUTY, AND THEY SENT A FRIEND.
DIRTY POOL.
I'LL REMEMBER THAT.
THIS IS S.H.I.E.L.D. AGENT DUGAN.
CAPTAIN AMERICA IS DEAD. WE'RE SWEEPING THE AREA. OVER.
OH MY GOD. YOU GOT HIM?
STAY THERE. WAIT FOR MY WORD.
SHOULD TAKE THEM TEN MINUTES TO FIGURE IT OUT.
FIVE MORE TO FIGURE OUT WHICH WAY I WENT.
HOPEFULLY, TEN MORE MINUTES DECIDING IF THIS ENTIRE TRICK IS BENEATH ME.
THEY SHOULD HAVE LEFT ME IN THE ICE.
I'D BE A HERO.

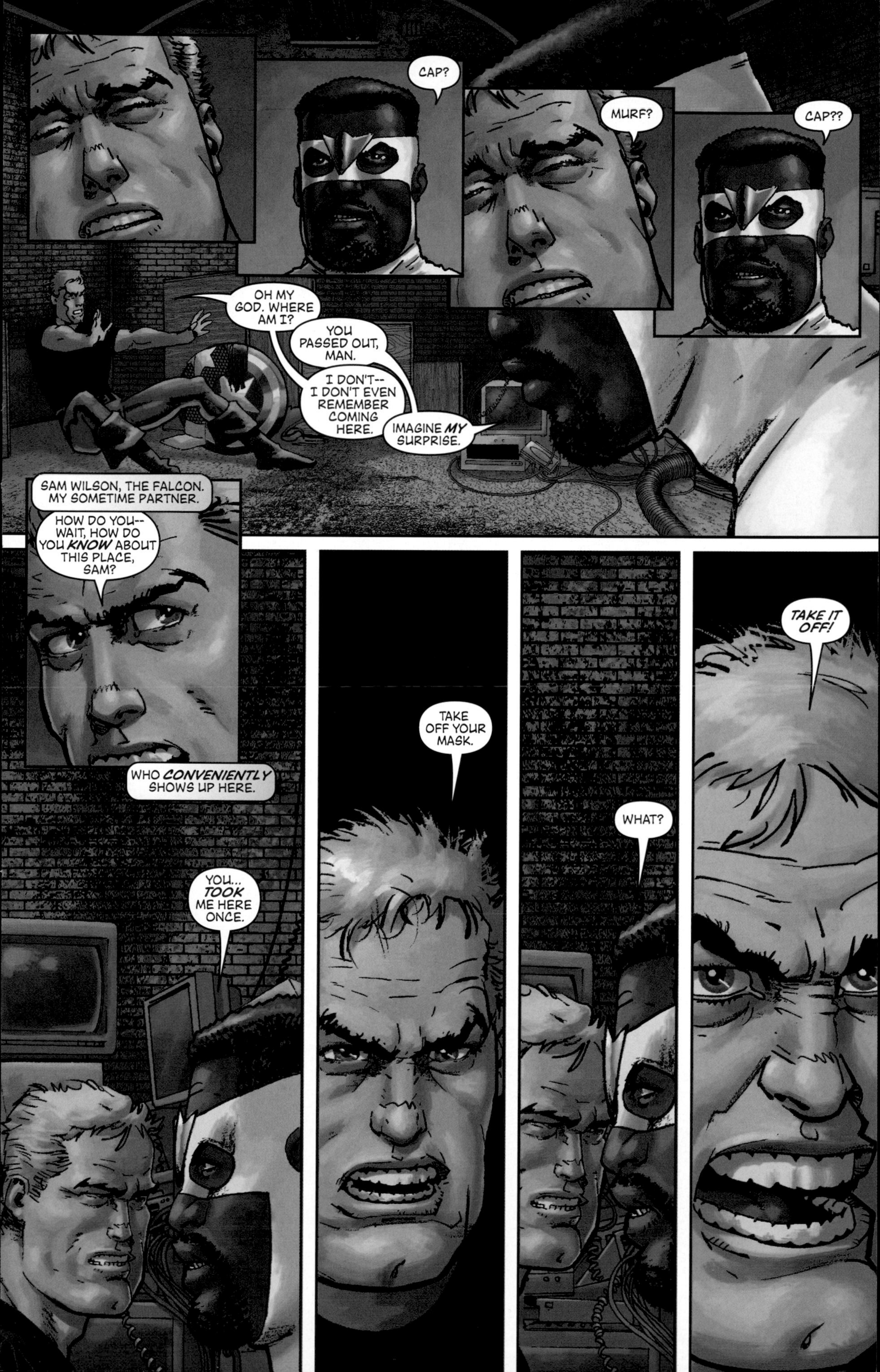
CAP?
MURF?
CAP??
OH MY GOD. WHERE AM I?
YOU PASSED OUT, MAN.
I DON'T-- I DON'T EVEN REMEMBER COMING HERE.
IMAGINE MY SURPRISE.
SAM WILSON, THE FALCON. MY SOMETIME PARTNER.
HOW DO YOU-- WAIT, HOW DO YOU KNOW ABOUT THIS PLACE, SAM?
WHO CONVENIENTLY SHOWS UP HERE.
YOU... TOOK ME HERE ONCE.
TAKE OFF YOUR MASK.
WHAT?
TAKE IT OFF!

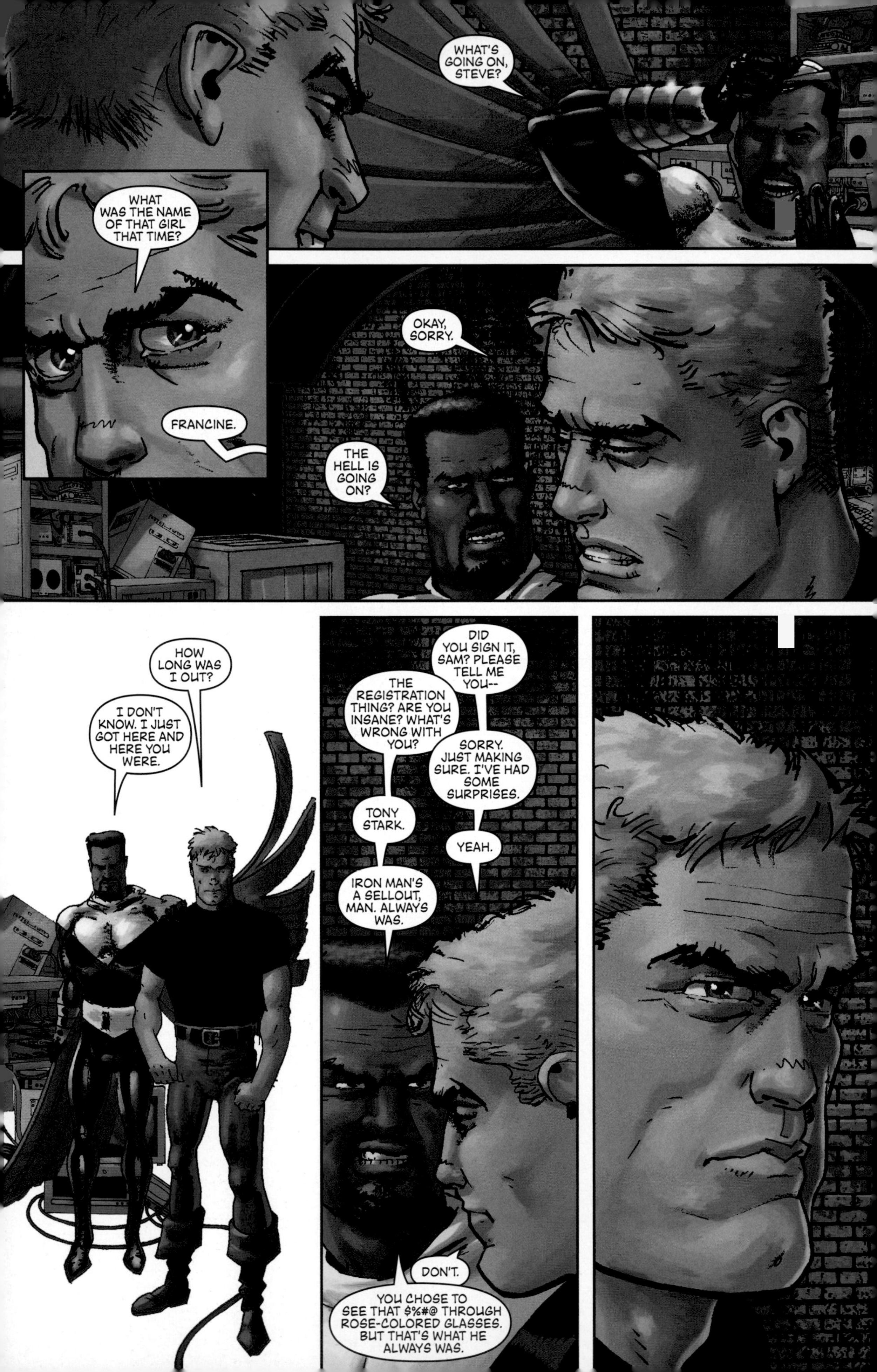
WHAT'S GOING ON, STEVE?
WHAT WAS THE NAME OF THAT GIRL THAT TIME?
FRANCINE.
OKAY, SORRY.
THE HELL IS GOING ON?
HOW LONG WAS I OUT?
I DON'T KNOW. I JUST GOT HERE AND HERE YOU WERE.
DID YOU SIGN IT, SAM? PLEASE TELL ME YOU--
THE REGISTRATION THING? ARE YOU INSANE? WHAT'S WRONG WITH YOU?
SORRY. JUST MAKING SURE. I'VE HAD SOME SURPRISES.
TONY STARK.
YEAH.
IRON MAN'S A SELLOUT, MAN. ALWAYS WAS.
DON'T.
YOU CHOSE TO SEE THAT $%#@ THROUGH ROSE-COLORED GLASSES. BUT THAT'S WHAT HE ALWAYS WAS.

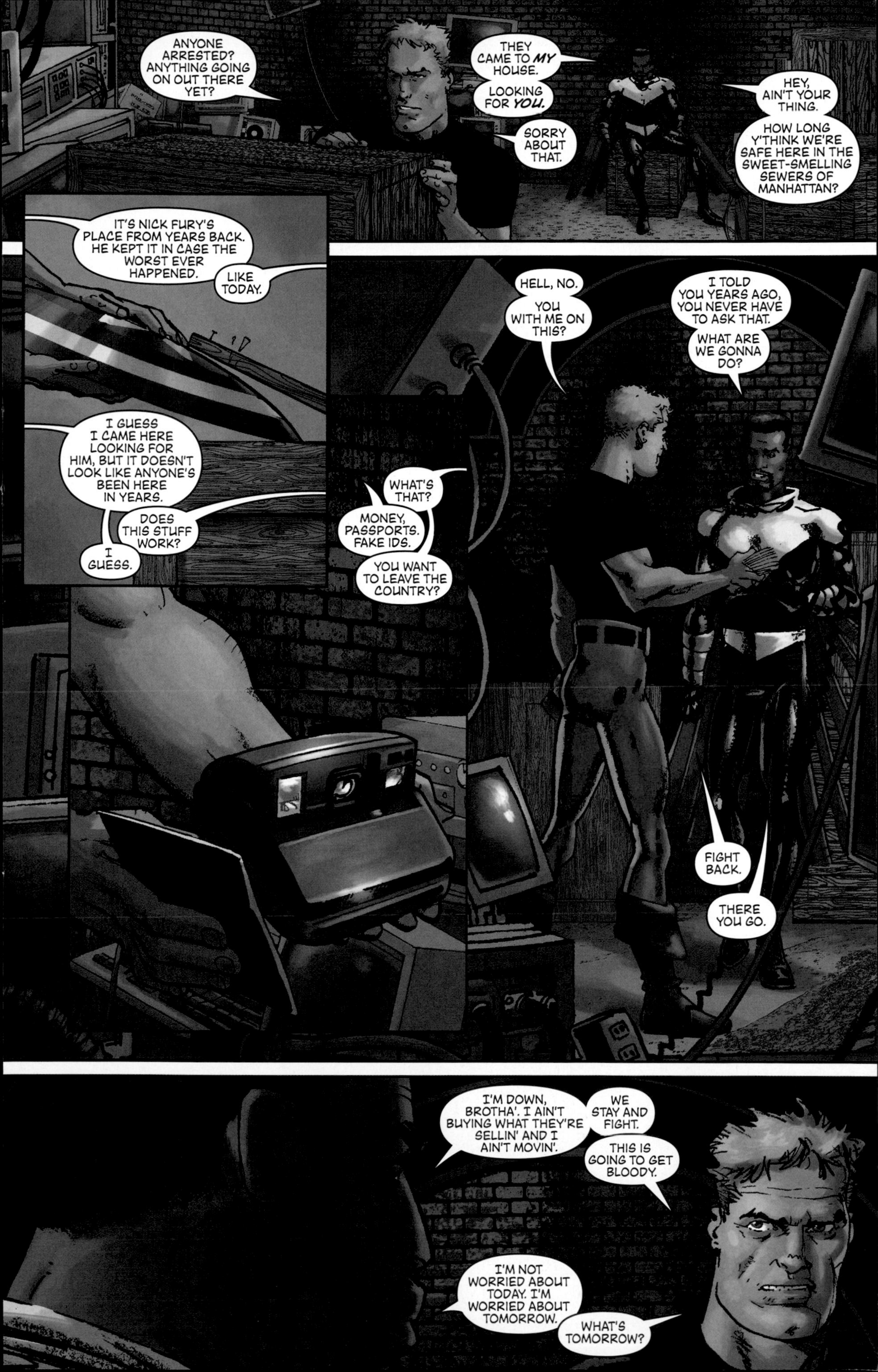
ANYONE ARRESTED? ANYTHING GOING ON OUT THERE YET?
THEY CAME TO *MY* HOUSE.
LOOKING FOR *YOU.*
SORRY ABOUT THAT.
HEY, AIN'T YOUR THING.
HOW LONG Y'THINK WE'RE SAFE HERE IN THE SWEET-SMELLING SEWERS OF MANHATTAN?
IT'S NICK FURY'S PLACE FROM YEARS BACK. HE KEPT IT IN CASE THE WORST EVER HAPPENED.
LIKE TODAY.
I GUESS I CAME HERE LOOKING FOR HIM, BUT IT DOESN'T LOOK LIKE ANYONE'S BEEN HERE IN YEARS.
DOES THIS STUFF WORK?
I GUESS.
WHAT'S THAT?
MONEY, PASSPORTS. FAKE IDS.
YOU WANT TO LEAVE THE COUNTRY?
HELL, NO.
YOU WITH ME ON THIS?
I TOLD YOU YEARS AGO, YOU NEVER HAVE TO ASK THAT.
WHAT ARE WE GONNA DO?
FIGHT BACK.
THERE YOU GO.
I'M DOWN, BROTHA'. I AIN'T BUYING WHAT THEY'RE SELLIN' AND I AIN'T MOVIN'.
WE STAY AND FIGHT.
THIS IS GOING TO GET BLOODY.
I'M NOT WORRIED ABOUT TODAY. I'M WORRIED ABOUT TOMORROW.
WHAT'S TOMORROW?

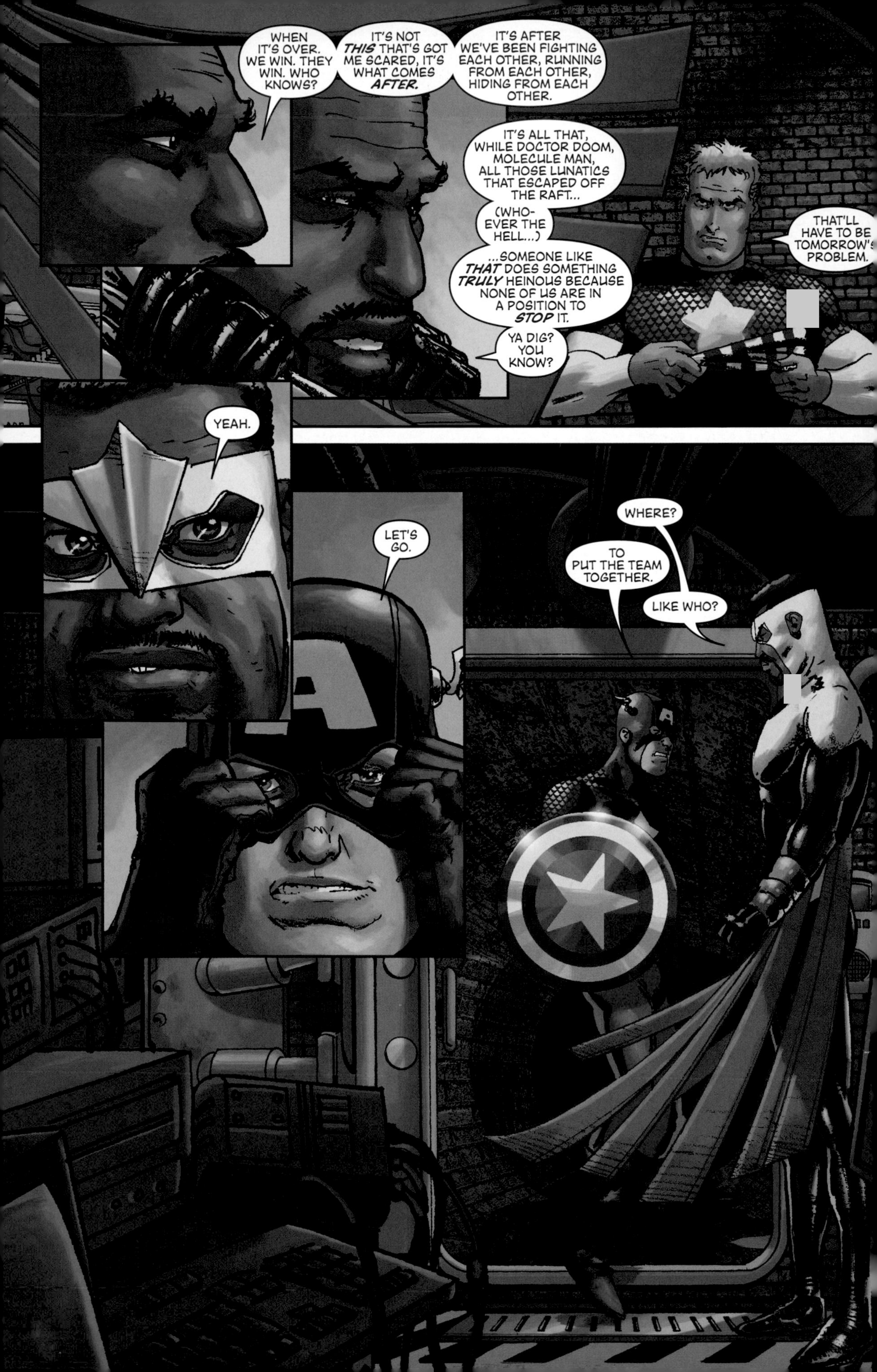
WHEN IT'S OVER. WE WIN. THEY WIN. WHO KNOWS?
IT'S NOT THIS THAT'S GOT ME SCARED, IT'S WHAT COMES AFTER.
IT'S AFTER WE'VE BEEN FIGHTING EACH OTHER, RUNNING FROM EACH OTHER, HIDING FROM EACH OTHER.
IT'S ALL THAT, WHILE DOCTOR DOOM, MOLECULE MAN, ALL THOSE LUNATICS THAT ESCAPED OFF THE RAFT...
(WHO-EVER THE HELL...)
...SOMEONE LIKE THAT DOES SOMETHING TRULY HEINOUS BECAUSE NONE OF US ARE IN A POSITION TO STOP IT.
YA DIG? YOU KNOW?
THAT'LL HAVE TO BE TOMORROW'S PROBLEM.
YEAH.
LET'S GO.
WHERE?
TO PUT THE TEAM TOGETHER.
LIKE WHO?

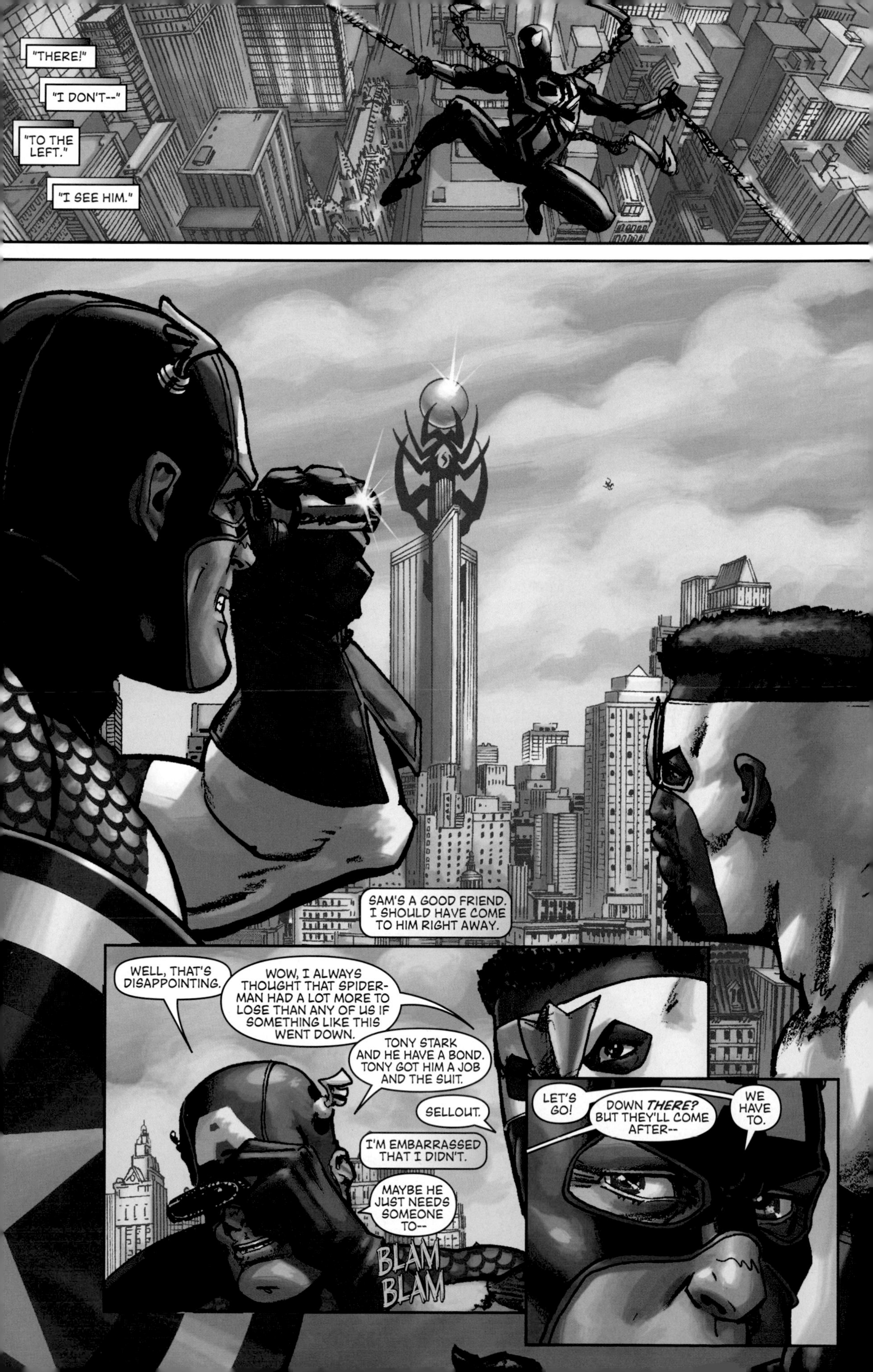
"THERE!"
"I DON'T--"
"TO THE LEFT."
"I SEE HIM."
SAM'S A GOOD FRIEND. I SHOULD HAVE COME TO HIM RIGHT AWAY.
WELL, THAT'S DISAPPOINTING.
WOW, I ALWAYS THOUGHT THAT SPIDER-MAN HAD A LOT MORE TO LOSE THAN ANY OF US IF SOMETHING LIKE THIS WENT DOWN.
TONY STARK AND HE HAVE A BOND. TONY GOT HIM A JOB AND THE SUIT.
SELLOUT.
I'M EMBARRASSED THAT I DIDN'T.
MAYBE HE JUST NEEDS SOMEONE TO--
BLAM
BLAM
LET'S GO!
DOWN *THERE?* BUT THEY'LL COME AFTER--
WE HAVE TO.

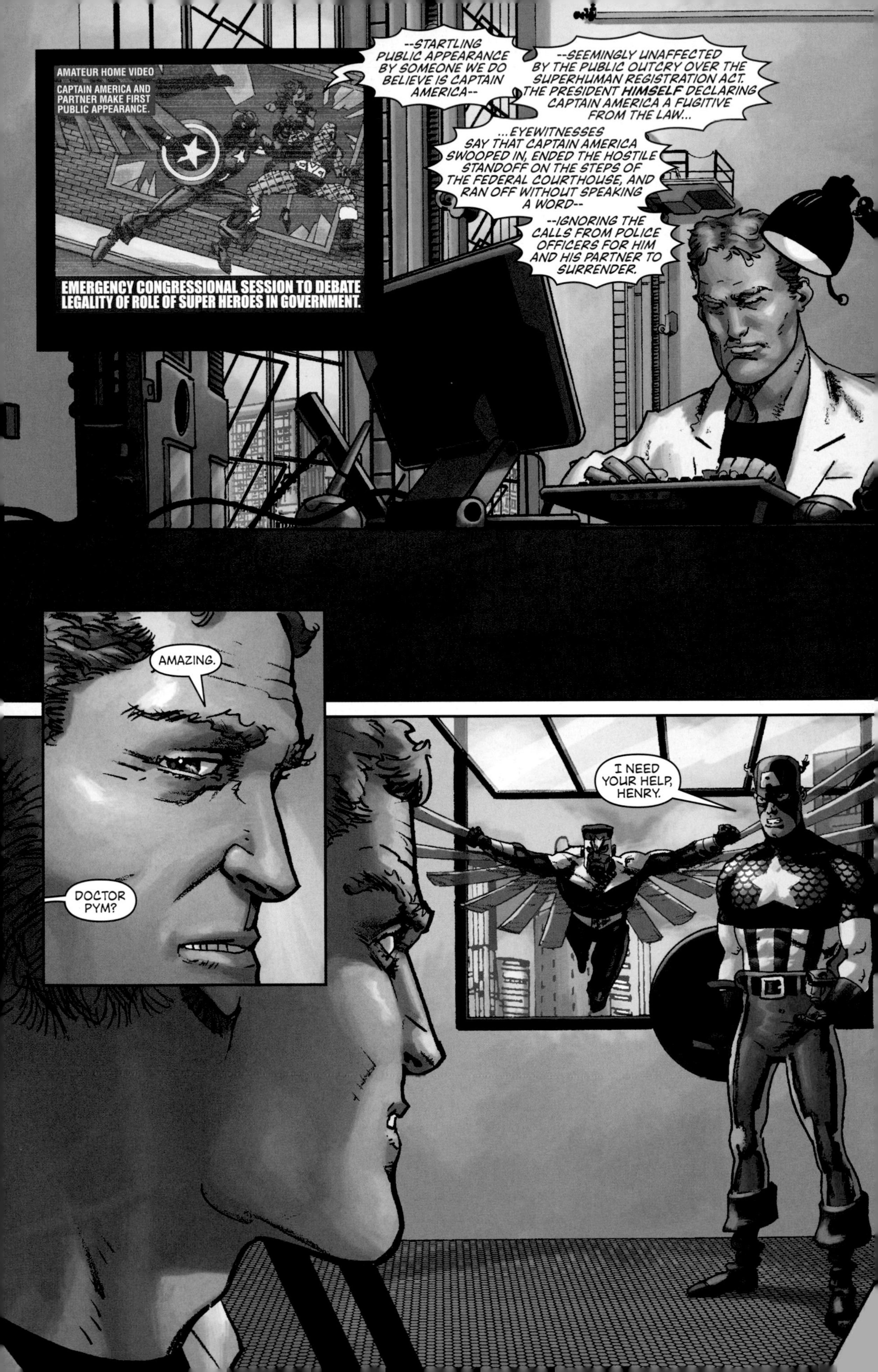
AMATEUR HOME VIDEO
CAPTAIN AMERICA AND PARTNER MAKE FIRST PUBLIC APPEARANCE.
EMERGENCY CONGRESSIONAL SESSION TO DEBATE LEGALITY OF ROLE OF SUPER HEROES IN GOVERNMENT.
--STARTLING PUBLIC APPEARANCE BY SOMEONE WE DO BELIEVE IS CAPTAIN AMERICA--
--SEEMINGLY UNAFFECTED BY THE PUBLIC OUTCRY OVER THE SUPERHUMAN REGISTRATION ACT. THE PRESIDENT HIMSELF DECLARING CAPTAIN AMERICA A FUGITIVE FROM THE LAW...
...EYEWITNESSES SAY THAT CAPTAIN AMERICA SWOOPED IN, ENDED THE HOSTILE STANDOFF ON THE STEPS OF THE FEDERAL COURTHOUSE, AND RAN OFF WITHOUT SPEAKING A WORD--
--IGNORING THE CALLS FROM POLICE OFFICERS FOR HIM AND HIS PARTNER TO SURRENDER.
AMAZING.
DOCTOR PYM?
I NEED YOUR HELP, HENRY.

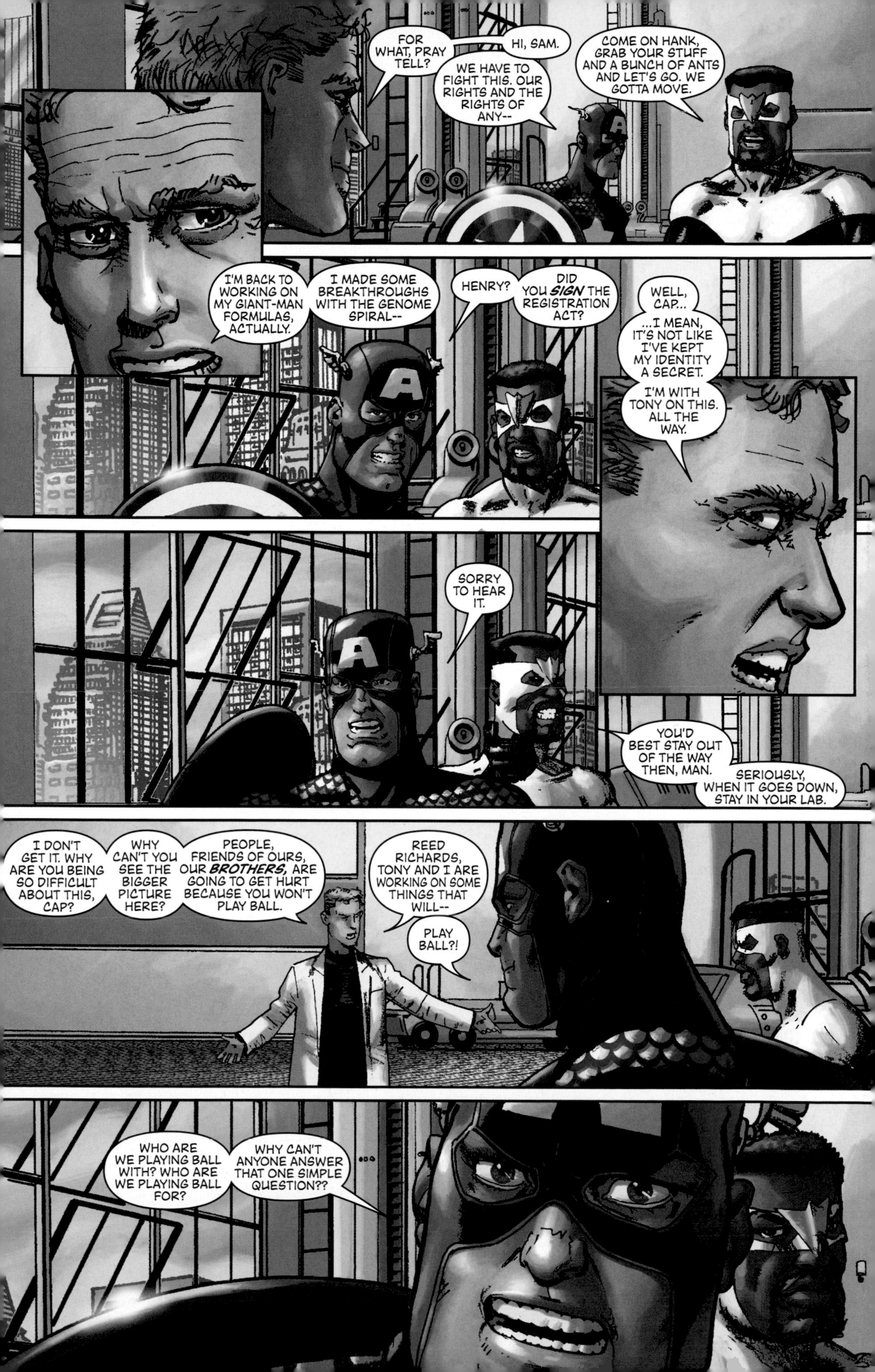
HI, SAM.
FOR WHAT, PRAY TELL?
WE HAVE TO FIGHT THIS. OUR RIGHTS AND THE RIGHTS OF ANY--
COME ON HANK, GRAB YOUR STUFF AND A BUNCH OF ANTS AND LET'S GO. WE GOTTA MOVE.
I'M BACK TO WORKING ON MY GIANT-MAN FORMULAS, ACTUALLY.
I MADE SOME BREAKTHROUGHS WITH THE GENOME SPIRAL--
HENRY?
DID YOU SIGN THE REGISTRATION ACT?
WELL, CAP...
...I MEAN, IT'S NOT LIKE I'VE KEPT MY IDENTITY A SECRET.
I'M WITH TONY ON THIS. ALL THE WAY.
SORRY TO HEAR IT.
YOU'D BEST STAY OUT OF THE WAY THEN, MAN.
SERIOUSLY, WHEN IT GOES DOWN, STAY IN YOUR LAB.
I DON'T GET IT. WHY ARE YOU BEING SO DIFFICULT ABOUT THIS, CAP?
WHY CAN'T YOU SEE THE BIGGER PICTURE HERE?
PEOPLE, FRIENDS OF OURS, OUR BROTHERS, ARE GOING TO GET HURT BECAUSE YOU WON'T PLAY BALL.
REED RICHARDS, TONY AND I ARE WORKING ON SOME THINGS THAT WILL--
PLAY BALL?!
WHO ARE WE PLAYING BALL WITH? WHO ARE WE PLAYING BALL FOR?
WHY CAN'T ANYONE ANSWER THAT ONE SIMPLE QUESTION??

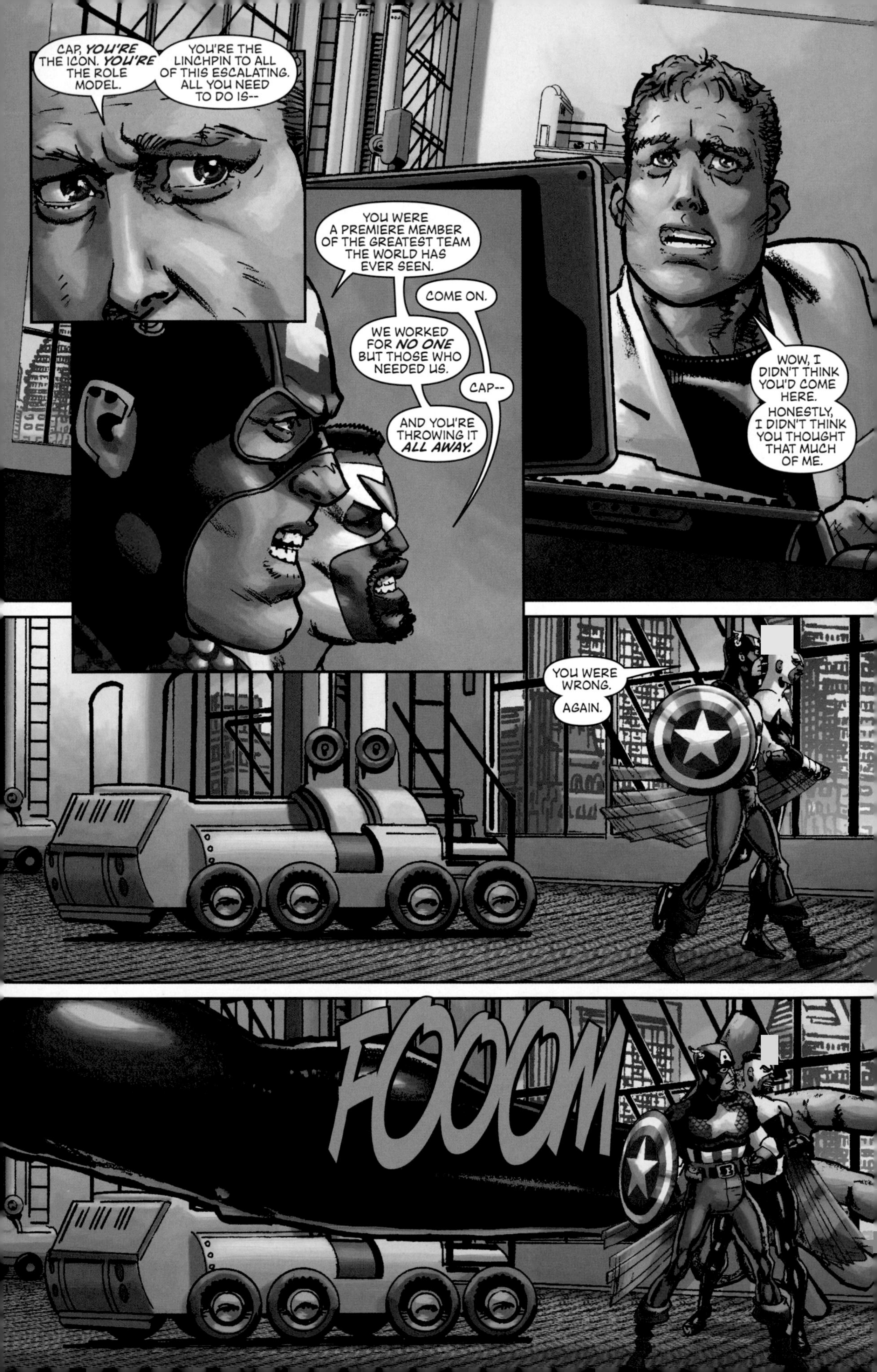
CAP, YOU'RE THE ICON. YOU'RE THE ROLE MODEL.
YOU'RE THE LINCHPIN TO ALL OF THIS ESCALATING. ALL YOU NEED TO DO IS--
WOW, I DIDN'T THINK YOU'D COME HERE.
HONESTLY, I DIDN'T THINK YOU THOUGHT THAT MUCH OF ME.
YOU WERE A PREMIERE MEMBER OF THE GREATEST TEAM THE WORLD HAS EVER SEEN.
COME ON.
WE WORKED FOR NO ONE BUT THOSE WHO NEEDED US.
CAP--
AND YOU'RE THROWING IT ALL AWAY.
YOU WERE WRONG.
AGAIN.
FOOOM

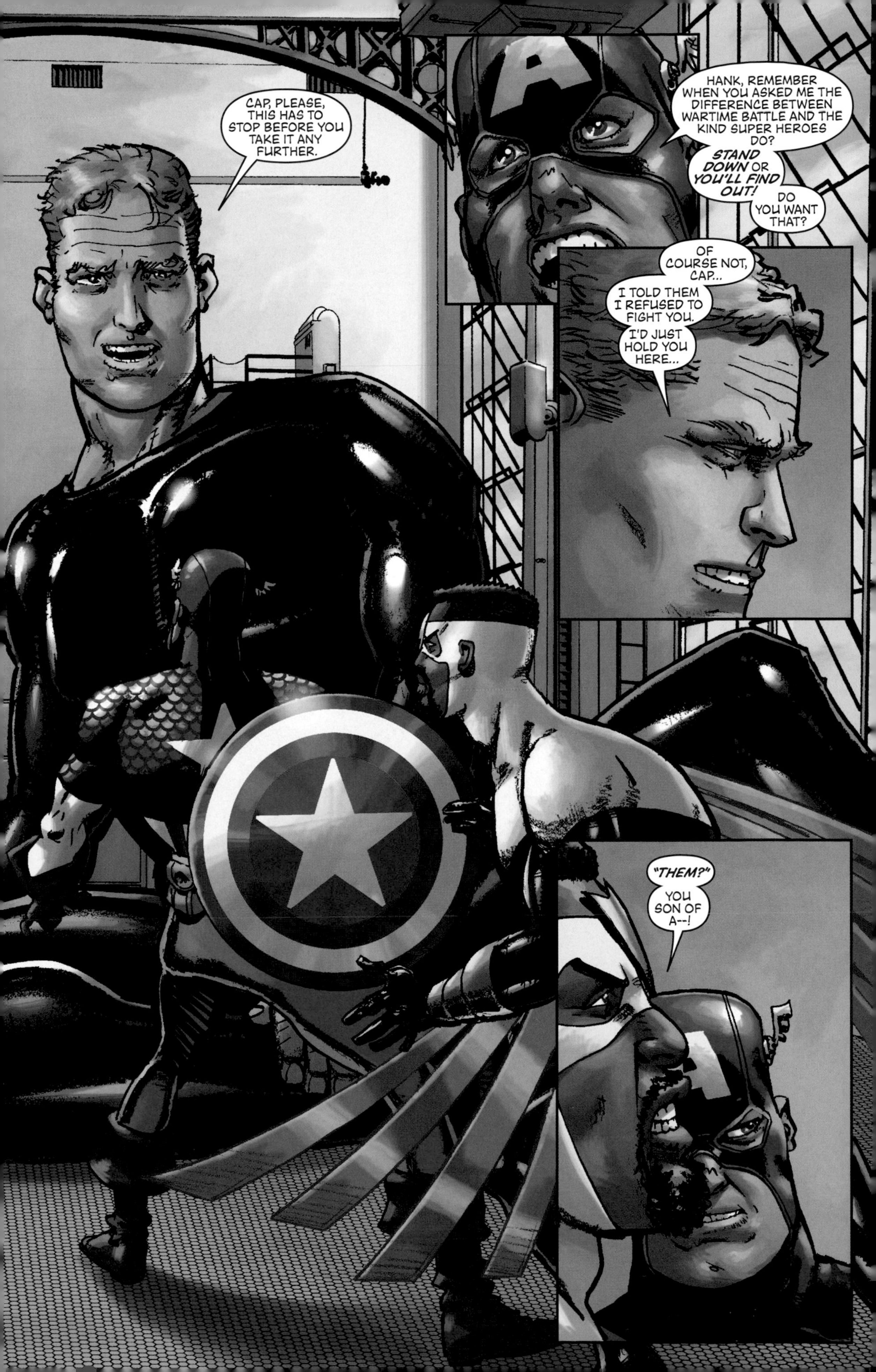
CAP, PLEASE, THIS HAS TO STOP BEFORE YOU TAKE IT ANY FURTHER.
HANK, REMEMBER WHEN YOU ASKED ME THE DIFFERENCE BETWEEN WARTIME BATTLE AND THE KIND SUPER HEROES DO?
STAND DOWN OR YOU'LL FIND OUT!
DO YOU WANT THAT?
OF COURSE NOT, CAP...
I TOLD THEM I REFUSED TO FIGHT YOU.
I'D JUST HOLD YOU HERE...
"THEM?"
YOU SON OF A--!

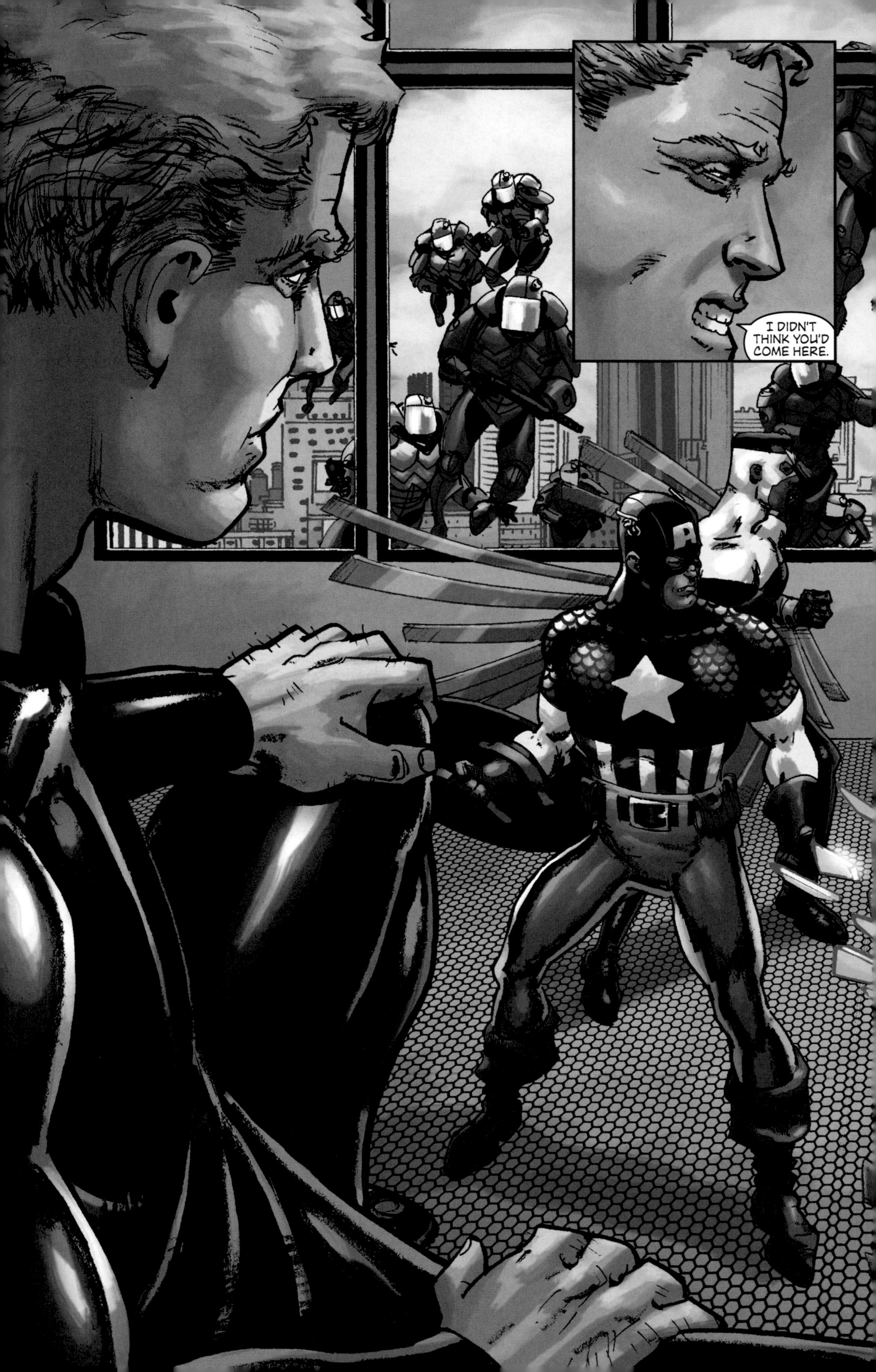
I DIDN'T THINK YOU'D COME HERE.

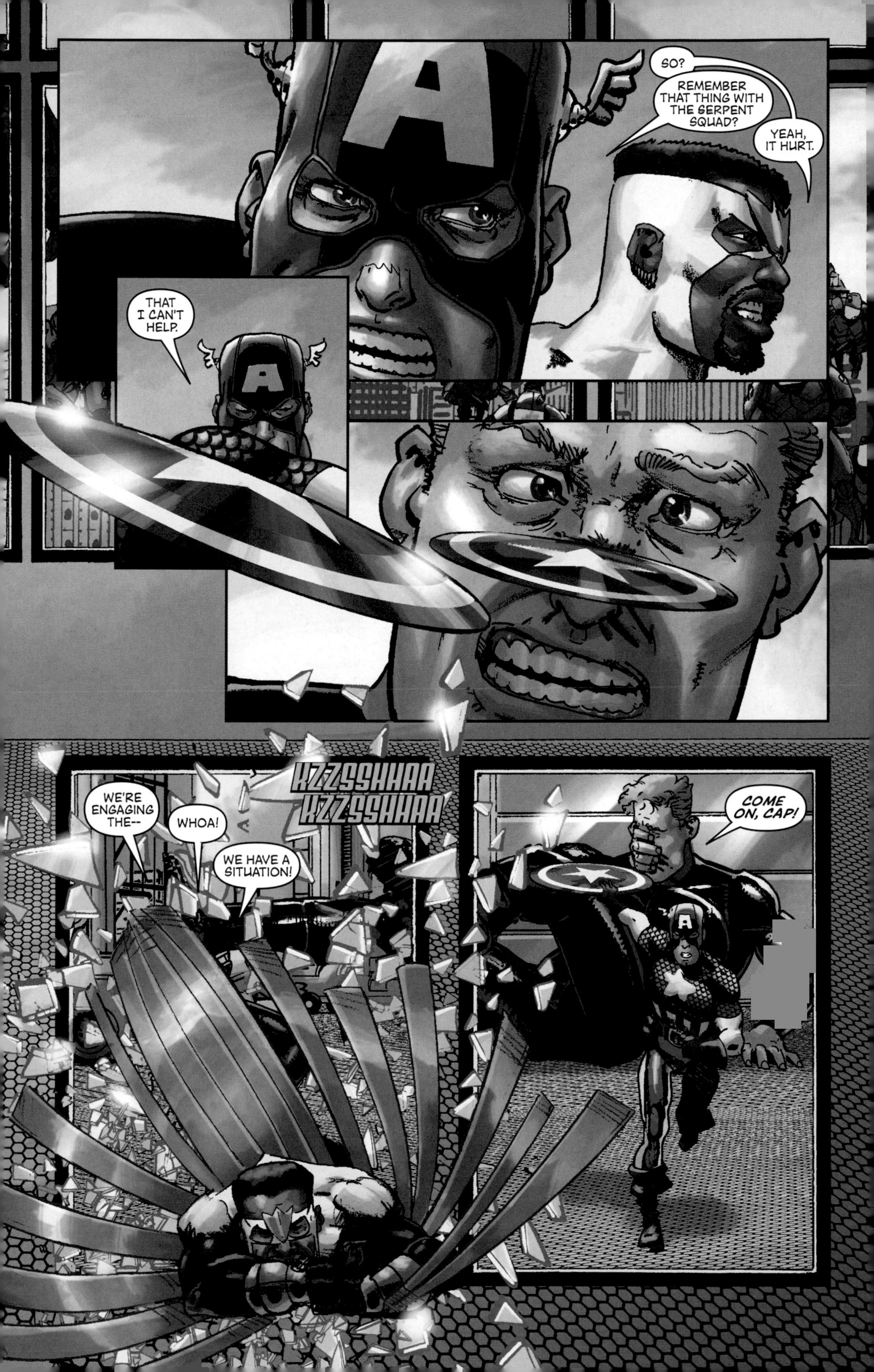

SO?
REMEMBER THAT THING WITH THE SERPENT SQUAD?
YEAH, IT HURT.
THAT I CAN'T HELP.
WE'RE ENGAGING THE--
WHOA!
WE HAVE A SITUATION!
KZZSSHHAA
KZZSSHHAA
COME ON, CAP!

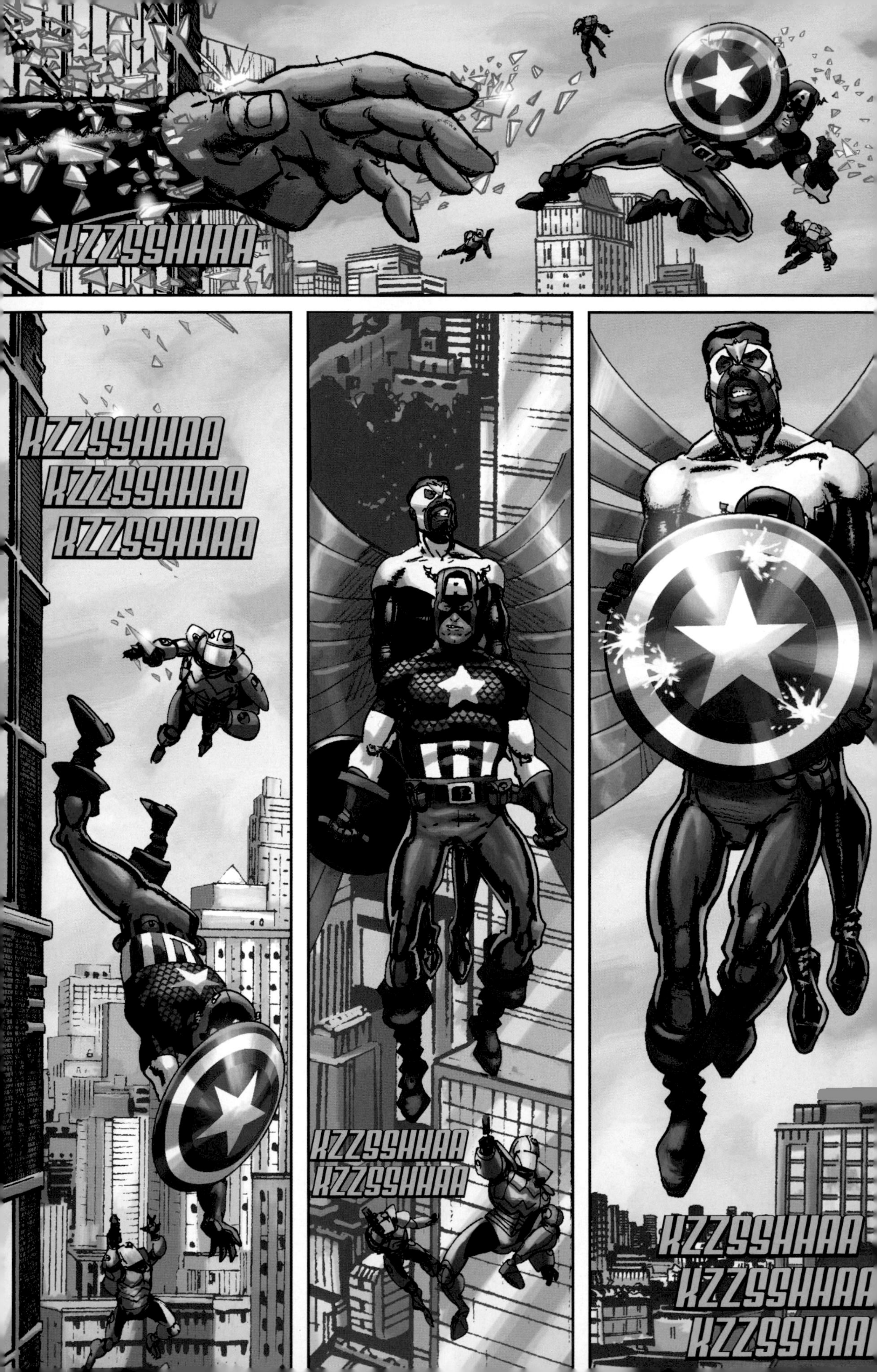
KZZSSHHAA
KZZSSHHAA
KZZSSHHAA
KZZSSHHAA
KZZSSHHAA
KZZSSHHAA
KZZSSHHAA
KZZSSHHAA
KZZSSHHAA

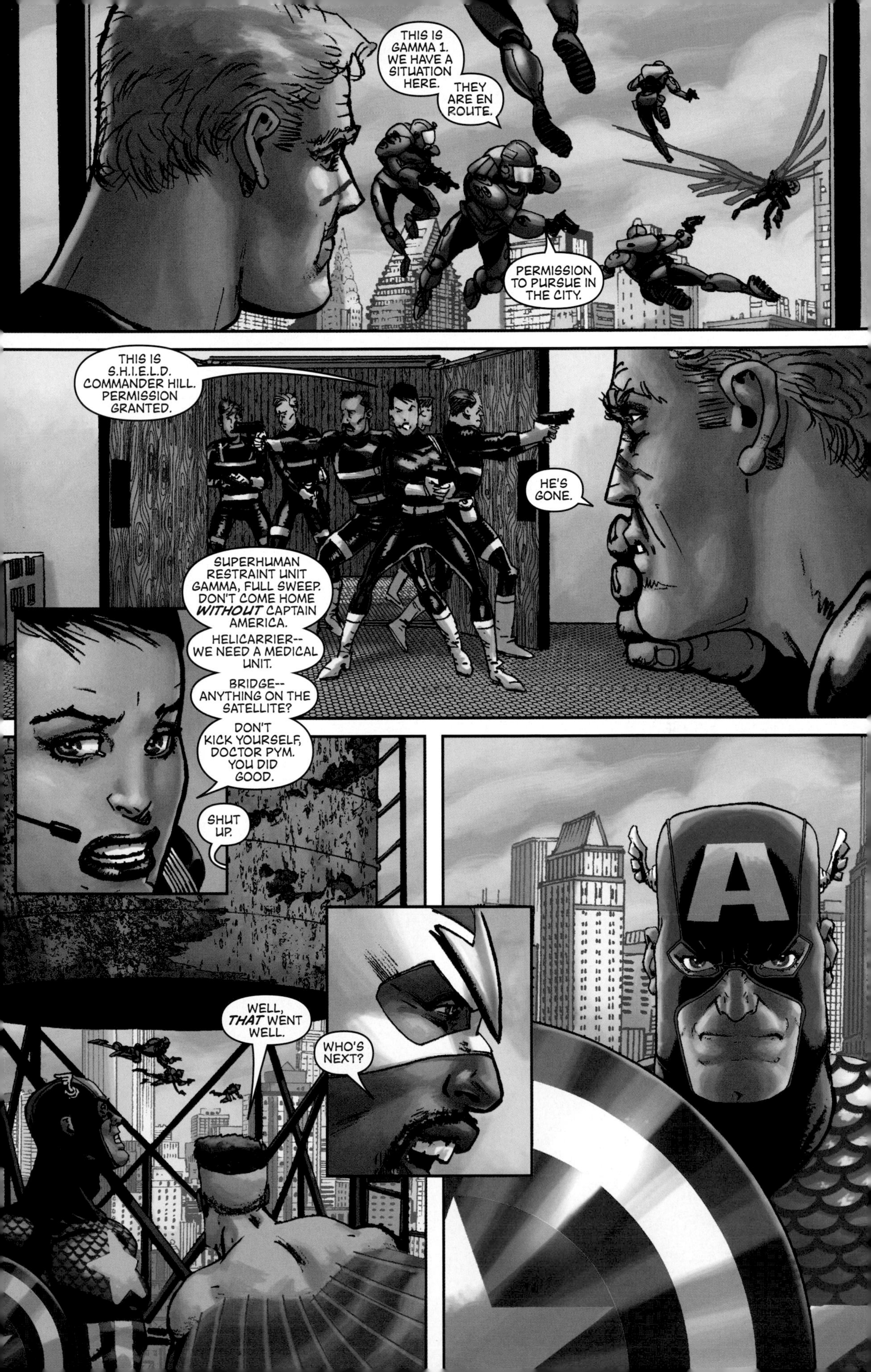

THIS IS GAMMA 1. WE HAVE A SITUATION HERE.
THEY ARE EN ROUTE.
PERMISSION TO PURSUE IN THE CITY.
THIS IS S.H.I.E.L.D. COMMANDER HILL. PERMISSION GRANTED.
HE'S GONE.
SUPERHUMAN RESTRAINT UNIT GAMMA, FULL SWEEP. DON'T COME HOME WITHOUT CAPTAIN AMERICA.
HELICARRIER-- WE NEED A MEDICAL UNIT.
BRIDGE-- ANYTHING ON THE SATELLITE?
DON'T KICK YOURSELF, DOCTOR PYM. YOU DID GOOD.
SHUT UP.
WELL, THAT WENT WELL.
WHO'S NEXT?

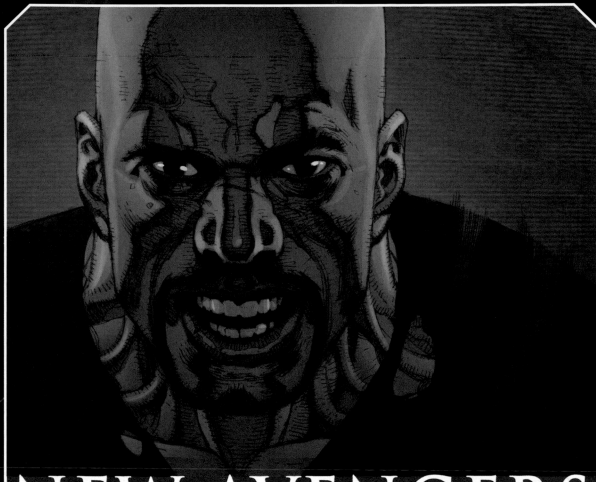

NEW AVENGERS
A MARVEL COMICS EVENT

CIVIL WAR

#22

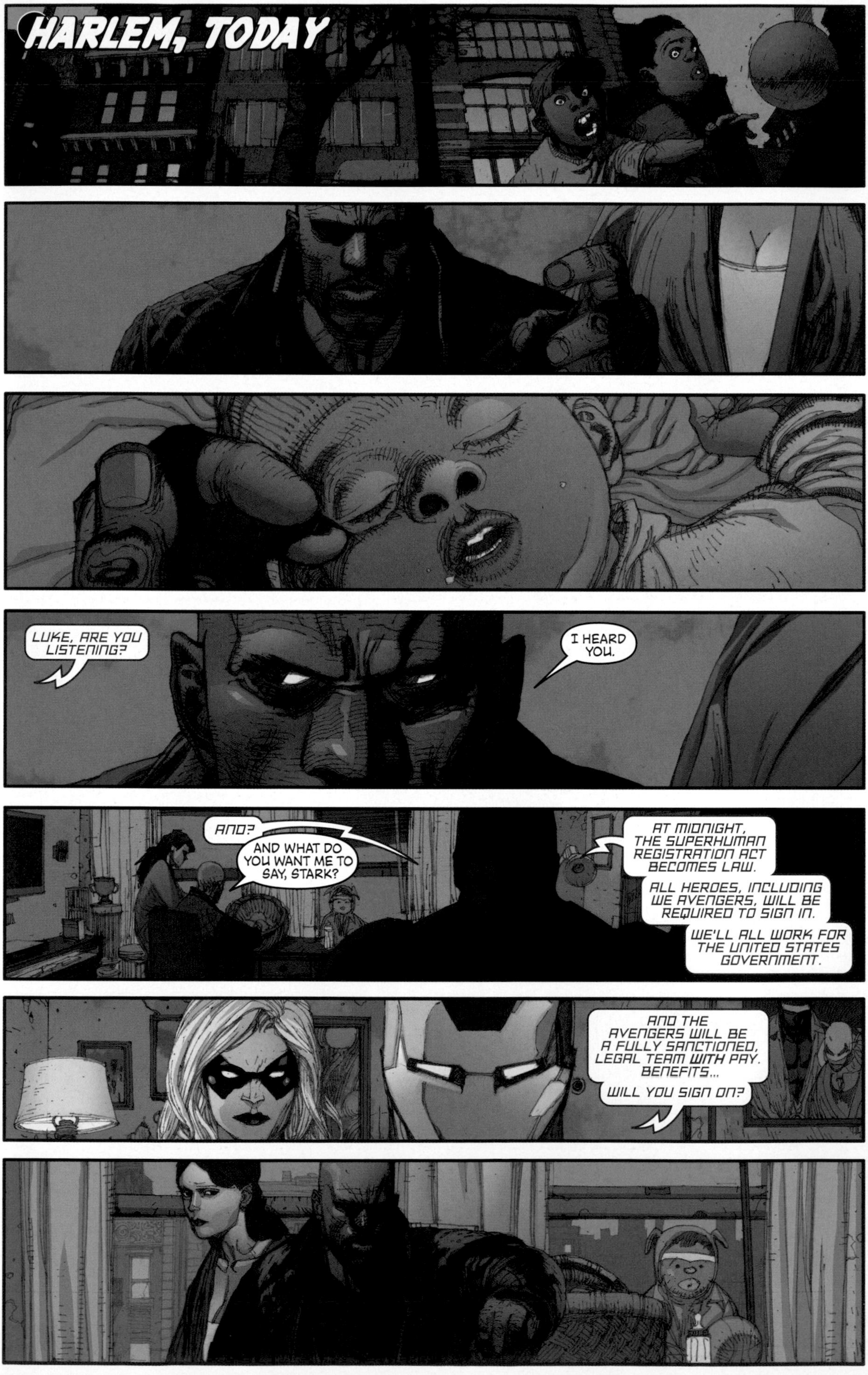
HARLEM, TODAY
LUKE, ARE YOU LISTENING?
I HEARD YOU.
AND?
AND WHAT DO YOU WANT ME TO SAY, STARK?
AT MIDNIGHT, THE SUPERHUMAN REGISTRATION ACT BECOMES LAW.
ALL HEROES, INCLUDING WE AVENGERS, WILL BE REQUIRED TO SIGN IN.
WE'LL ALL WORK FOR THE UNITED STATES GOVERNMENT.
AND THE AVENGERS WILL BE A FULLY SANCTIONED, LEGAL TEAM WITH PAY. BENEFITS...
WILL YOU SIGN ON?

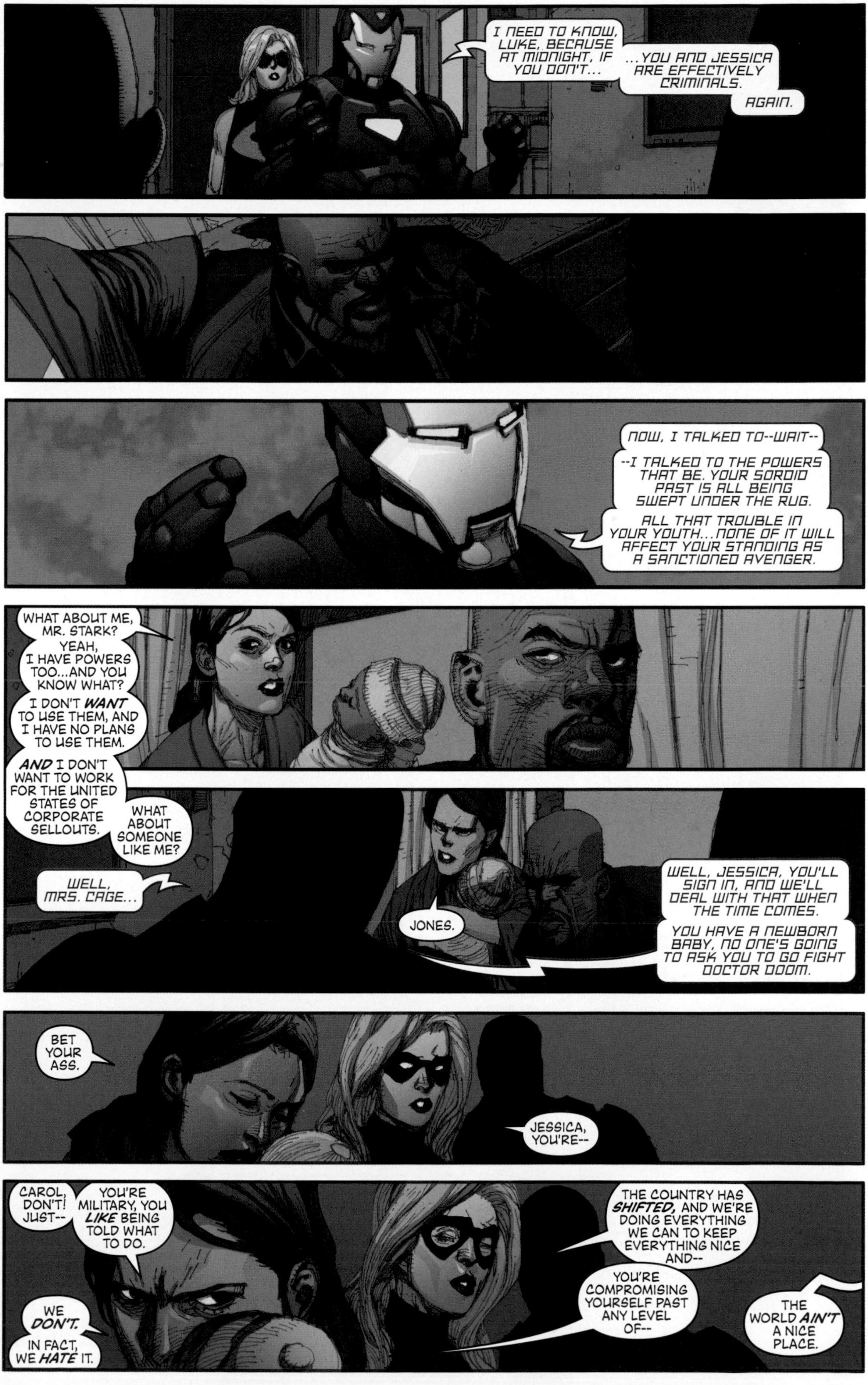
I NEED TO KNOW, LUKE, BECAUSE AT MIDNIGHT, IF YOU DON'T...
...YOU AND JESSICA ARE EFFECTIVELY CRIMINALS.
AGAIN.
NOW, I TALKED TO--WAIT--
--I TALKED TO THE POWERS THAT BE. YOUR SORDID PAST IS ALL BEING SWEPT UNDER THE RUG.
ALL THAT TROUBLE IN YOUR YOUTH...NONE OF IT WILL AFFECT YOUR STANDING AS A SANCTIONED AVENGER.
WHAT ABOUT ME, MR. STARK?
YEAH, I HAVE POWERS TOO...AND YOU KNOW WHAT?
I DON'T WANT TO USE THEM, AND I HAVE NO PLANS TO USE THEM.
AND I DON'T WANT TO WORK FOR THE UNITED STATES OF CORPORATE SELLOUTS.
WHAT ABOUT SOMEONE LIKE ME?
WELL, MRS. CAGE...
JONES.
WELL, JESSICA, YOU'LL SIGN IN, AND WE'LL DEAL WITH THAT WHEN THE TIME COMES.
YOU HAVE A NEWBORN BABY, NO ONE'S GOING TO ASK YOU TO GO FIGHT DOCTOR DOOM.
BET YOUR ASS.
JESSICA, YOU'RE--
CAROL, DON'T! JUST--
YOU'RE MILITARY, YOU LIKE BEING TOLD WHAT TO DO.
WE DON'T.
IN FACT, WE HATE IT.
THE COUNTRY HAS SHIFTED, AND WE'RE DOING EVERYTHING WE CAN TO KEEP EVERYTHING NICE AND--
YOU'RE COMPROMISING YOURSELF PAST ANY LEVEL OF--
THE WORLD AIN'T A NICE PLACE.

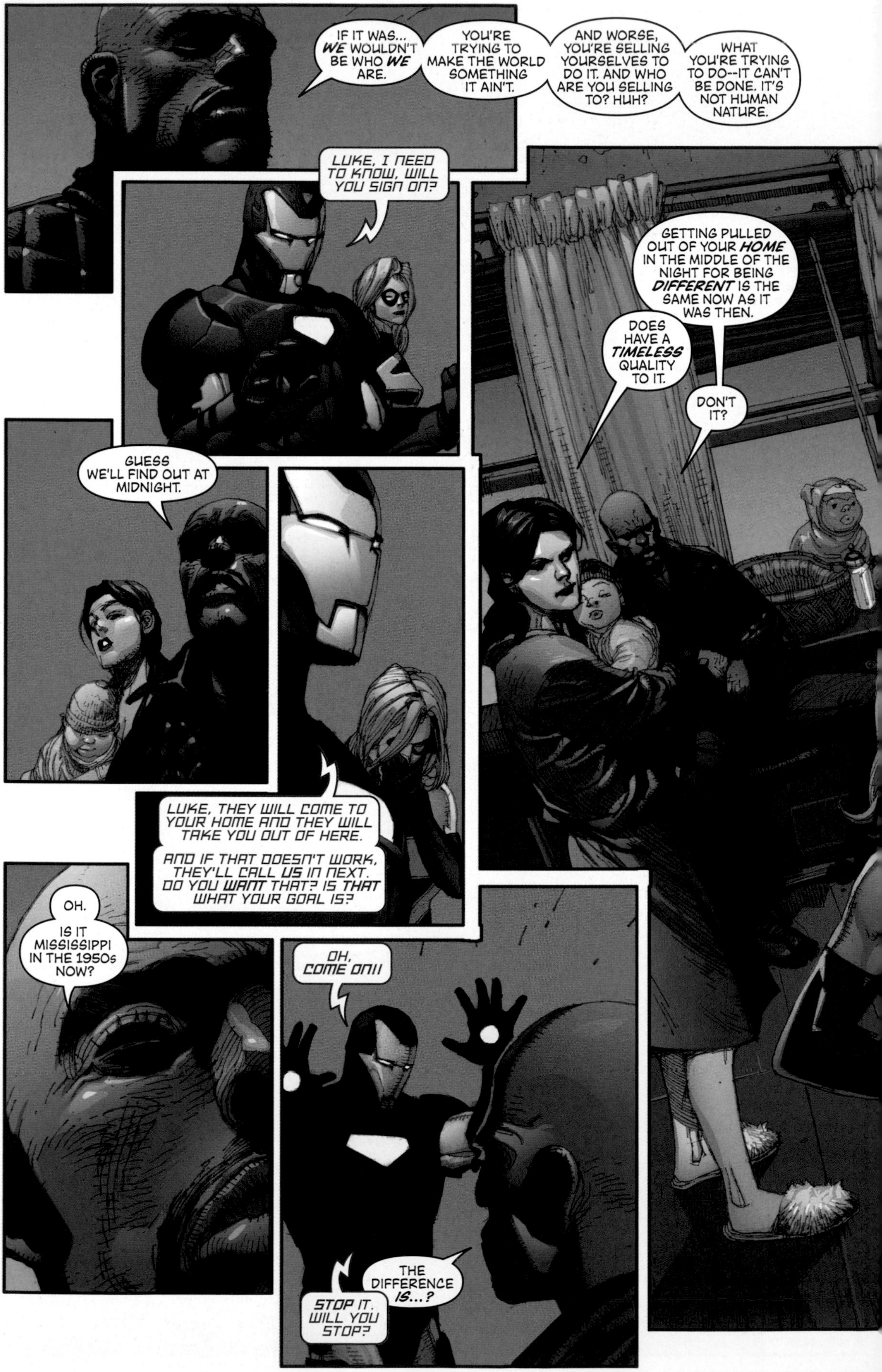
IF IT WAS... WE WOULDN'T BE WHO WE ARE.
YOU'RE TRYING TO MAKE THE WORLD SOMETHING IT AIN'T.
AND WORSE, YOU'RE SELLING YOURSELVES TO DO IT. AND WHO ARE YOU SELLING TO? HUH?
WHAT YOU'RE TRYING TO DO--IT CAN'T BE DONE. IT'S NOT HUMAN NATURE.
LUKE, I NEED TO KNOW, WILL YOU SIGN ON?
GETTING PULLED OUT OF YOUR HOME IN THE MIDDLE OF THE NIGHT FOR BEING DIFFERENT IS THE SAME NOW AS IT WAS THEN.
DOES HAVE A TIMELESS QUALITY TO IT.
DON'T IT?
GUESS WE'LL FIND OUT AT MIDNIGHT.
LUKE, THEY WILL COME TO YOUR HOME AND THEY WILL TAKE YOU OUT OF HERE.
AND IF THAT DOESN'T WORK, THEY'LL CALL US IN NEXT. DO YOU WANT THAT? IS THAT WHAT YOUR GOAL IS?
OH.
IS IT MISSISSIPPI IN THE 1950s NOW?
OH, COME ON!!
THE DIFFERENCE IS...?
STOP IT. WILL YOU STOP?

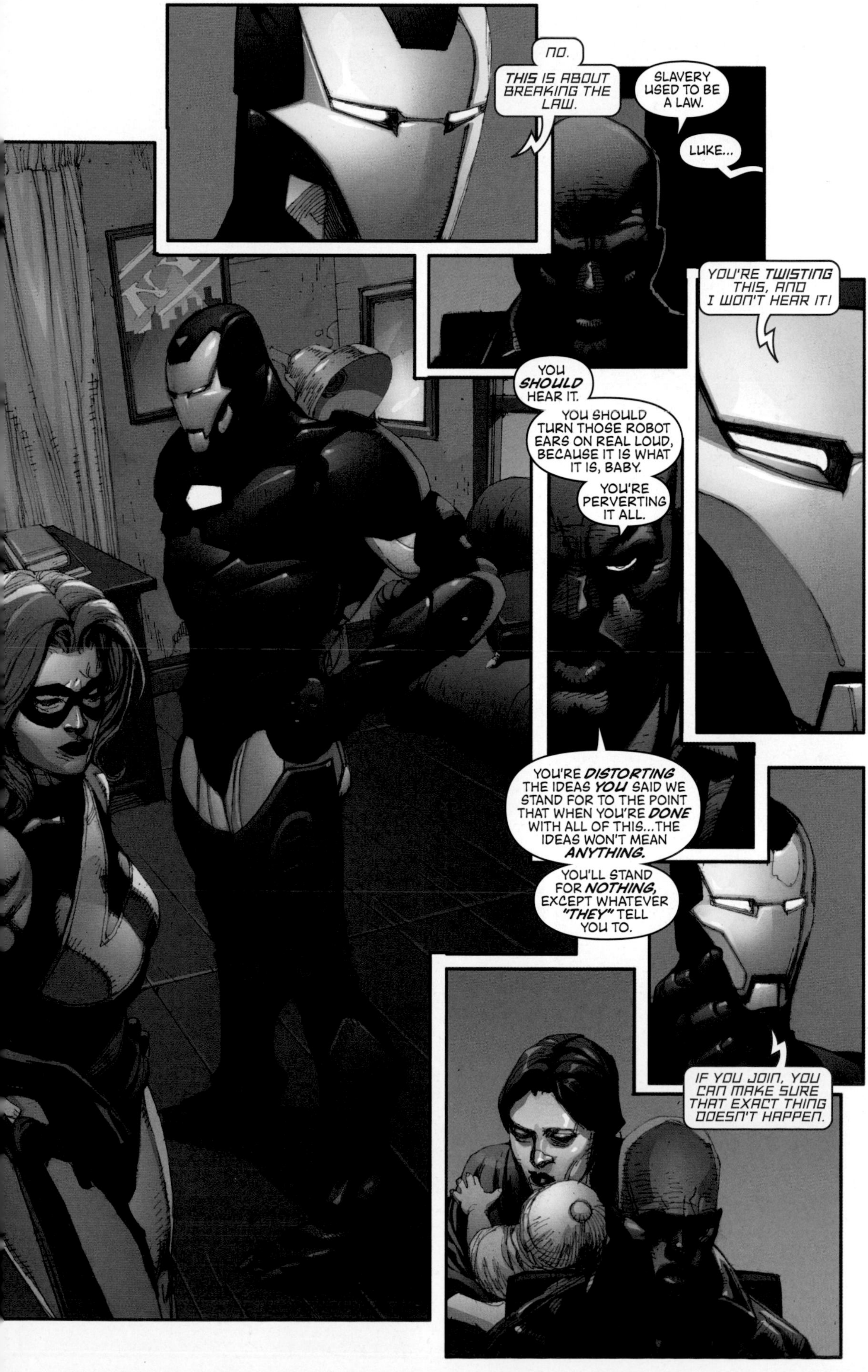
NO.
THIS IS ABOUT BREAKING THE LAW.
SLAVERY USED TO BE A LAW.
LUKE...
YOU'RE TWISTING THIS, AND I WON'T HEAR IT!
YOU SHOULD HEAR IT.
YOU SHOULD TURN THOSE ROBOT EARS ON REAL LOUD, BECAUSE IT IS WHAT IT IS, BABY.
YOU'RE PERVERTING IT ALL.
YOU'RE DISTORTING THE IDEAS YOU SAID WE STAND FOR TO THE POINT THAT WHEN YOU'RE DONE WITH ALL OF THIS...THE IDEAS WON'T MEAN ANYTHING.
YOU'LL STAND FOR NOTHING, EXCEPT WHATEVER "THEY" TELL YOU TO.
IF YOU JOIN, YOU CAN MAKE SURE THAT EXACT THING DOESN'T HAPPEN.

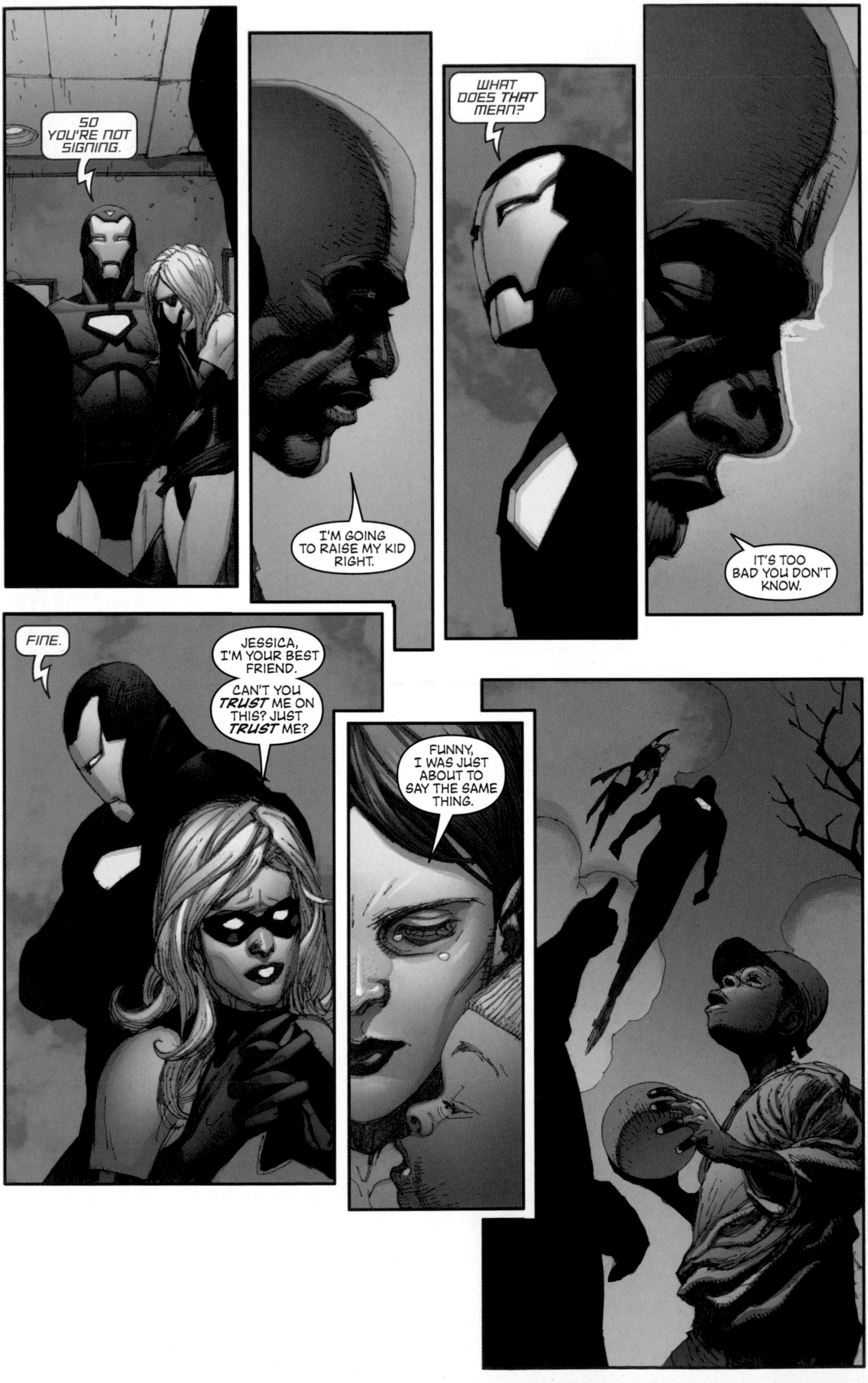
SO YOU'RE NOT SIGNING.
I'M GOING TO RAISE MY KID RIGHT.
WHAT DOES THAT MEAN?
IT'S TOO BAD YOU DON'T KNOW.
FINE.
JESSICA, I'M YOUR BEST FRIEND.
CAN'T YOU TRUST ME ON THIS? JUST TRUST ME?
FUNNY, I WAS JUST ABOUT TO SAY THE SAME THING.

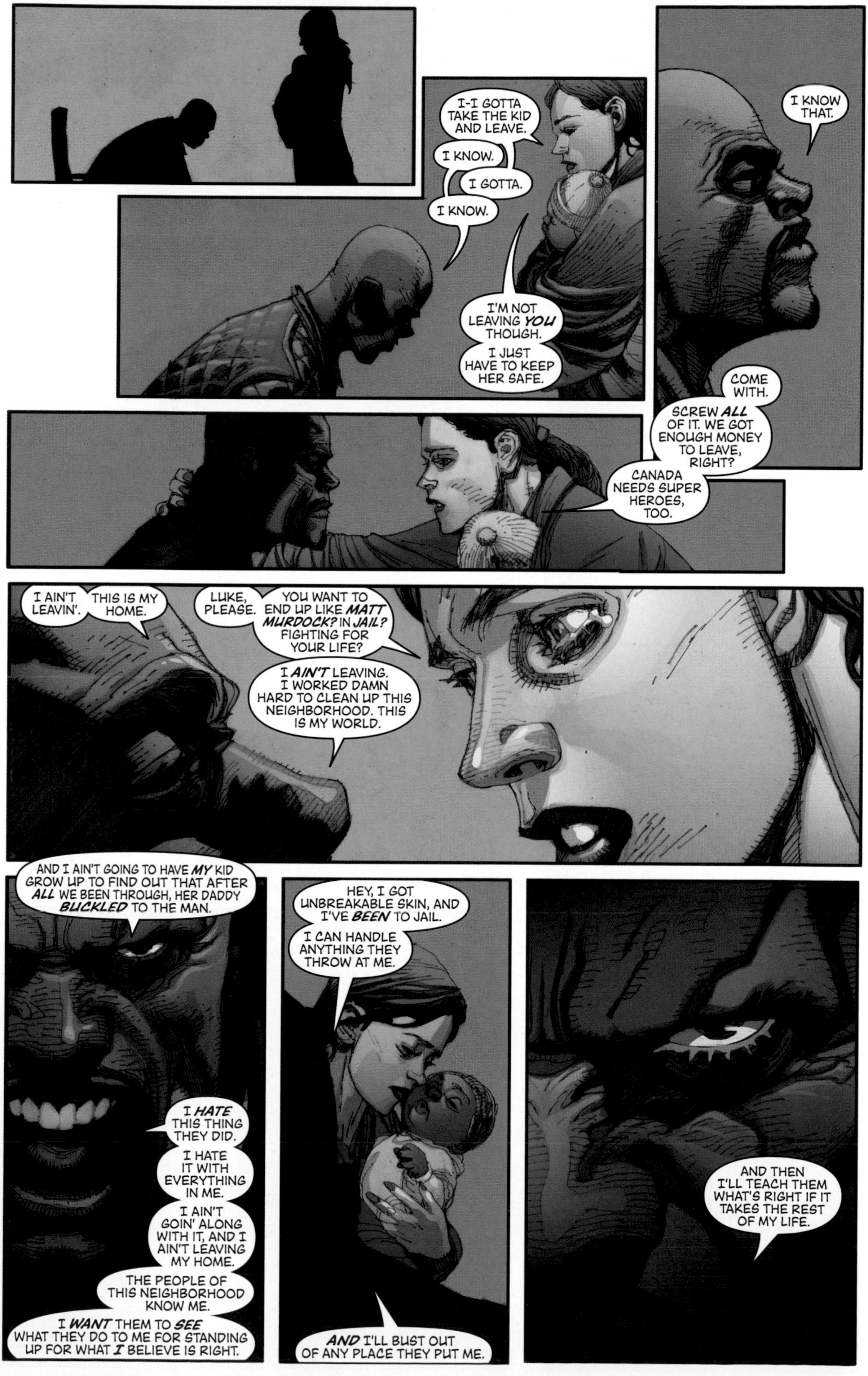
I-I GOTTA TAKE THE KID AND LEAVE.
I KNOW.
I GOTTA.
I KNOW.
I'M NOT LEAVING YOU THOUGH.
I JUST HAVE TO KEEP HER SAFE.
I KNOW THAT.
COME WITH.
SCREW ALL OF IT. WE GOT ENOUGH MONEY TO LEAVE, RIGHT?
CANADA NEEDS SUPER HEROES, TOO.
I AIN'T LEAVIN'.
THIS IS MY HOME.
LUKE, PLEASE.
YOU WANT TO END UP LIKE MATT MURDOCK? IN JAIL? FIGHTING FOR YOUR LIFE?
I AIN'T LEAVING. I WORKED DAMN HARD TO CLEAN UP THIS NEIGHBORHOOD. THIS IS MY WORLD.
AND I AIN'T GOING TO HAVE MY KID GROW UP TO FIND OUT THAT AFTER ALL WE BEEN THROUGH, HER DADDY BUCKLED TO THE MAN.
I HATE THIS THING THEY DID.
I HATE IT WITH EVERYTHING IN ME.
I AIN'T GOIN' ALONG WITH IT, AND I AIN'T LEAVING MY HOME.
THE PEOPLE OF THIS NEIGHBORHOOD KNOW ME.
I WANT THEM TO SEE WHAT THEY DO TO ME FOR STANDING UP FOR WHAT I BELIEVE IS RIGHT.
HEY, I GOT UNBREAKABLE SKIN, AND I'VE BEEN TO JAIL.
I CAN HANDLE ANYTHING THEY THROW AT ME.
AND I'LL BUST OUT OF ANY PLACE THEY PUT ME.
AND THEN I'LL TEACH THEM WHAT'S RIGHT IF IT TAKES THE REST OF MY LIFE.

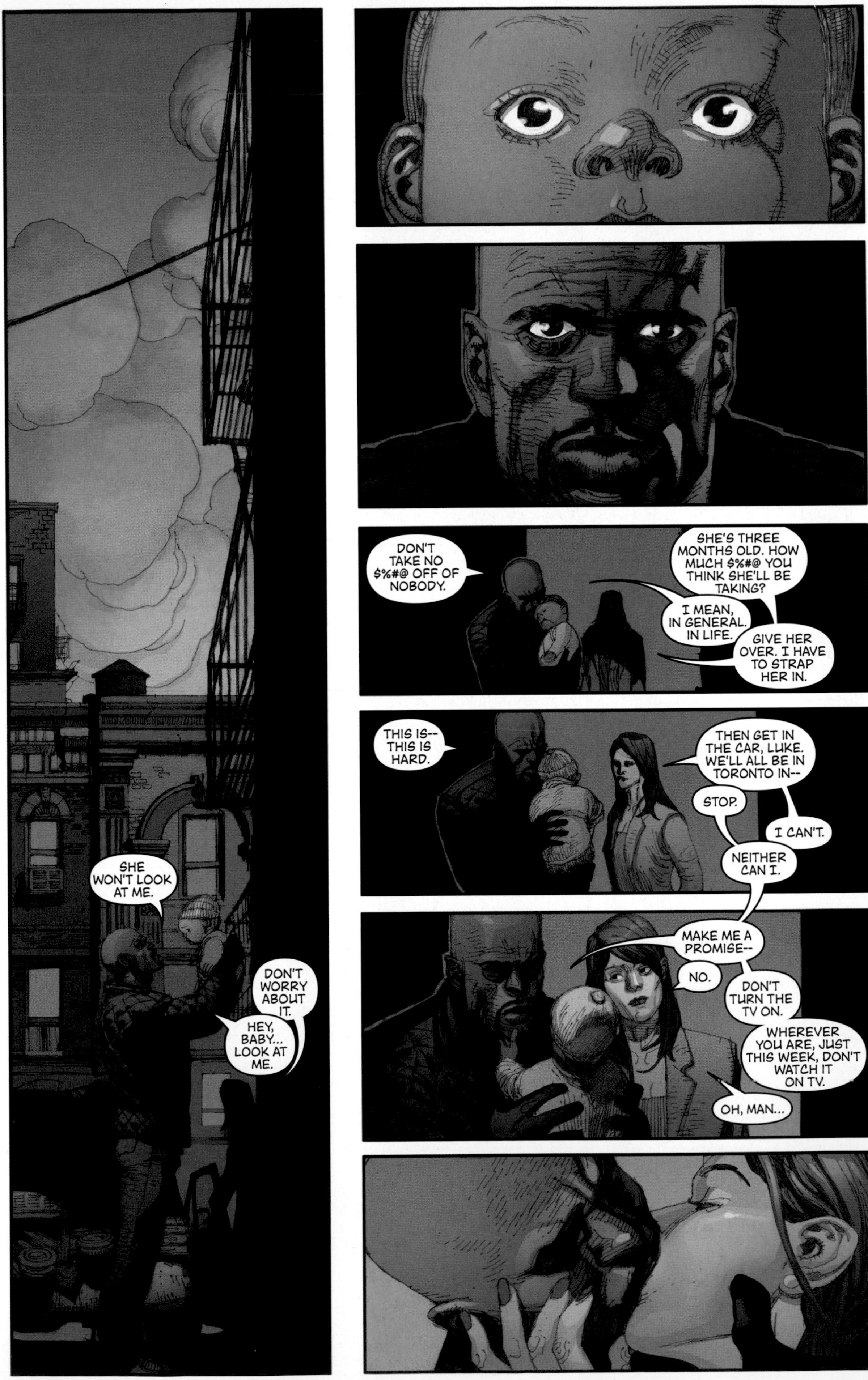

SHE WON'T LOOK AT ME.
DON'T WORRY ABOUT IT.
HEY, BABY... LOOK AT ME.
DON'T TAKE NO $%#@ OFF OF NOBODY.
SHE'S THREE MONTHS OLD. HOW MUCH $%#@ YOU THINK SHE'LL BE TAKING?
I MEAN, IN GENERAL. IN LIFE.
GIVE HER OVER. I HAVE TO STRAP HER IN.
THIS IS-- THIS IS HARD.
THEN GET IN THE CAR, LUKE. WE'LL ALL BE IN TORONTO IN--
STOP.
I CAN'T.
NEITHER CAN I.
MAKE ME A PROMISE--
NO.
DON'T TURN THE TV ON.
WHEREVER YOU ARE, JUST THIS WEEK, DON'T WATCH IT ON TV.
OH, MAN...

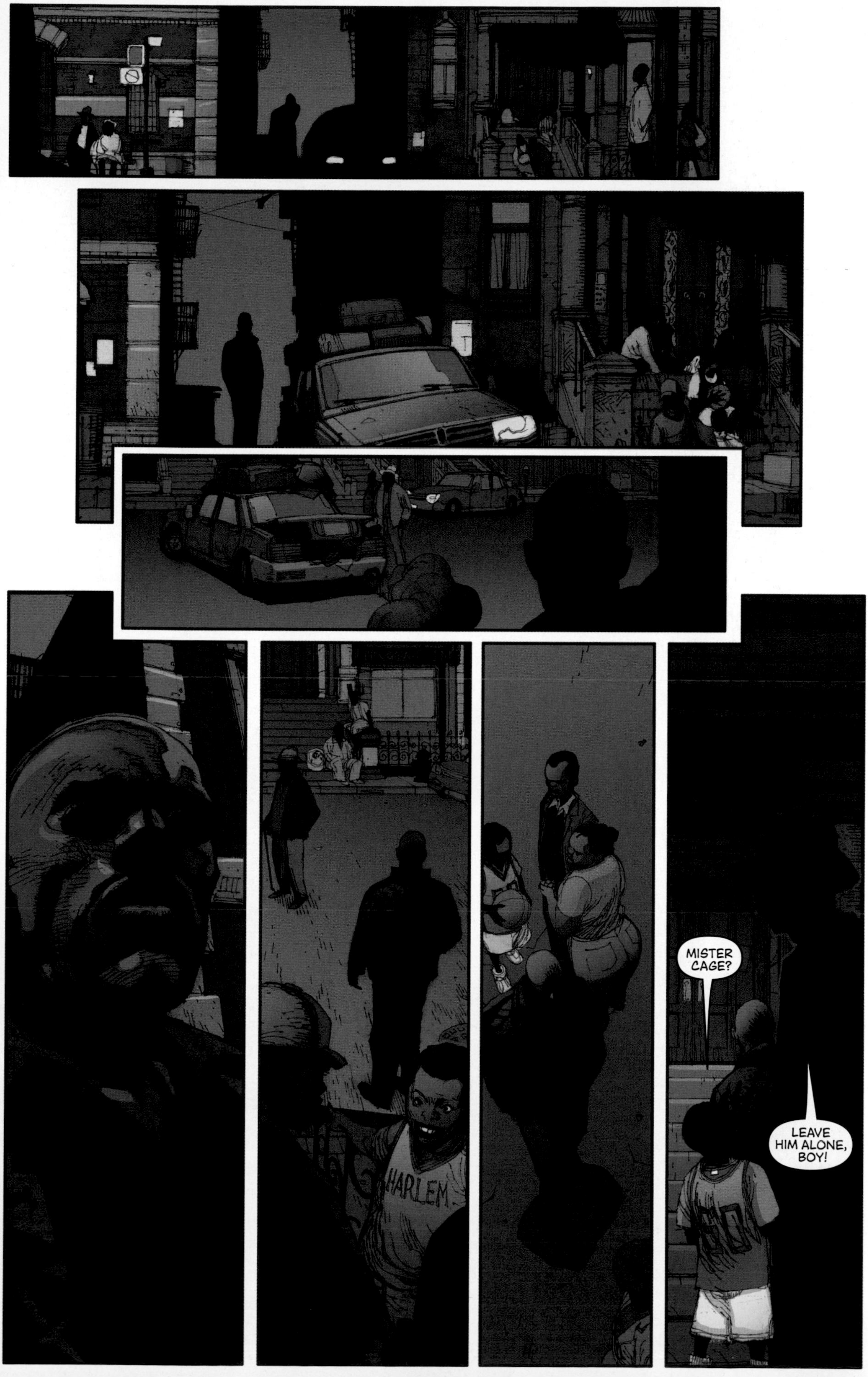
HARLEM
MISTER CAGE?
LEAVE HIM ALONE, BOY!

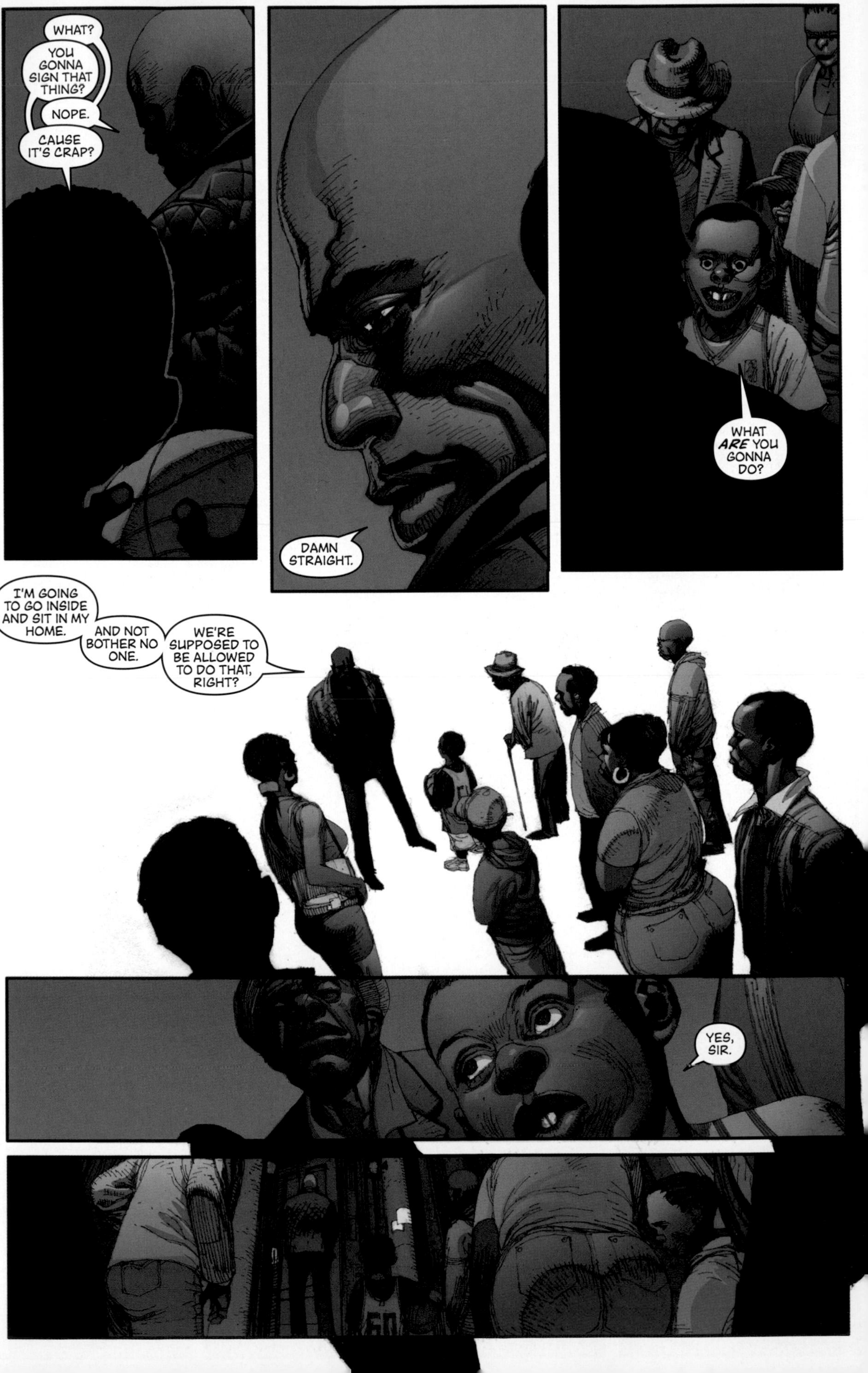
WHAT?
YOU GONNA SIGN THAT THING?
NOPE.
CAUSE IT'S CRAP?
DAMN STRAIGHT.
WHAT ARE YOU GONNA DO?
I'M GOING TO GO INSIDE AND SIT IN MY HOME.
AND NOT BOTHER NO ONE.
WE'RE SUPPOSED TO BE ALLOWED TO DO THAT, RIGHT?
YES, SIR.

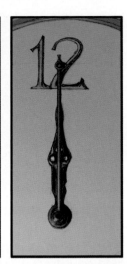

MISTER CAGE?

INCREDIBLE.

MISTER CAGE, THIS IS S.H.I.E.L.D. AGENT GABRIEL JONES. CAN I HAVE A WORD WITH YOU, PLEASE?

I'M KIND OF IN THE MIDDLE OF SOMETHING.

CAN YOU COME BACK ANOTHER TIME?

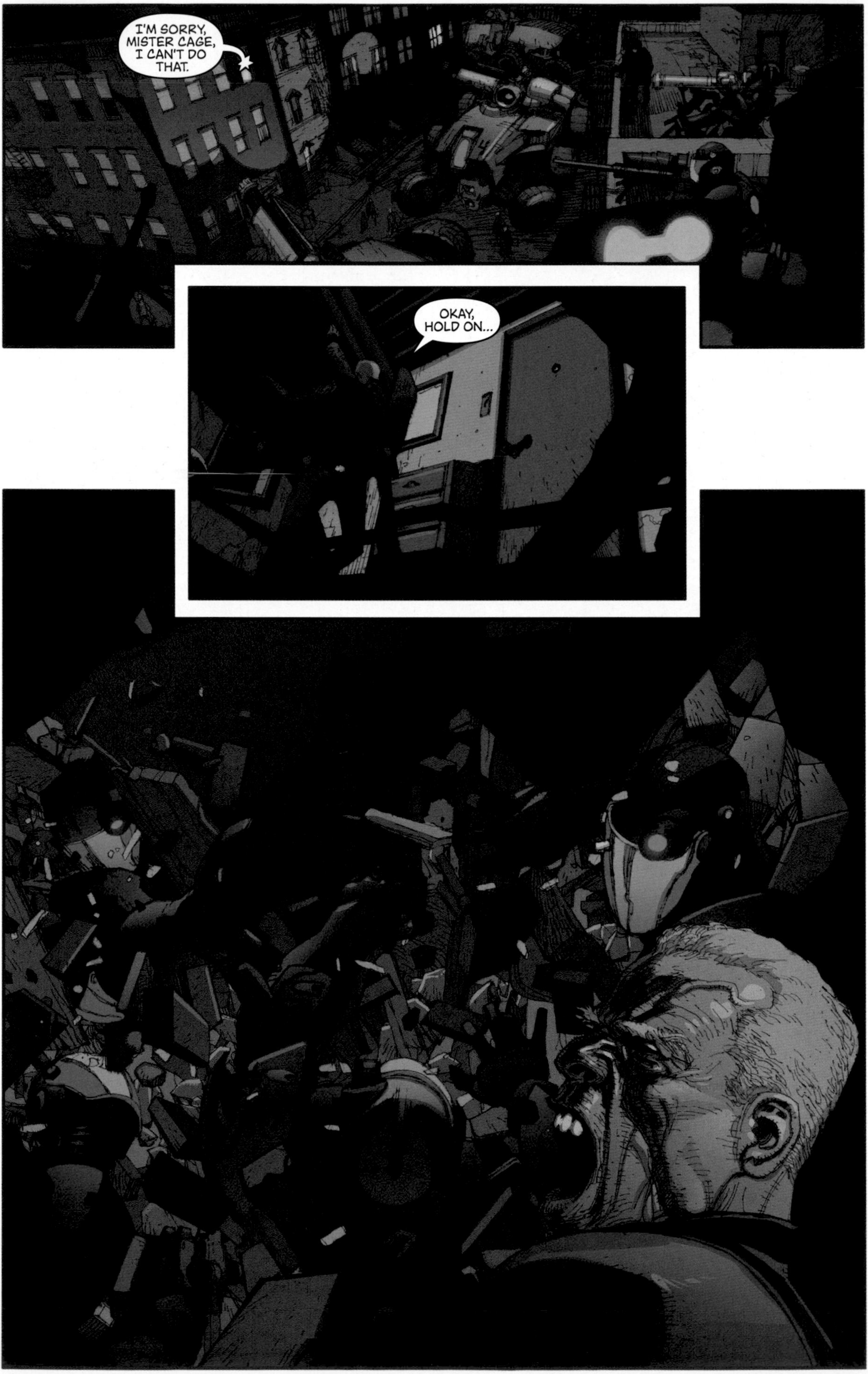
I'M SORRY, MISTER CAGE, I CAN'T DO THAT.
OKAY, HOLD ON...

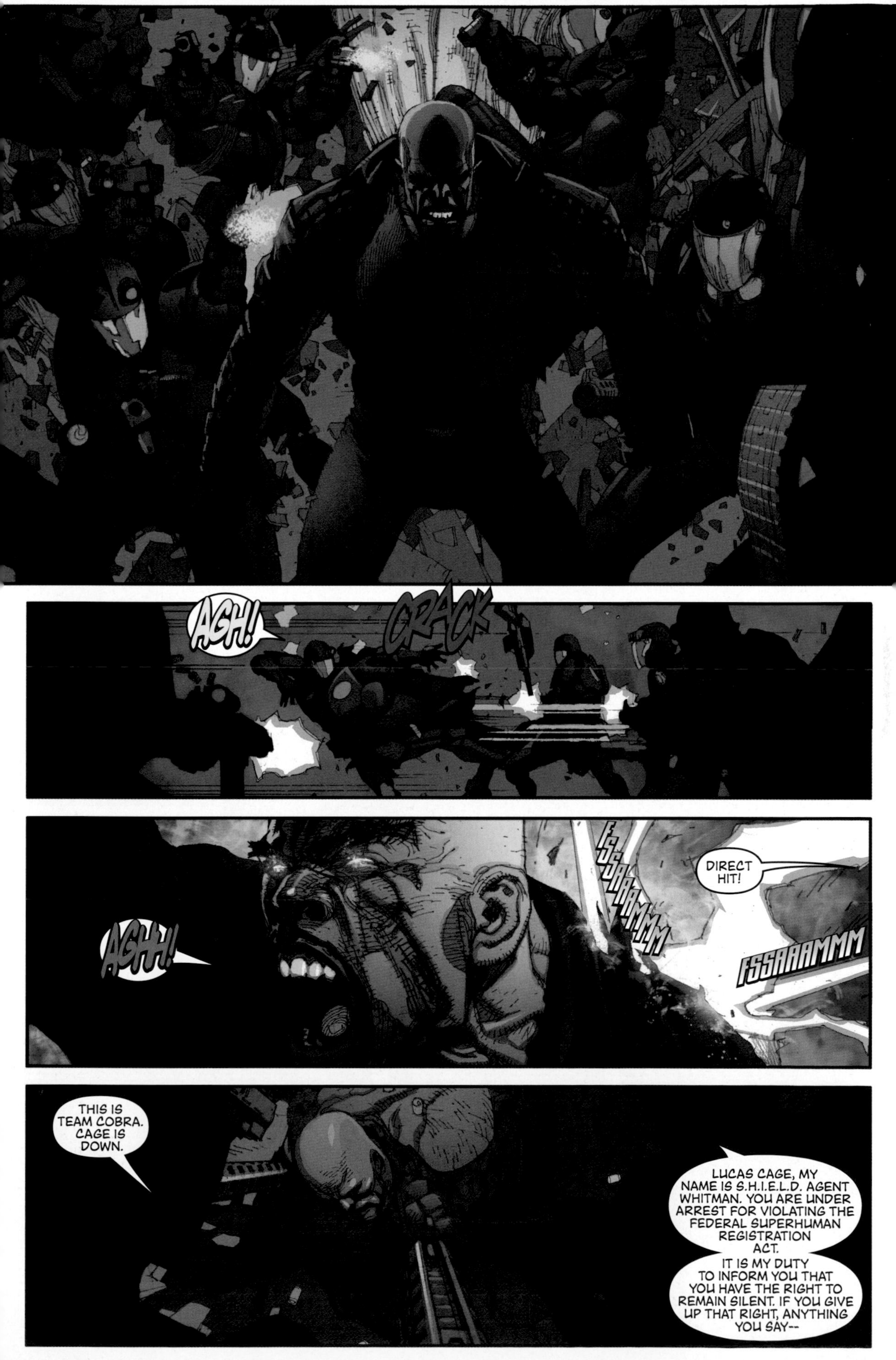
AGH!
CRACK
AGHH!
FSSAAAMMM
DIRECT HIT!
FSSAAAMMM
THIS IS TEAM COBRA. CAGE IS DOWN.
LUCAS CAGE, MY NAME IS S.H.I.E.L.D. AGENT WHITMAN. YOU ARE UNDER ARREST FOR VIOLATING THE FEDERAL SUPERHUMAN REGISTRATION ACT.
IT IS MY DUTY TO INFORM YOU THAT YOU HAVE THE RIGHT TO REMAIN SILENT. IF YOU GIVE UP THAT RIGHT, ANYTHING YOU SAY--

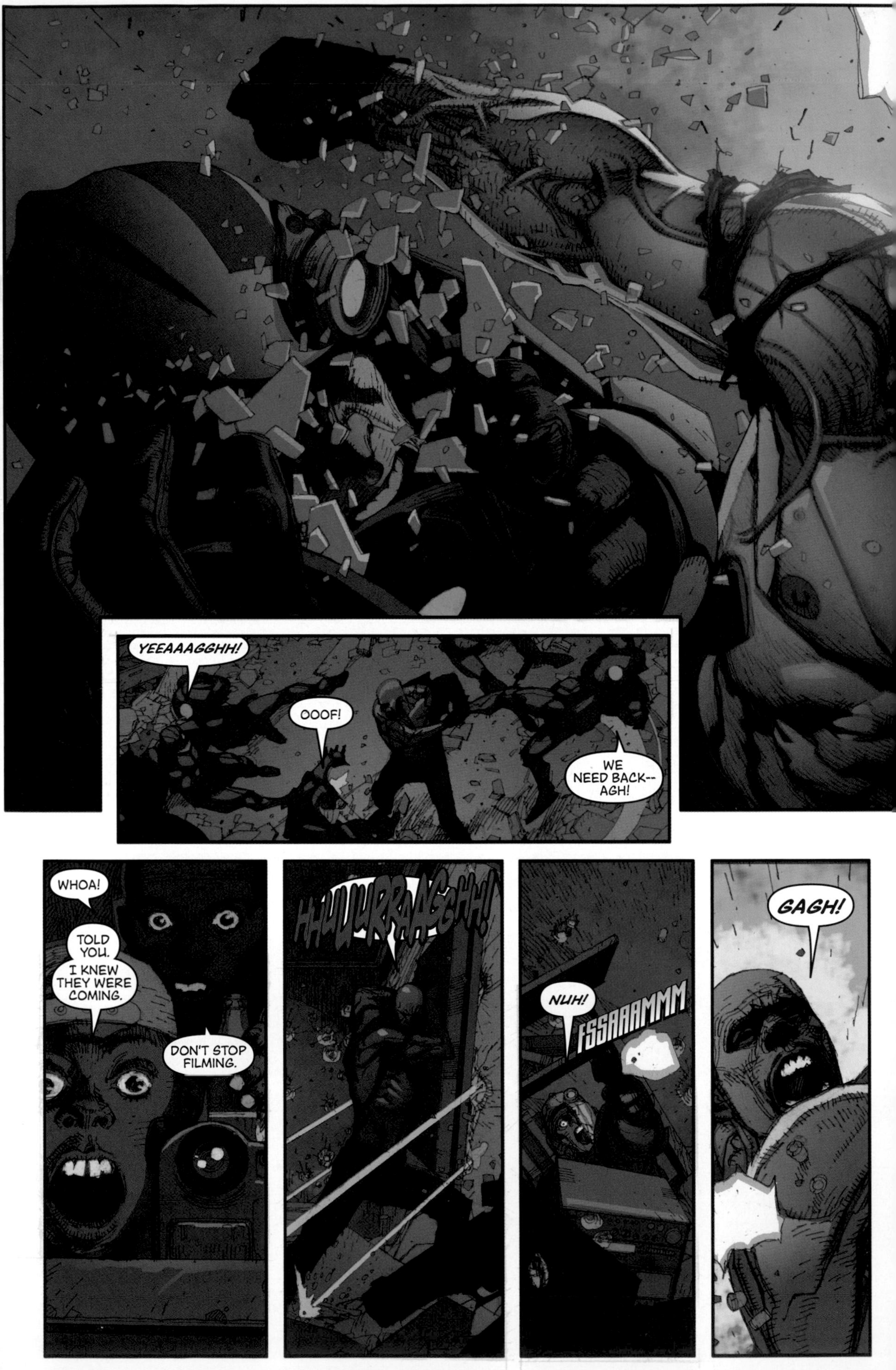
YEEAAAGGHH!
OOOF!
WE NEED BACK-- AGH!
WHOA!
TOLD YOU. I KNEW THEY WERE COMING.
DON'T STOP FILMING.
HHUUURRAAGGHH!
NUH!
FSSAAAMMM
GAGH!

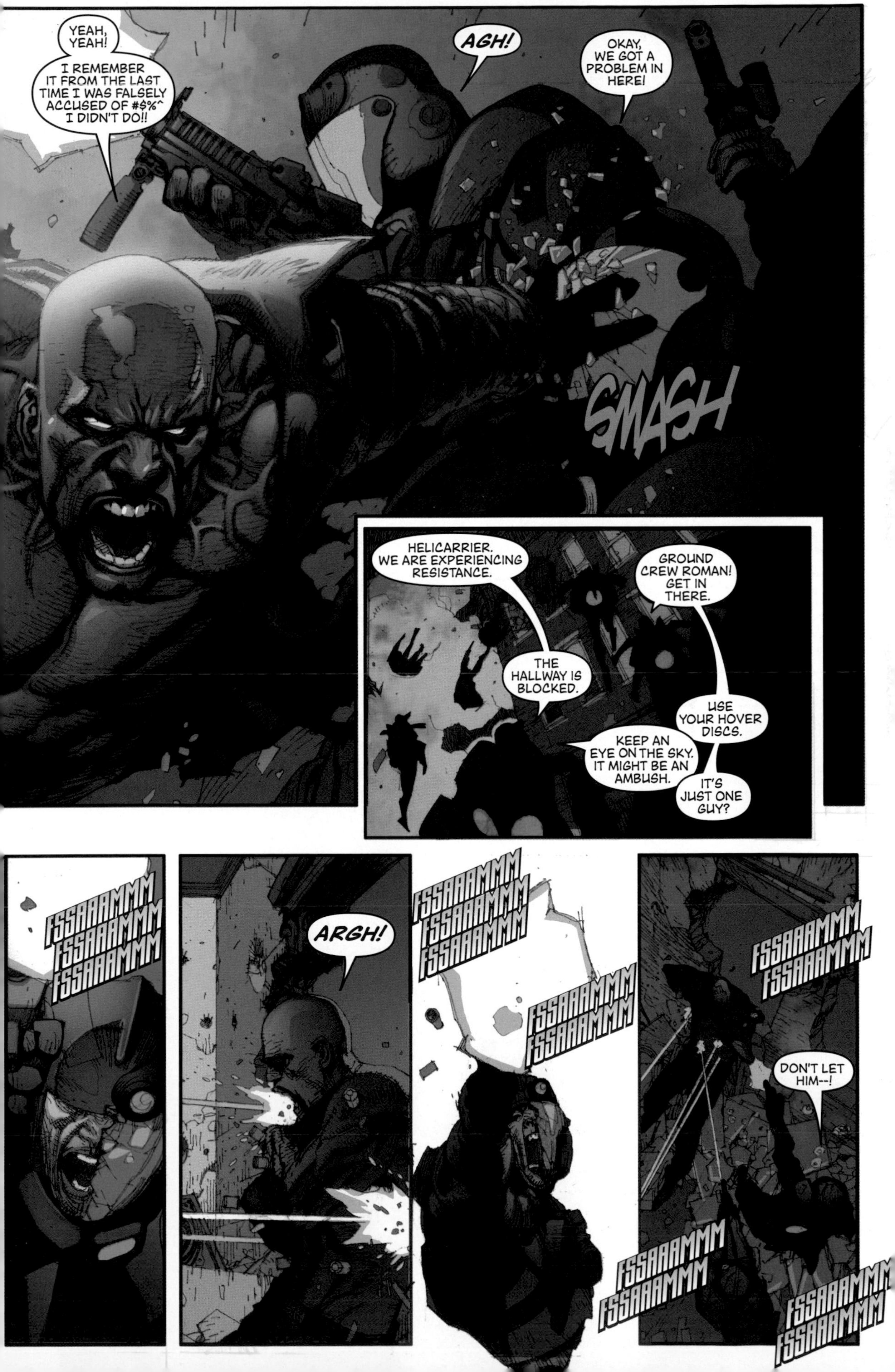
YEAH, YEAH!
I REMEMBER IT FROM THE LAST TIME I WAS FALSELY ACCUSED OF #$%^ I DIDN'T DO!!
AGH!
OKAY, WE GOT A PROBLEM IN HERE!
SMASH
HELICARRIER. WE ARE EXPERIENCING RESISTANCE.
GROUND CREW ROMAN! GET IN THERE.
THE HALLWAY IS BLOCKED.
USE YOUR HOVER DISCS.
KEEP AN EYE ON THE SKY. IT MIGHT BE AN AMBUSH.
IT'S JUST ONE GUY?
FSSAAAMMM FSSAAAMMM FSSAAAMMM
ARGH!
FSSAAAMMM FSSAAAMMM FSSAAAMMM
FSSAAAMMM FSSAAAMMM
FSSAAAMMM FSSAAAMMM
DON'T LET HIM--!
FSSAAAMMM FSSAAAMMM
FSSAAAMMM FSSAAAMMM

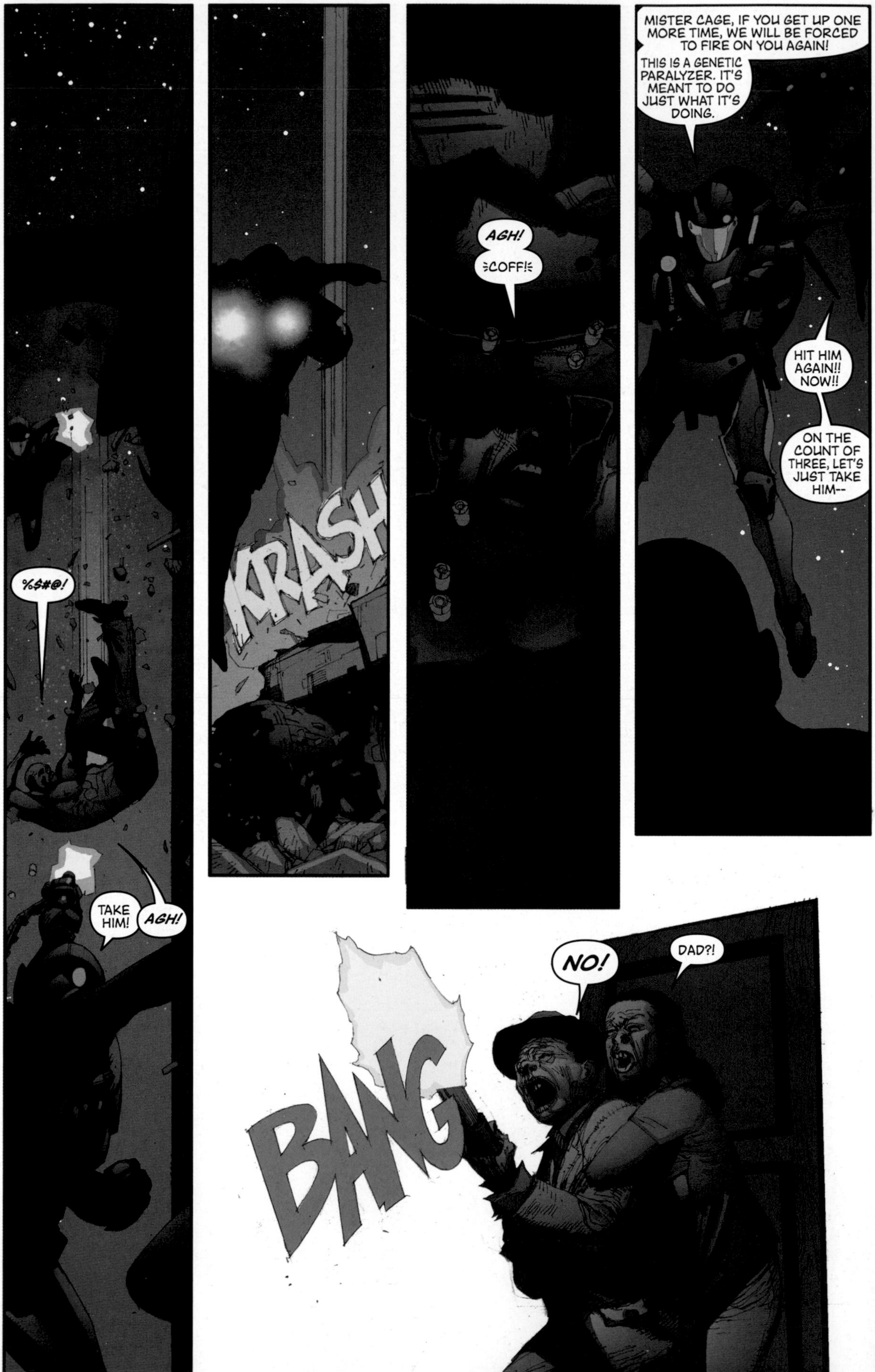
%$#@!
TAKE HIM!
AGH!
KRASH
AGH!
COFF!
MISTER CAGE, IF YOU GET UP ONE MORE TIME, WE WILL BE FORCED TO FIRE ON YOU AGAIN!
THIS IS A GENETIC PARALYZER. IT'S MEANT TO DO JUST WHAT IT'S DOING.
HIT HIM AGAIN!! NOW!!
ON THE COUNT OF THREE, LET'S JUST TAKE HIM--
BANG
NO!
DAD?!

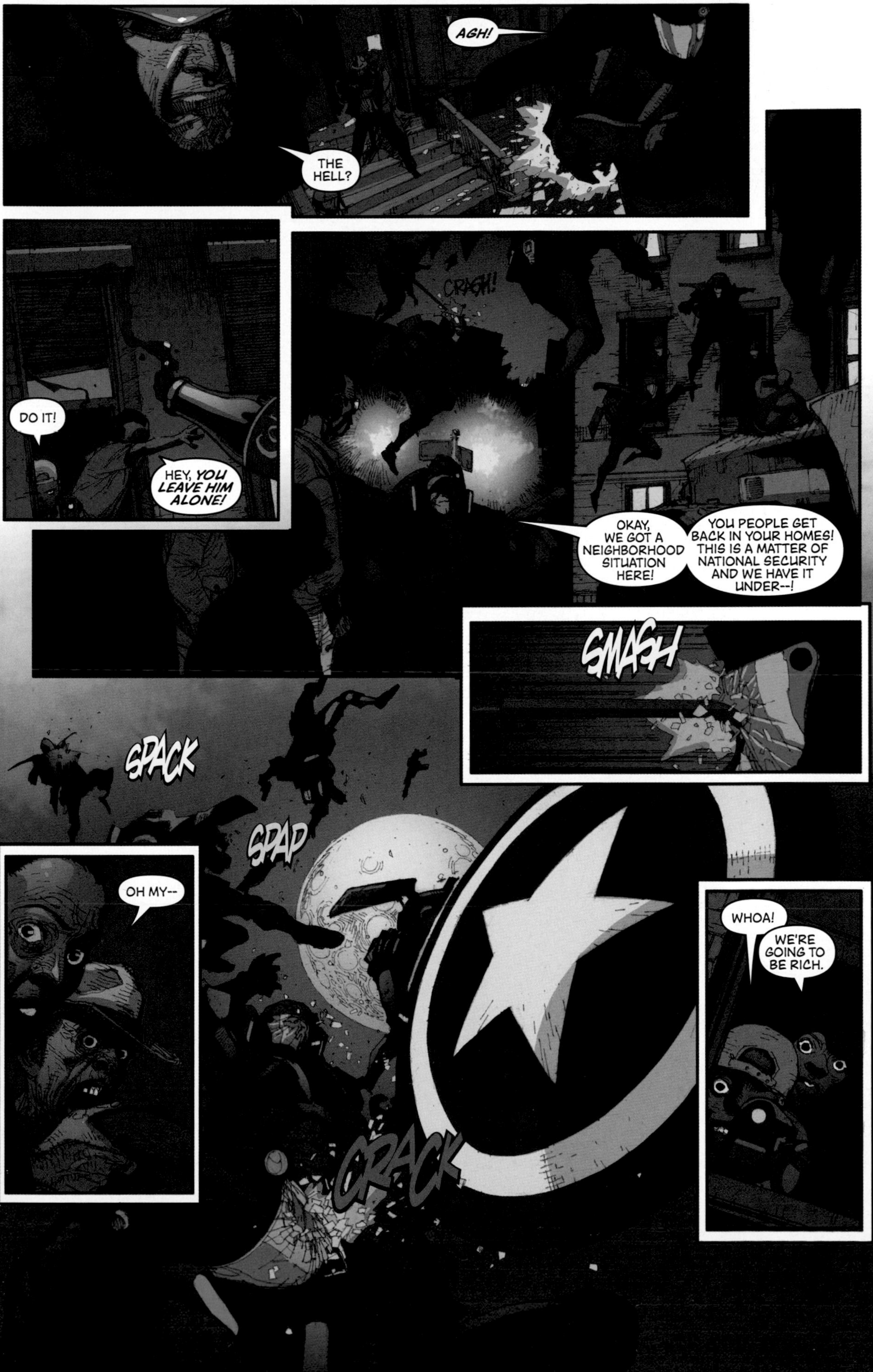
AGH!
THE HELL?
DO IT!
HEY, YOU LEAVE HIM ALONE!
CRASH!
OKAY, WE GOT A NEIGHBORHOOD SITUATION HERE!
YOU PEOPLE GET BACK IN YOUR HOMES! THIS IS A MATTER OF NATIONAL SECURITY AND WE HAVE IT UNDER--!
SMASH
SPACK
SPAP
OH MY--
WHOA!
WE'RE GOING TO BE RICH.
CRACK

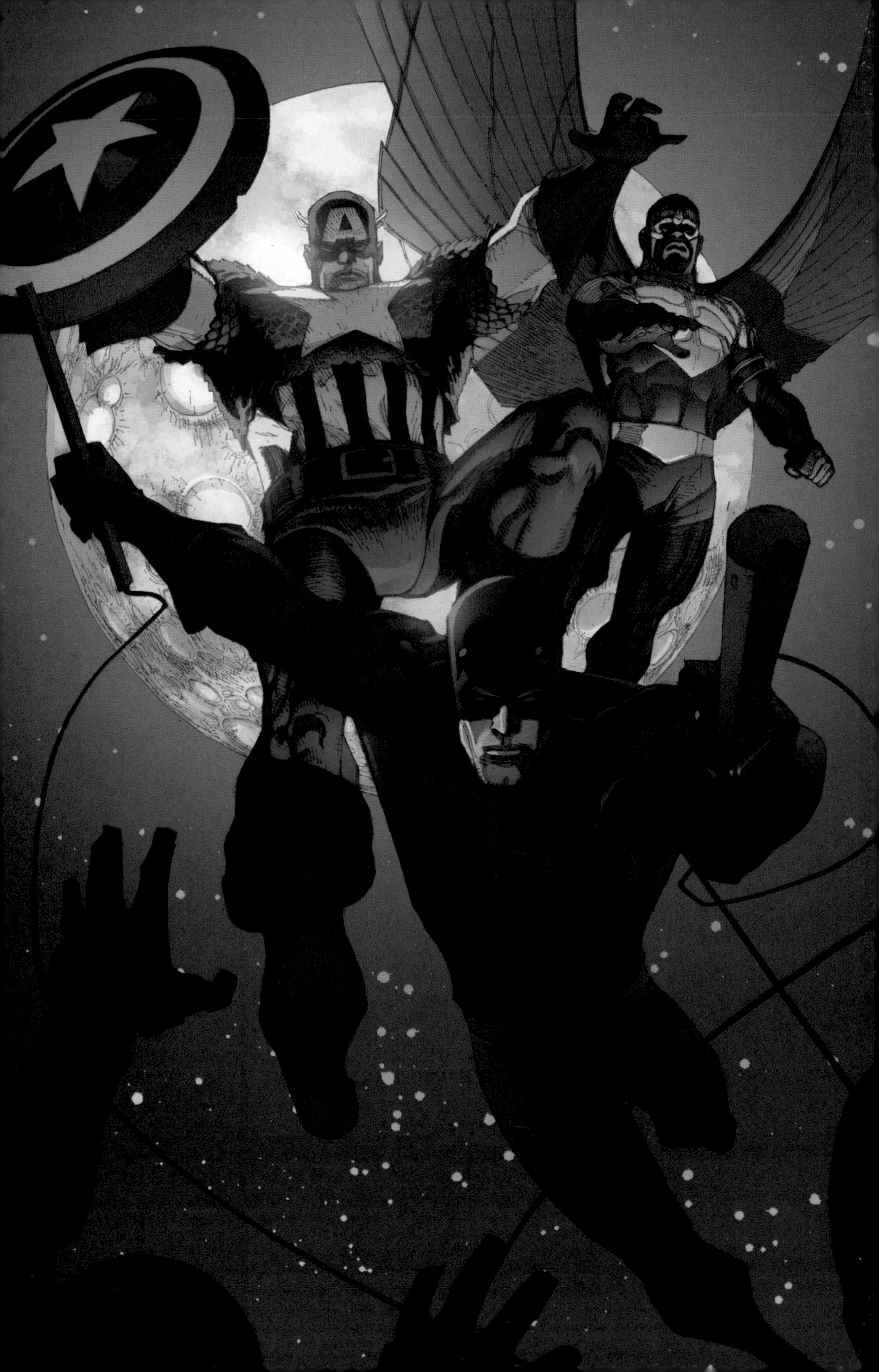

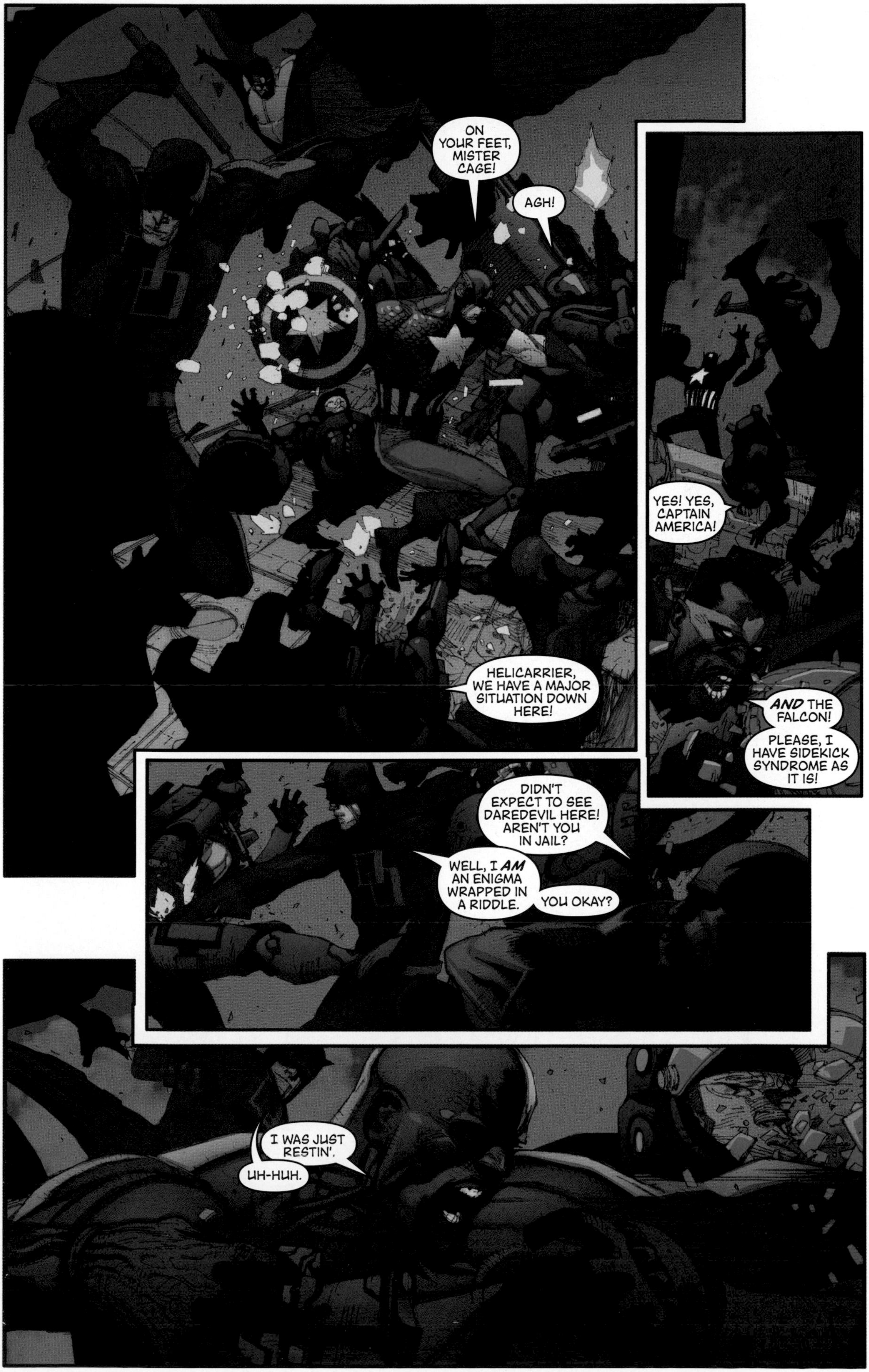
ON YOUR FEET, MISTER CAGE!
AGH!
HELICARRIER, WE HAVE A MAJOR SITUATION DOWN HERE!
YES! YES, CAPTAIN AMERICA!
AND THE FALCON!
PLEASE, I HAVE SIDEKICK SYNDROME AS IT IS!
DIDN'T EXPECT TO SEE DAREDEVIL HERE! AREN'T YOU IN JAIL?
WELL, I AM AN ENIGMA WRAPPED IN A RIDDLE.
YOU OKAY?
I WAS JUST RESTIN'.
UH-HUH.

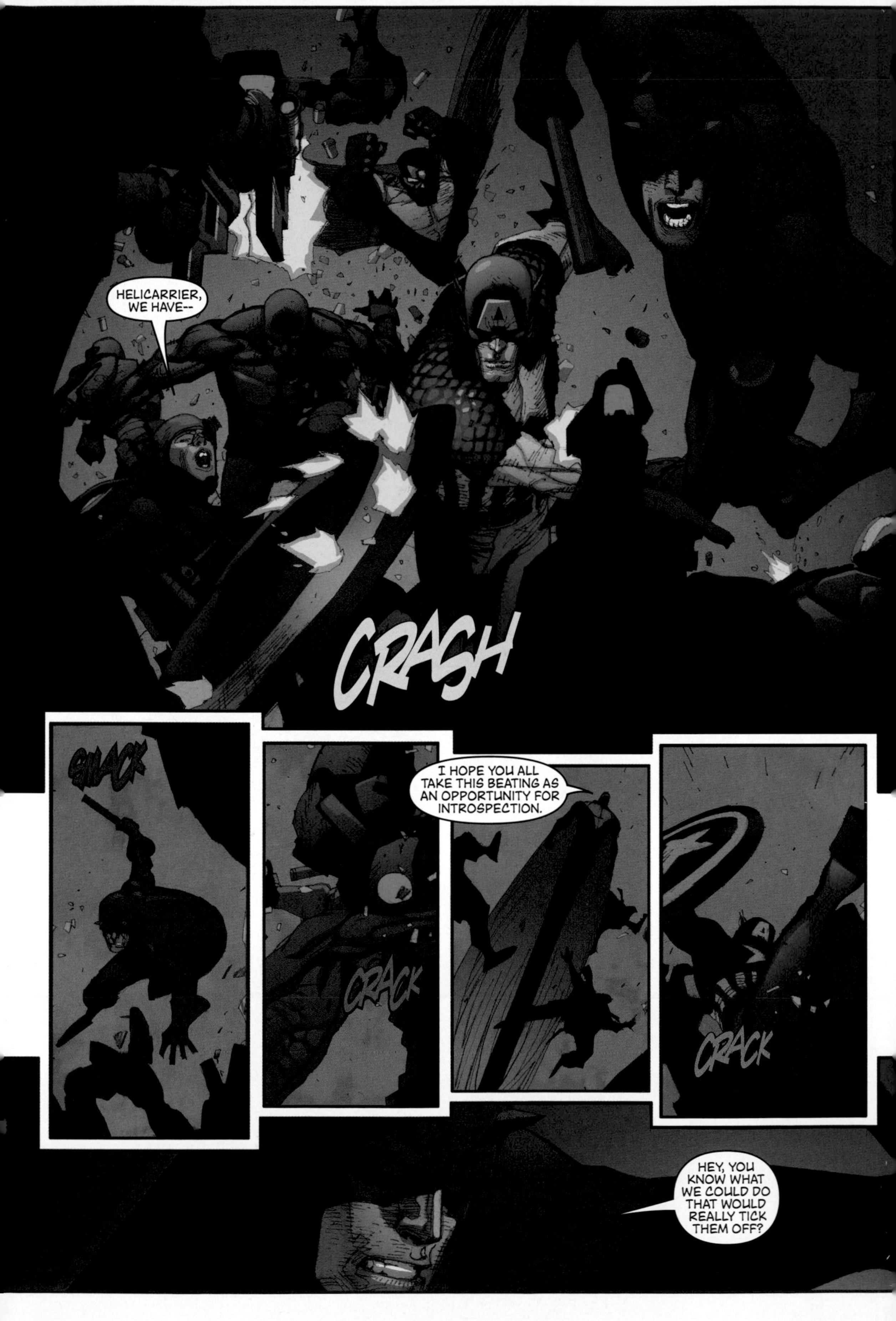
HELICARRIER, WE HAVE--
CRASH
SMACK
CRACK
I HOPE YOU ALL TAKE THIS BEATING AS AN OPPORTUNITY FOR INTROSPECTION.
CRACK
HEY, YOU KNOW WHAT WE COULD DO THAT WOULD REALLY TICK THEM OFF?

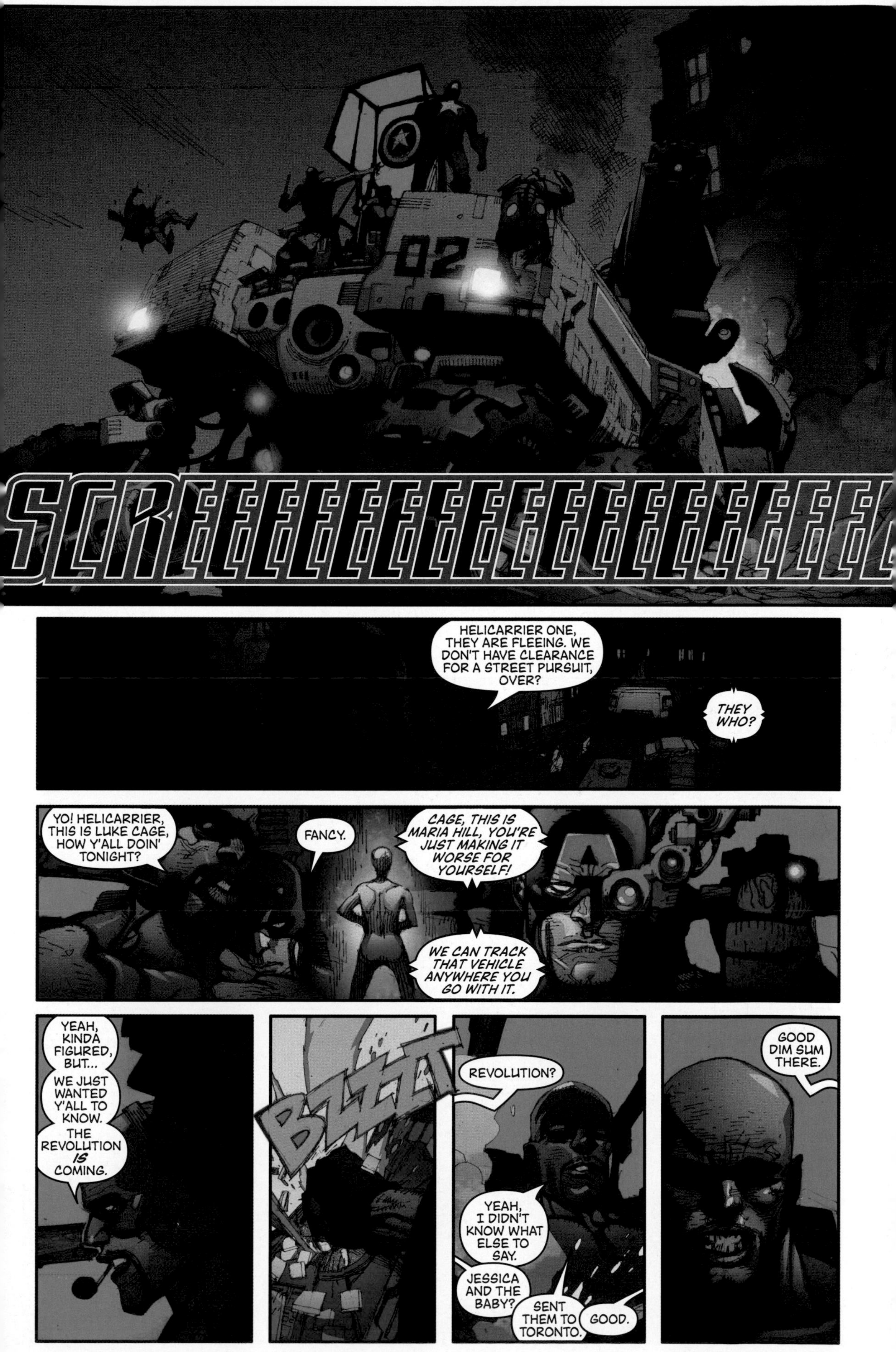
SCREEEEEEEEEEEEEEEEEEEE
HELICARRIER ONE, THEY ARE FLEEING. WE DON'T HAVE CLEARANCE FOR A STREET PURSUIT, OVER?
THEY WHO?
YO! HELICARRIER, THIS IS LUKE CAGE, HOW Y'ALL DOIN' TONIGHT?
FANCY.
CAGE, THIS IS MARIA HILL, YOU'RE JUST MAKING IT WORSE FOR YOURSELF!
WE CAN TRACK THAT VEHICLE ANYWHERE YOU GO WITH IT.
YEAH, KINDA FIGURED, BUT...
WE JUST WANTED Y'ALL TO KNOW.
THE REVOLUTION *IS* COMING.
BZZZT
REVOLUTION?
YEAH, I DIDN'T KNOW WHAT ELSE TO SAY.
JESSICA AND THE BABY?
SENT THEM TO TORONTO.
GOOD.
GOOD DIM SUM THERE.

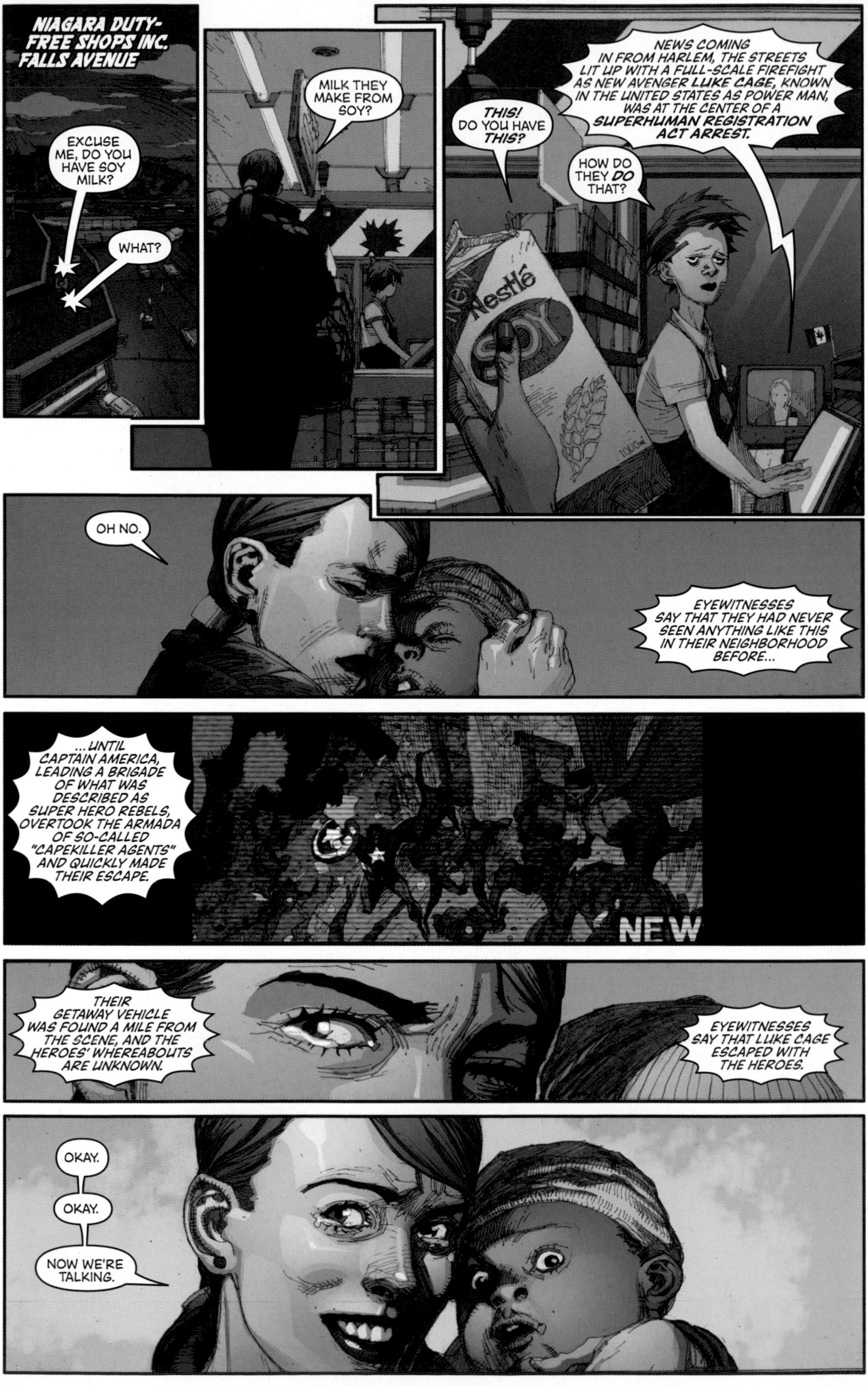
NIAGARA DUTY-FREE SHOPS INC. FALLS AVENUE
EXCUSE ME, DO YOU HAVE SOY MILK?
WHAT?
MILK THEY MAKE FROM SOY?
THIS! DO YOU HAVE THIS?
HOW DO THEY DO THAT?
NEWS COMING IN FROM HARLEM, THE STREETS LIT UP WITH A FULL-SCALE FIREFIGHT AS NEW AVENGER LUKE CAGE, KNOWN IN THE UNITED STATES AS POWER MAN, WAS AT THE CENTER OF A SUPERHUMAN REGISTRATION ACT ARREST.
Nestlé SOY
OH NO.
EYEWITNESSES SAY THAT THEY HAD NEVER SEEN ANYTHING LIKE THIS IN THEIR NEIGHBORHOOD BEFORE...
...UNTIL CAPTAIN AMERICA, LEADING A BRIGADE OF WHAT WAS DESCRIBED AS SUPER HERO REBELS, OVERTOOK THE ARMADA OF SO-CALLED "CAPEKILLER AGENTS" AND QUICKLY MADE THEIR ESCAPE.
NEW
THEIR GETAWAY VEHICLE WAS FOUND A MILE FROM THE SCENE, AND THE HEROES' WHEREABOUTS ARE UNKNOWN.
EYEWITNESSES SAY THAT LUKE CAGE ESCAPED WITH THE HEROES.
OKAY.
OKAY.
NOW WE'RE TALKING.

NEW AVENGERS

A MARVEL COMICS EVENT

CIVIL WAR

#23

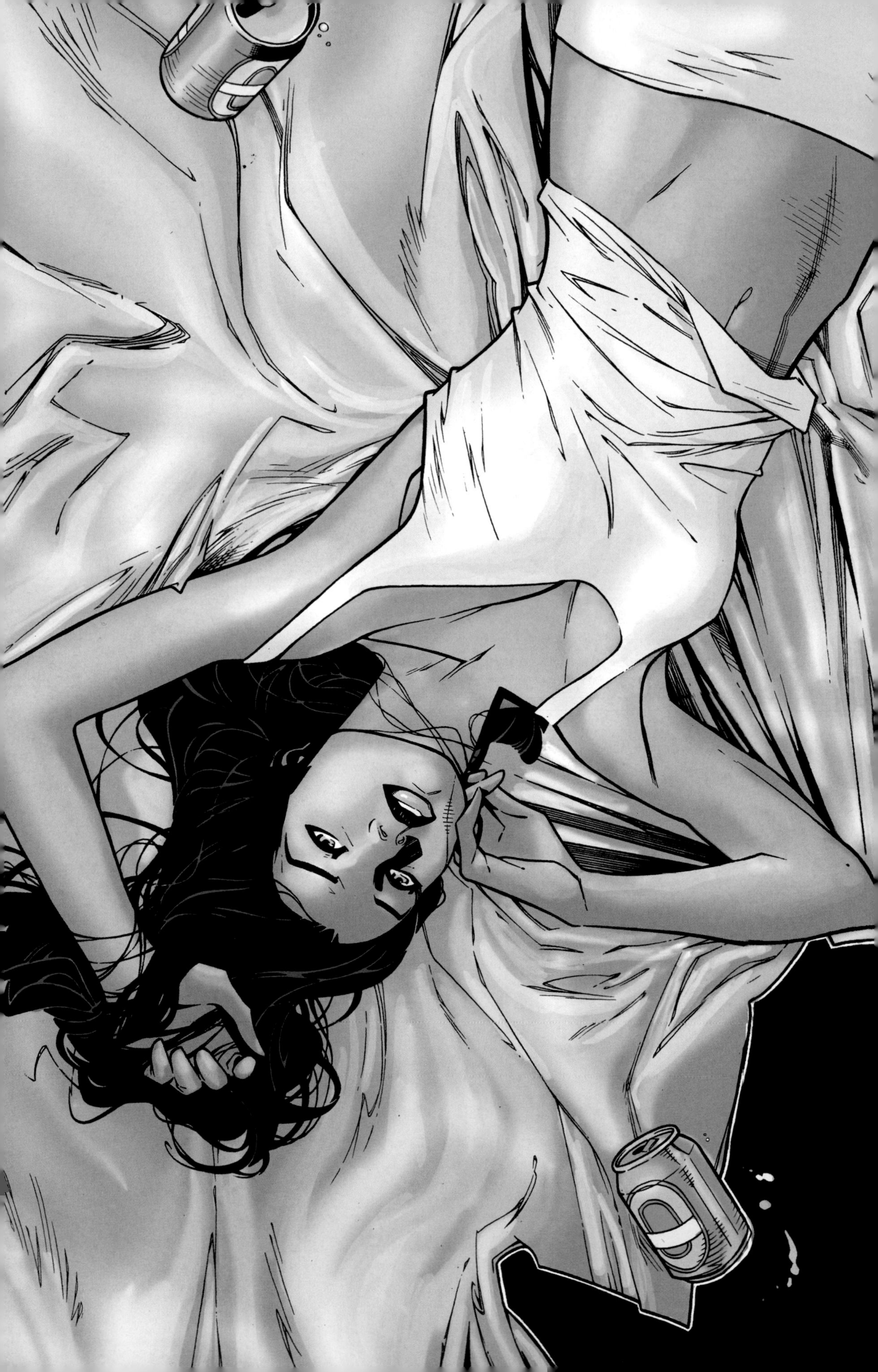

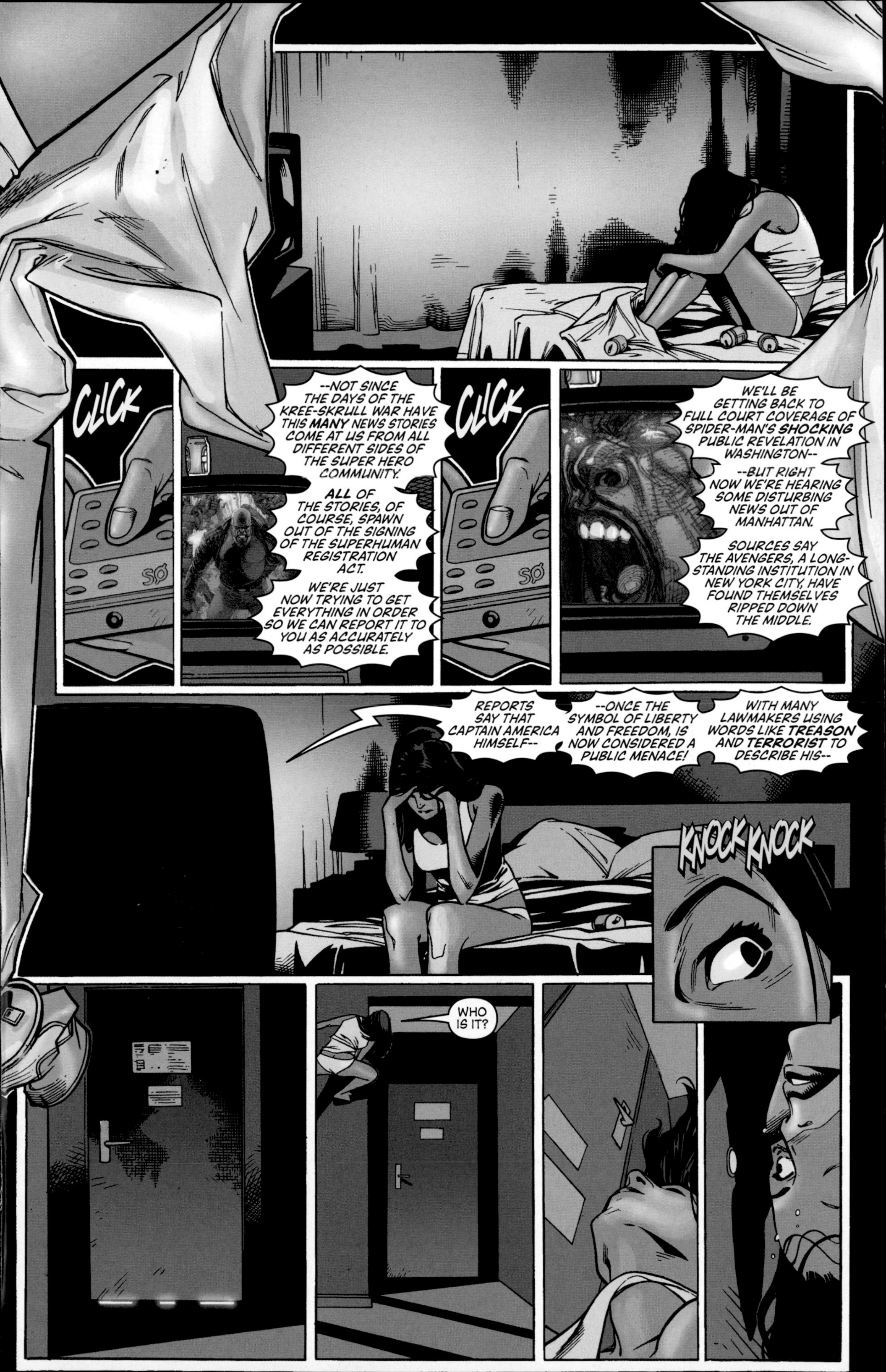
CLICK
--NOT SINCE THE DAYS OF THE KREE-SKRULL WAR HAVE THIS MANY NEWS STORIES COME AT US FROM ALL DIFFERENT SIDES OF THE SUPER HERO COMMUNITY.
ALL OF THE STORIES, OF COURSE, SPAWN OUT OF THE SIGNING OF THE SUPERHUMAN REGISTRATION ACT.
WE'RE JUST NOW TRYING TO GET EVERYTHING IN ORDER SO WE CAN REPORT IT TO YOU AS ACCURATELY AS POSSIBLE.
CLICK
WE'LL BE GETTING BACK TO FULL COURT COVERAGE OF SPIDER-MAN'S SHOCKING PUBLIC REVELATION IN WASHINGTON--
--BUT RIGHT NOW WE'RE HEARING SOME DISTURBING NEWS OUT OF MANHATTAN.
SOURCES SAY THE AVENGERS, A LONG-STANDING INSTITUTION IN NEW YORK CITY, HAVE FOUND THEMSELVES RIPPED DOWN THE MIDDLE.
REPORTS SAY THAT CAPTAIN AMERICA HIMSELF--
--ONCE THE SYMBOL OF LIBERTY AND FREEDOM, IS NOW CONSIDERED A PUBLIC MENACE!
WITH MANY LAWMAKERS USING WORDS LIKE TREASON AND TERRORIST TO DESCRIBE HIS--
KNOCK KNOCK
WHO IS IT?

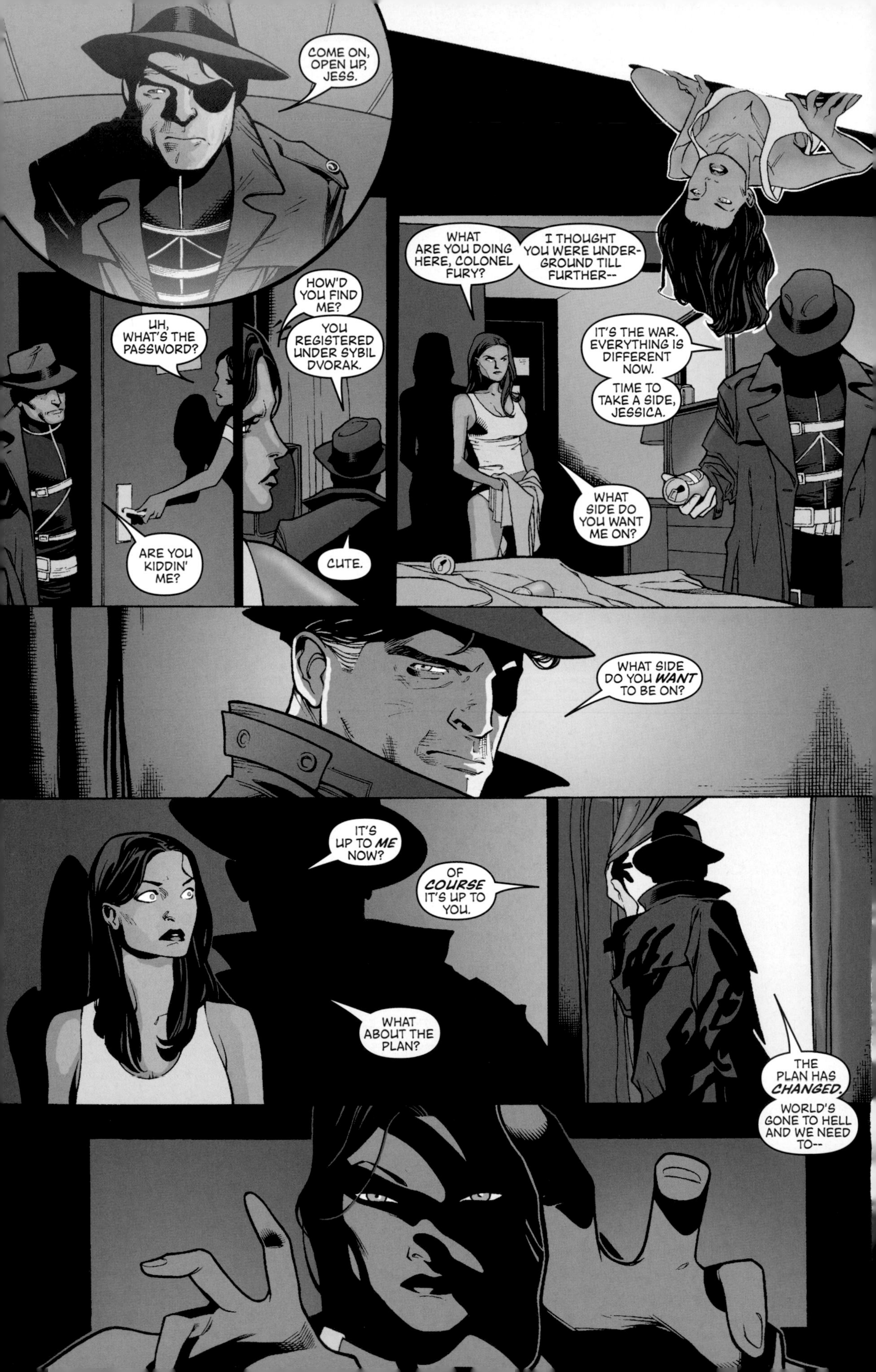
COME ON, OPEN UP, JESS.
UH, WHAT'S THE PASSWORD?
ARE YOU KIDDIN' ME?
HOW'D YOU FIND ME?
YOU REGISTERED UNDER SYBIL DVORAK.
CUTE.
WHAT ARE YOU DOING HERE, COLONEL FURY?
I THOUGHT YOU WERE UNDER-GROUND TILL FURTHER--
IT'S THE WAR. EVERYTHING IS DIFFERENT NOW.
TIME TO TAKE A SIDE, JESSICA.
WHAT SIDE DO YOU WANT ME ON?
WHAT SIDE DO YOU *WANT* TO BE ON?
IT'S UP TO *ME* NOW?
OF *COURSE* IT'S UP TO YOU.
WHAT ABOUT THE PLAN?
THE PLAN HAS *CHANGED.*
WORLD'S GONE TO HELL AND WE NEED TO--

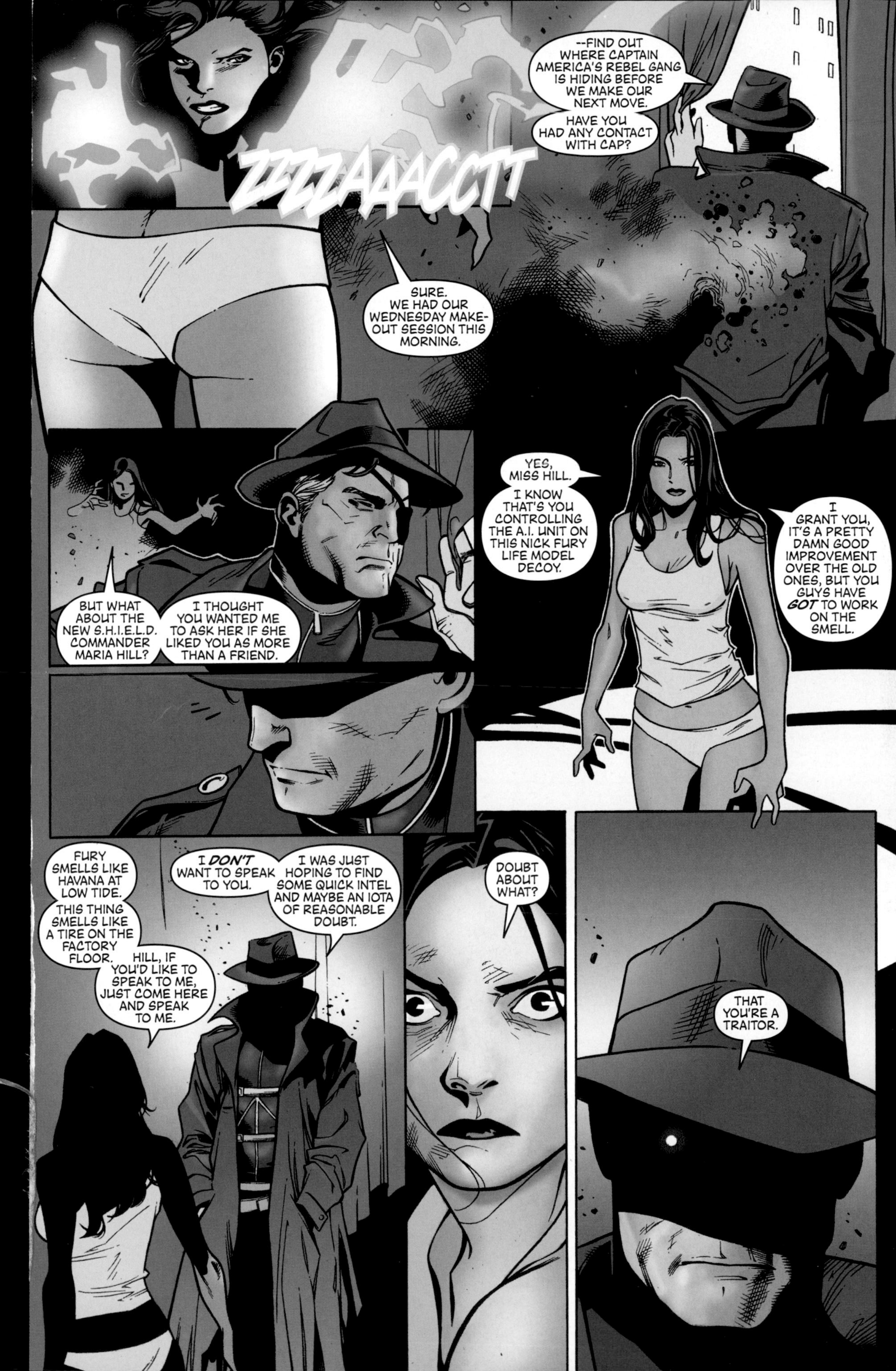

--FIND OUT WHERE CAPTAIN AMERICA'S REBEL GANG IS HIDING BEFORE WE MAKE OUR NEXT MOVE.
HAVE YOU HAD ANY CONTACT WITH CAP?
ZZZZAAACCTT
SURE. WE HAD OUR WEDNESDAY MAKE-OUT SESSION THIS MORNING.
BUT WHAT ABOUT THE NEW S.H.I.E.L.D. COMMANDER MARIA HILL?
I THOUGHT YOU WANTED ME TO ASK HER IF SHE LIKED YOU AS MORE THAN A FRIEND.
YES, MISS HILL.
I KNOW THAT'S YOU CONTROLLING THE A.I. UNIT ON THIS NICK FURY LIFE MODEL DECOY.
I GRANT YOU, IT'S A PRETTY DAMN GOOD IMPROVEMENT OVER THE OLD ONES, BUT YOU GUYS HAVE *GOT* TO WORK ON THE SMELL.
FURY SMELLS LIKE HAVANA AT LOW TIDE.
THIS THING SMELLS LIKE A TIRE ON THE FACTORY FLOOR.
HILL, IF YOU'D LIKE TO SPEAK TO ME, JUST COME HERE AND SPEAK TO ME.
I *DON'T* WANT TO SPEAK TO YOU.
I WAS JUST HOPING TO FIND SOME QUICK INTEL AND MAYBE AN IOTA OF REASONABLE DOUBT.
DOUBT ABOUT WHAT?
THAT YOU'RE A TRAITOR.

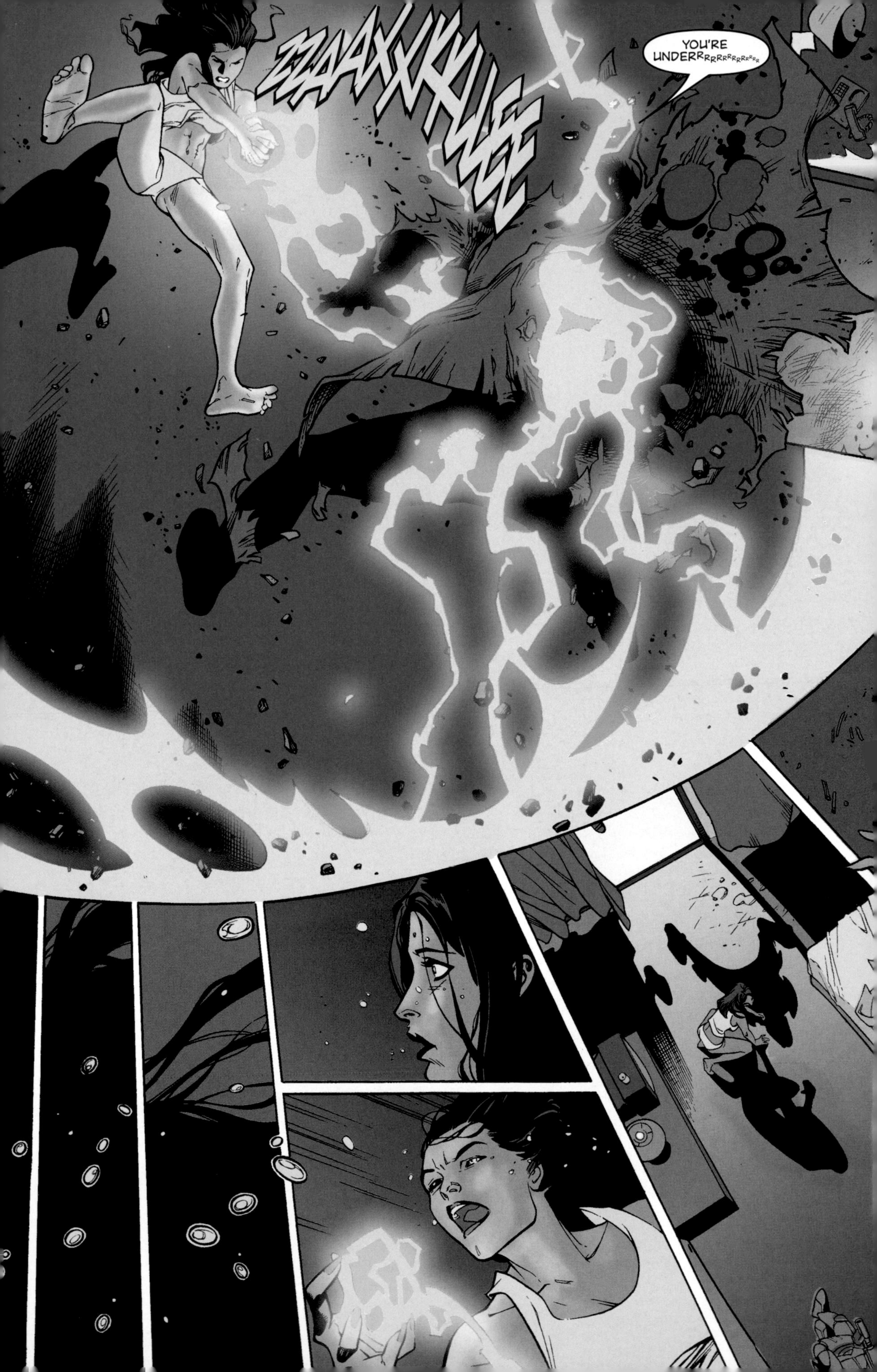
ZZAAXXKKLLEE
YOU'RE UNDERRRRRRRRRRRR

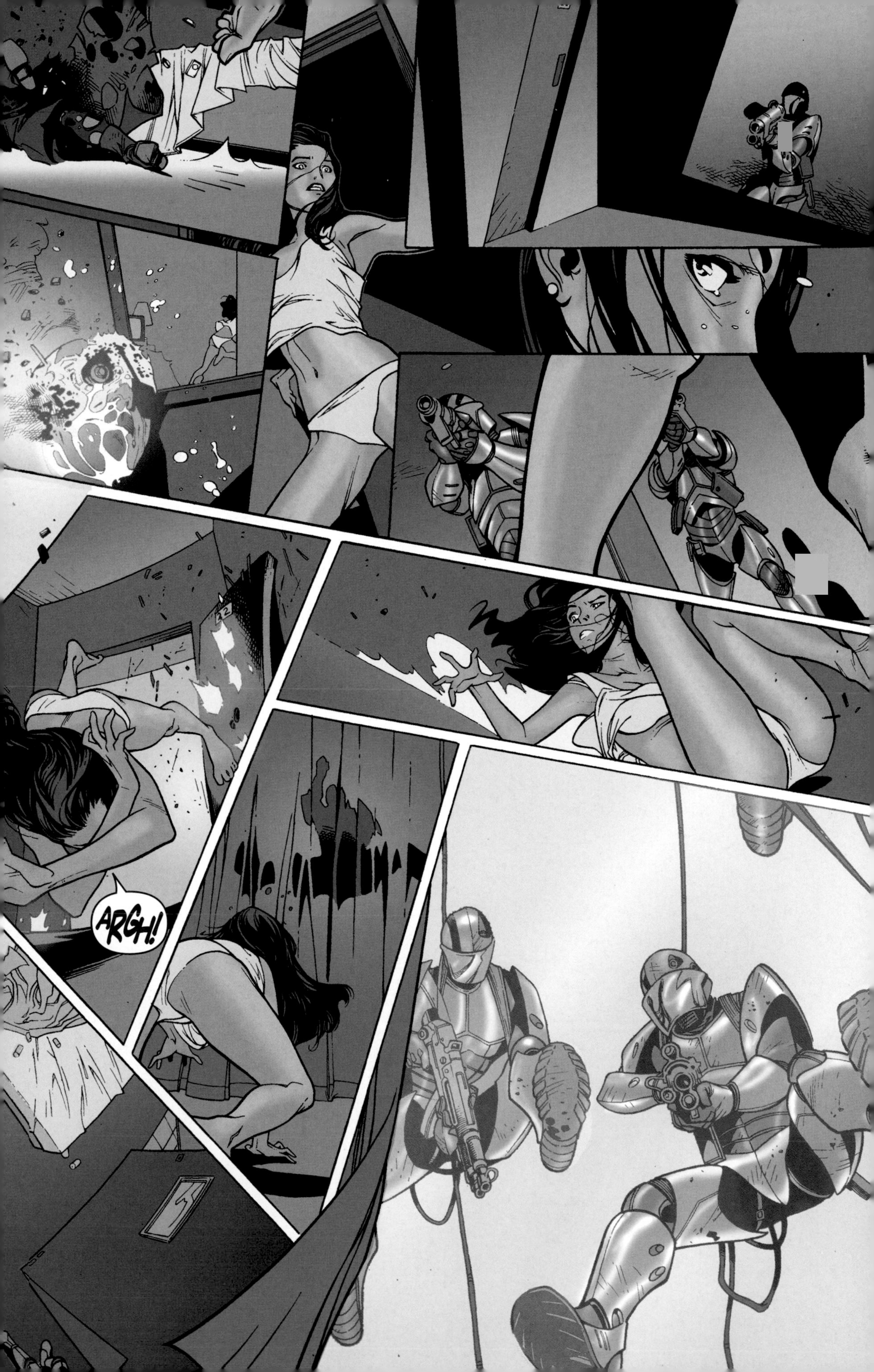
ARGH!

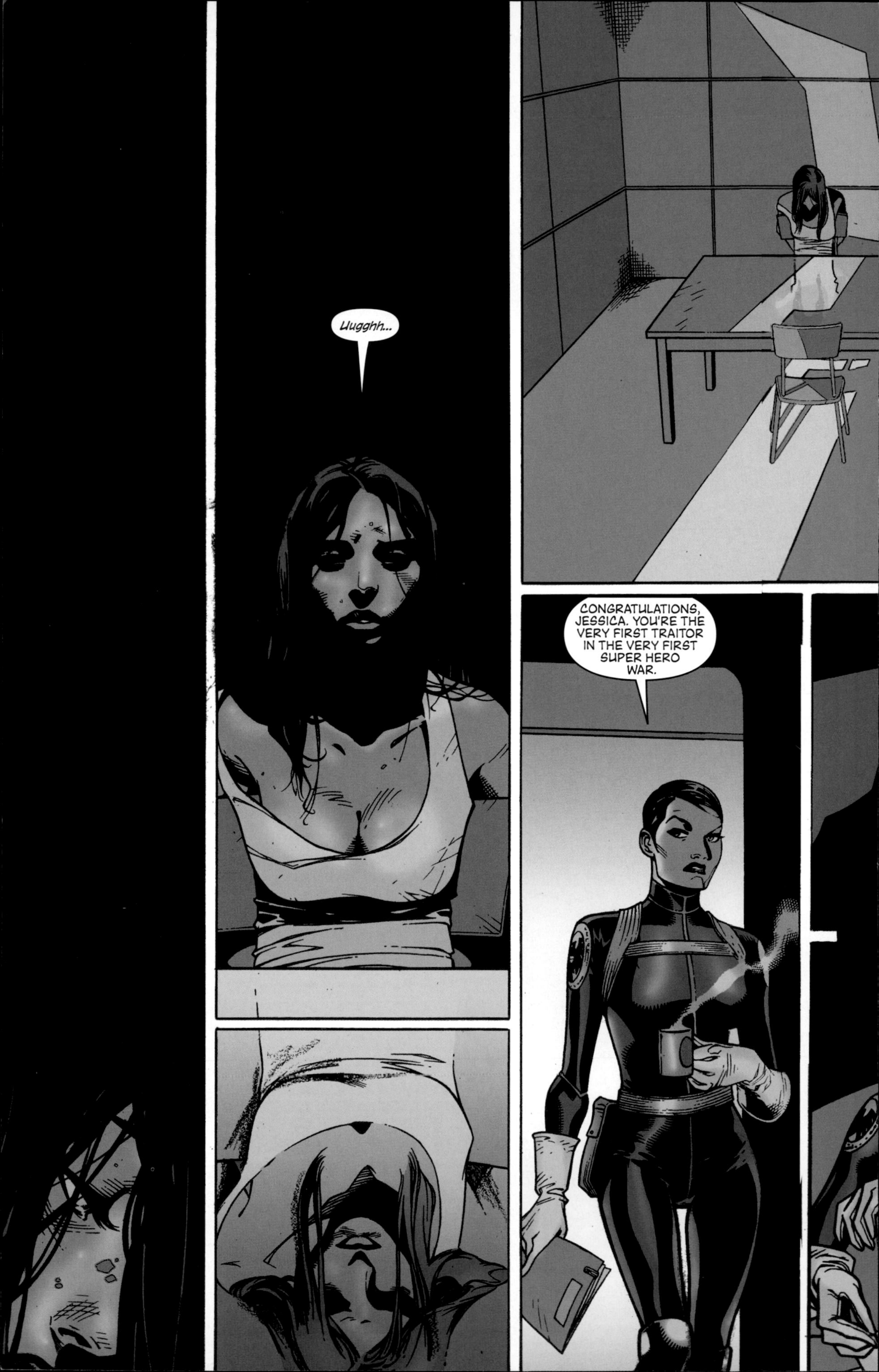
Uugghh...
CONGRATULATIONS, JESSICA. YOU'RE THE VERY FIRST TRAITOR IN THE VERY FIRST SUPER HERO WAR.

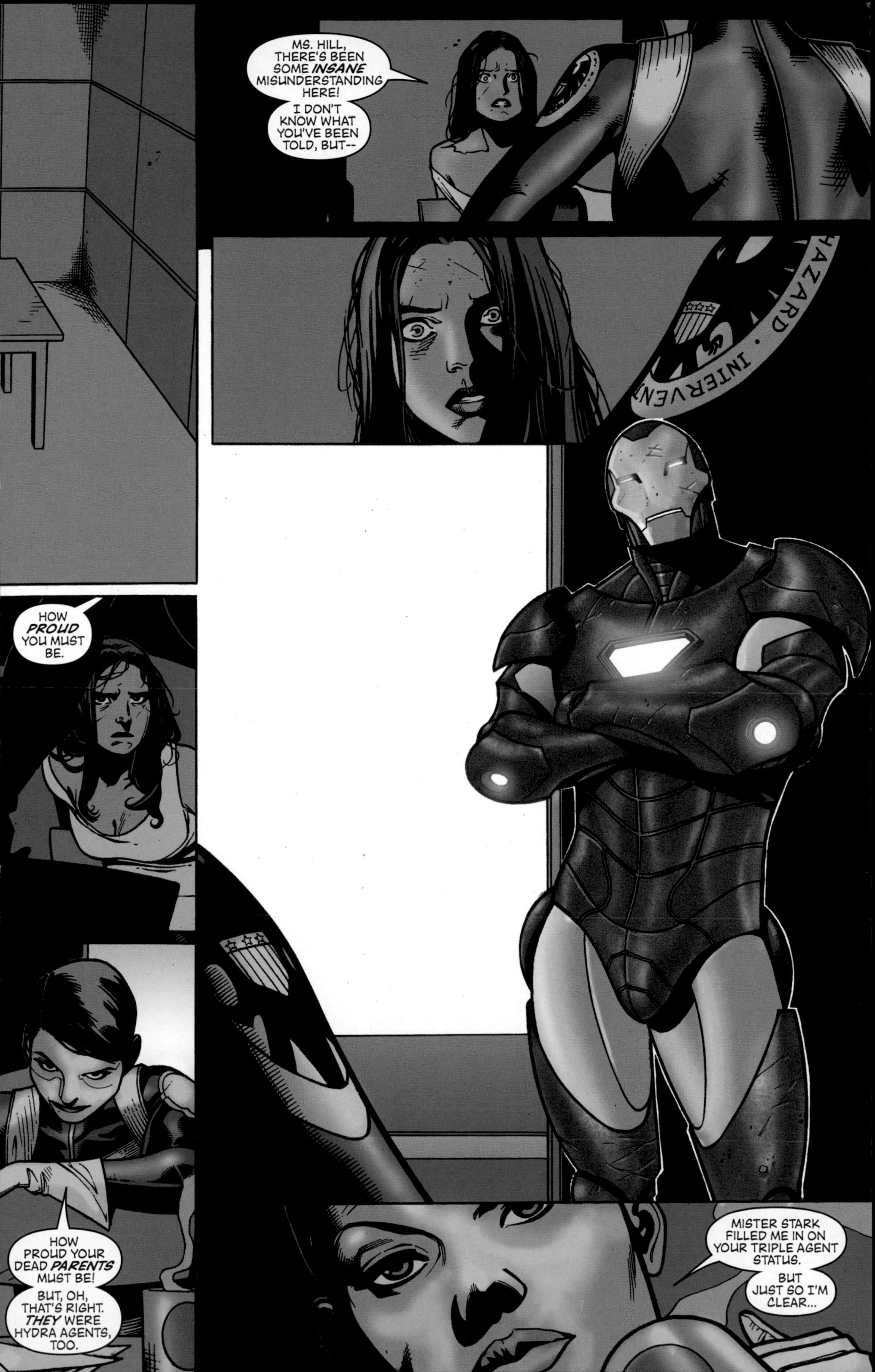
MS. HILL, THERE'S BEEN SOME *INSANE* MISUNDERSTANDING HERE!
I DON'T KNOW WHAT YOU'VE BEEN TOLD, BUT--
HAZARD · INTERVEN
HOW *PROUD* YOU MUST BE.
HOW PROUD YOUR DEAD *PARENTS* MUST BE!
BUT, OH, THAT'S RIGHT. *THEY* WERE HYDRA AGENTS, TOO.
MISTER STARK FILLED ME IN ON YOUR TRIPLE AGENT STATUS.
BUT JUST SO I'M CLEAR...

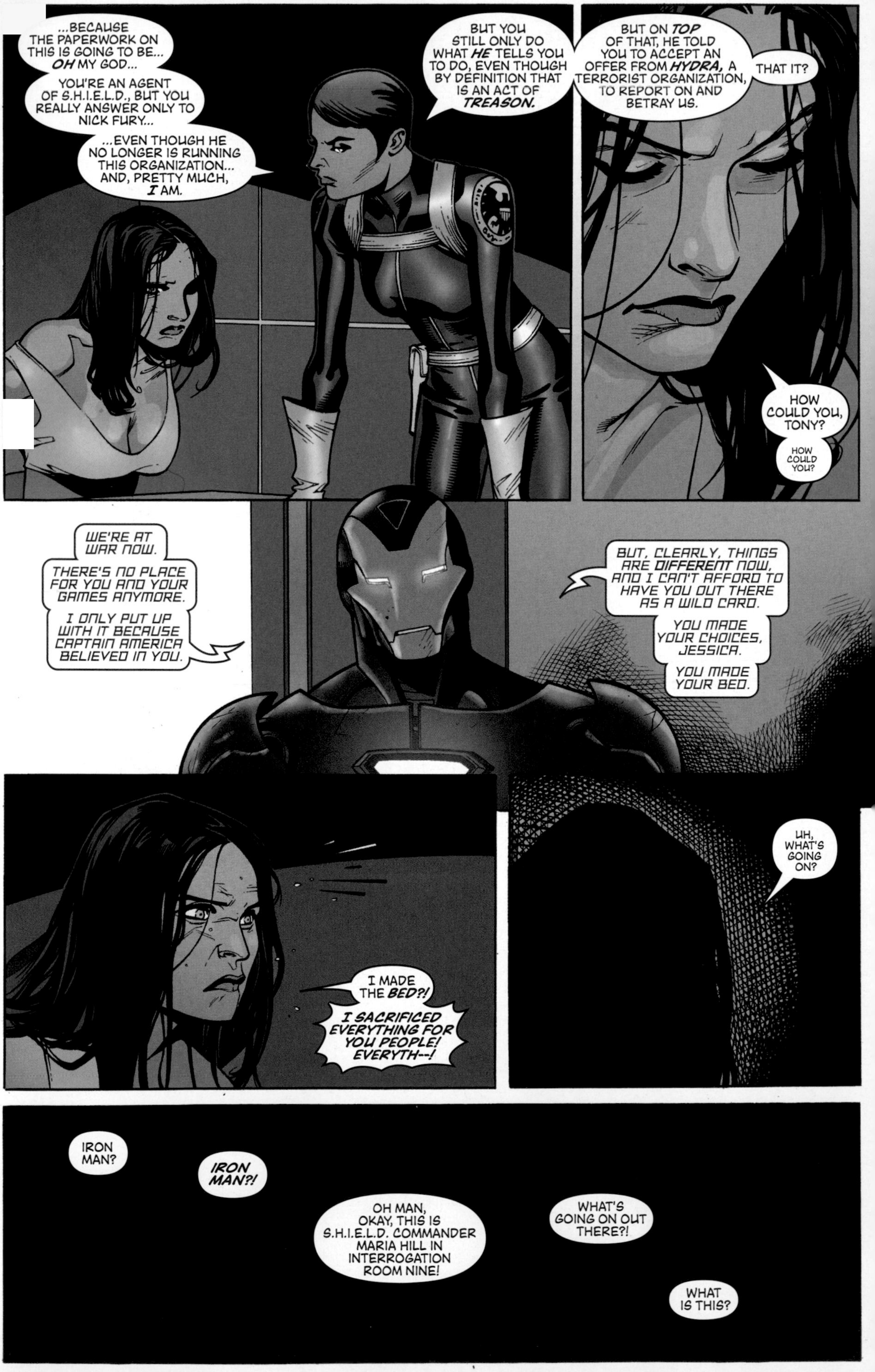
...BECAUSE THE PAPERWORK ON THIS IS GOING TO BE... OH MY GOD...
YOU'RE AN AGENT OF S.H.I.E.L.D., BUT YOU REALLY ANSWER ONLY TO NICK FURY...
...EVEN THOUGH HE NO LONGER IS RUNNING THIS ORGANIZATION... AND, PRETTY MUCH, I AM.
BUT YOU STILL ONLY DO WHAT HE TELLS YOU TO DO, EVEN THOUGH BY DEFINITION THAT IS AN ACT OF TREASON.
BUT ON TOP OF THAT, HE TOLD YOU TO ACCEPT AN OFFER FROM HYDRA, A TERRORIST ORGANIZATION, TO REPORT ON AND BETRAY US.
THAT IT?
HOW COULD YOU, TONY?
HOW COULD YOU?
WE'RE AT WAR NOW.
THERE'S NO PLACE FOR YOU AND YOUR GAMES ANYMORE.
I ONLY PUT UP WITH IT BECAUSE CAPTAIN AMERICA BELIEVED IN YOU.
BUT, CLEARLY, THINGS ARE DIFFERENT NOW, AND I CAN'T AFFORD TO HAVE YOU OUT THERE AS A WILD CARD.
YOU MADE YOUR CHOICES, JESSICA.
YOU MADE YOUR BED.
I MADE THE BED?!
I SACRIFICED EVERYTHING FOR YOU PEOPLE! EVERYTH--!
UH, WHAT'S GOING ON?
IRON MAN?
IRON MAN?!
OH MAN, OKAY, THIS IS S.H.I.E.L.D. COMMANDER MARIA HILL IN INTERROGATION ROOM NINE!
WHAT'S GOING ON OUT THERE?!
WHAT IS THIS?

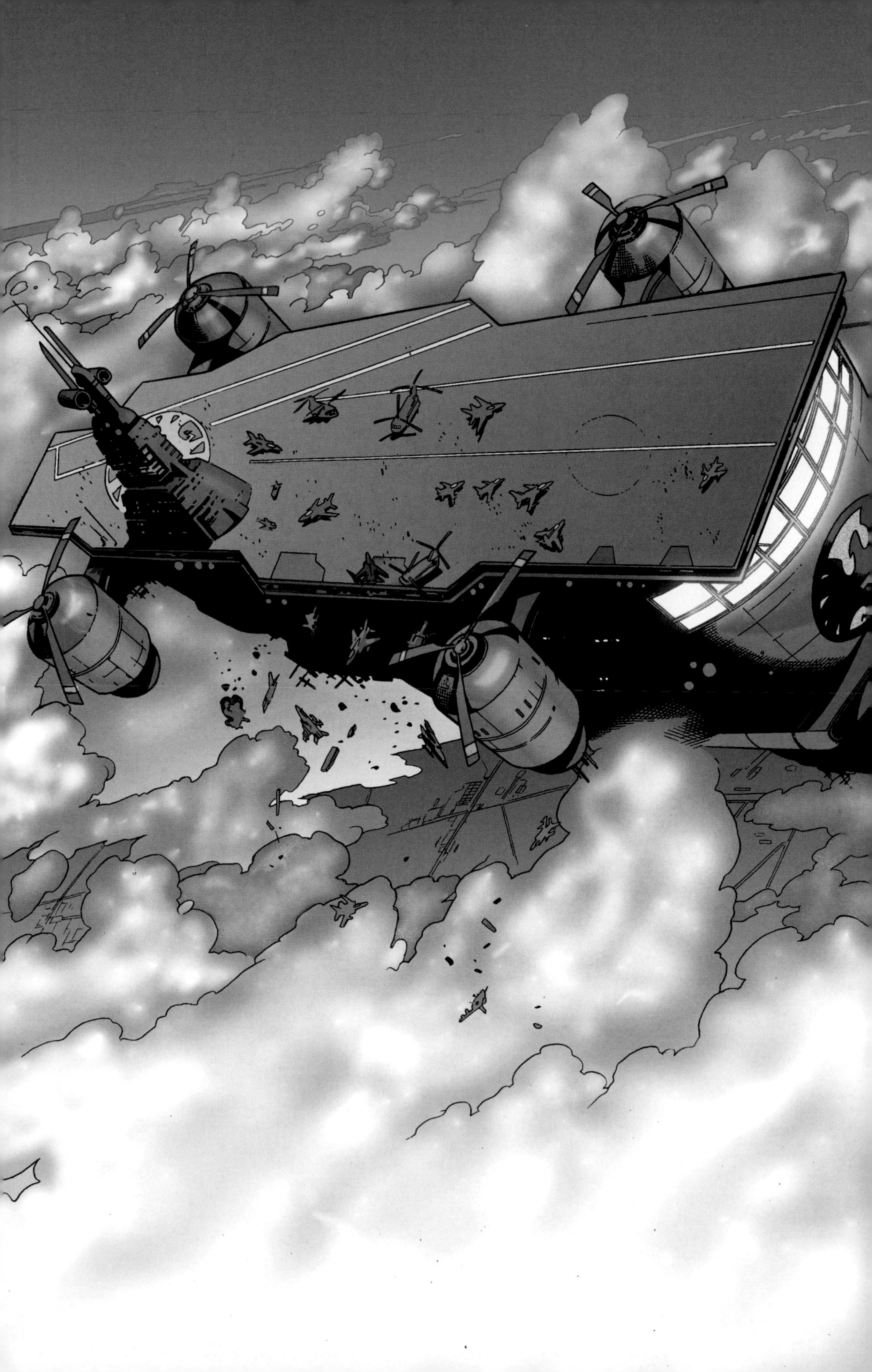

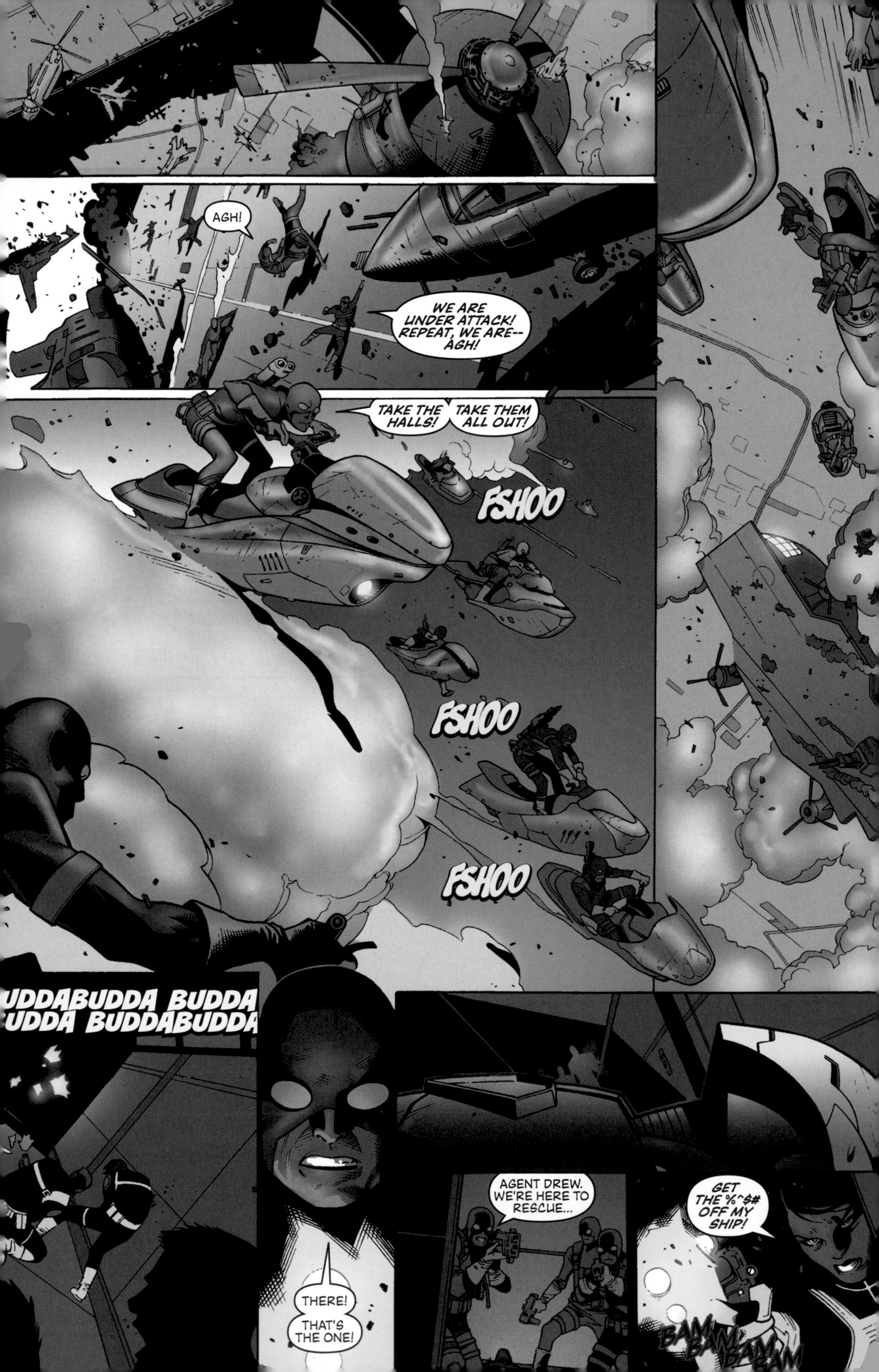
AGH!
WE ARE UNDER ATTACK! REPEAT, WE ARE-- AGH!
TAKE THE HALLS!
TAKE THEM ALL OUT!
FSHOO
FSHOO
FSHOO
UDDABUDDA BUDDA UDDA BUDDABUDDA
THERE!
THAT'S THE ONE!
AGENT DREW. WE'RE HERE TO RESCUE...
GET THE %^$# OFF MY SHIP!
BAM BAM BAM BAM

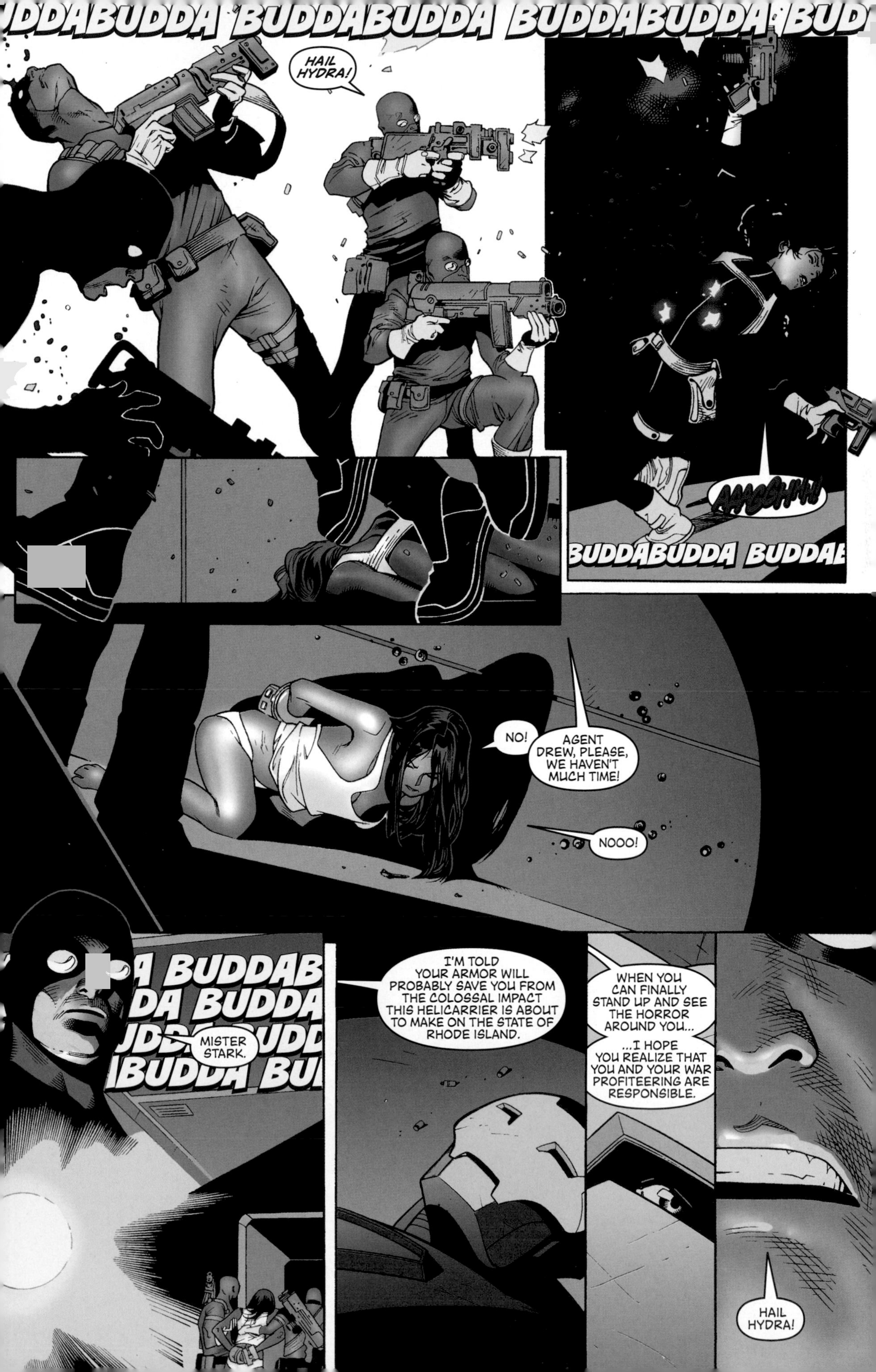
DDABUDDA BUDDABUDDA BUDDABUDDA
HAIL HYDRA!
AAAGGHHH!
BUDDABUDDA BUDDA
NO!
AGENT DREW, PLEASE, WE HAVEN'T MUCH TIME!
NOOO!
A BUDDAB
DA BUDDA
BUDDA BU
MISTER STARK.
I'M TOLD YOUR ARMOR WILL PROBABLY SAVE YOU FROM THE COLOSSAL IMPACT THIS HELICARRIER IS ABOUT TO MAKE ON THE STATE OF RHODE ISLAND.
WHEN YOU CAN FINALLY STAND UP AND SEE THE HORROR AROUND YOU...
...I HOPE YOU REALIZE THAT YOU AND YOUR WAR PROFITEERING ARE RESPONSIBLE.
HAIL HYDRA!

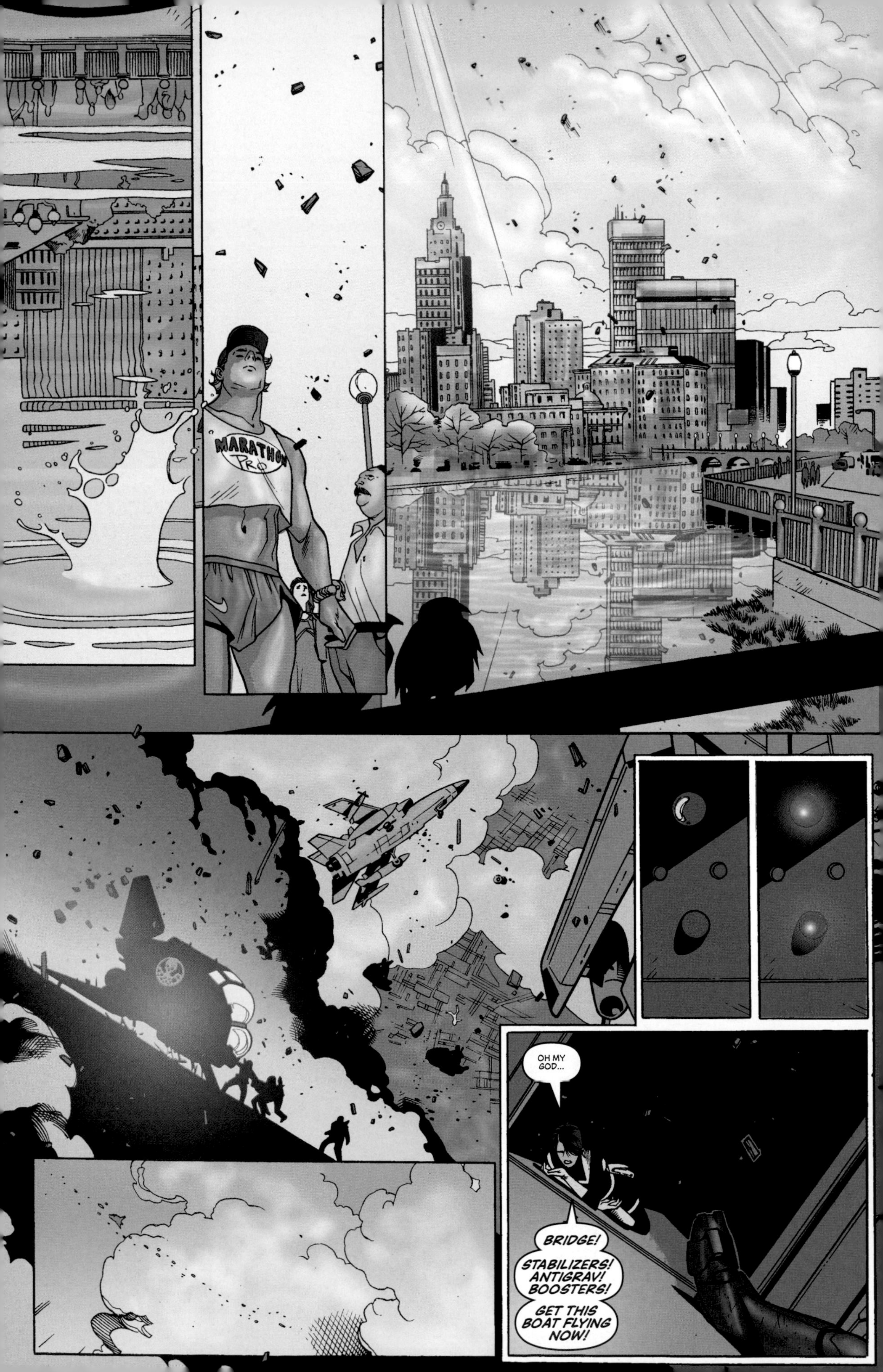
MARATHON
PRO
OH MY GOD...
BRIDGE!
STABILIZERS! ANTIGRAV! BOOSTERS!
GET THIS BOAT FLYING NOW!

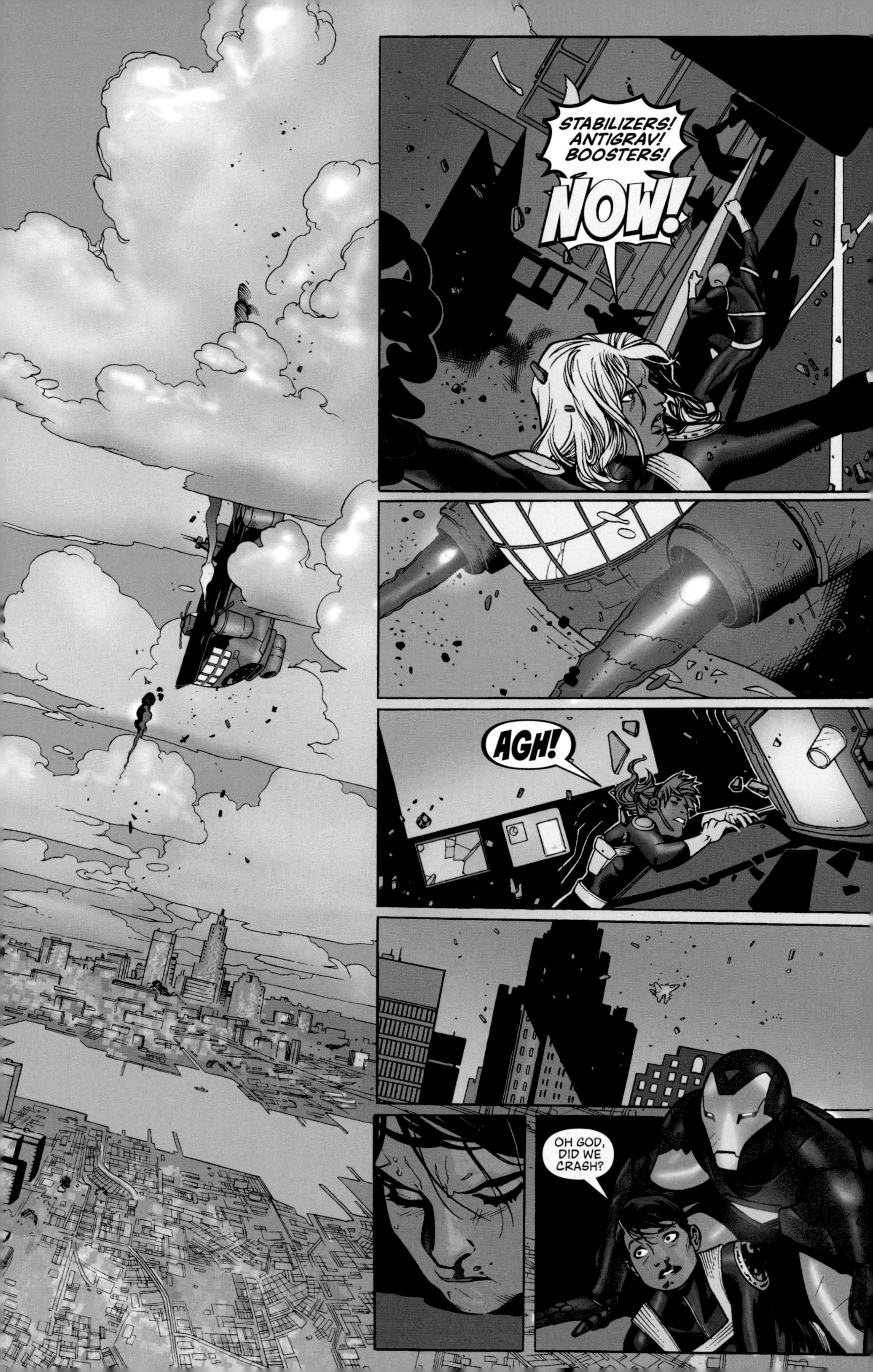
STABILIZERS! ANTIGRAV! BOOSTERS!
NOW!
AGH!
OH GOD, DID WE CRASH?

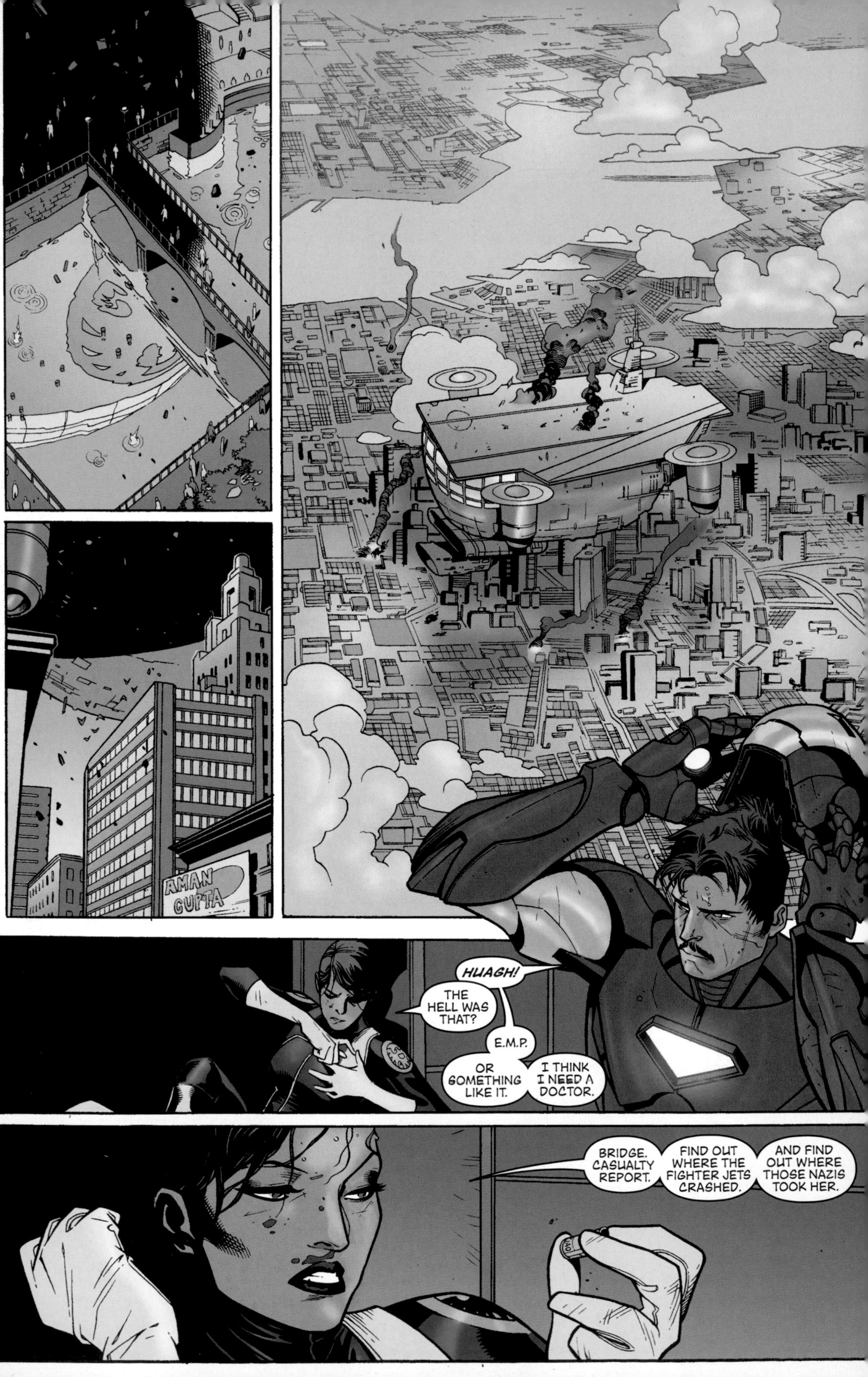
AMAN GUPTA
HUAGH!
THE HELL WAS THAT?
E.M.P.
OR SOMETHING LIKE IT.
I THINK I NEED A DOCTOR.
BRIDGE. CASUALTY REPORT.
FIND OUT WHERE THE FIGHTER JETS CRASHED.
AND FIND OUT WHERE THOSE NAZIS TOOK HER.

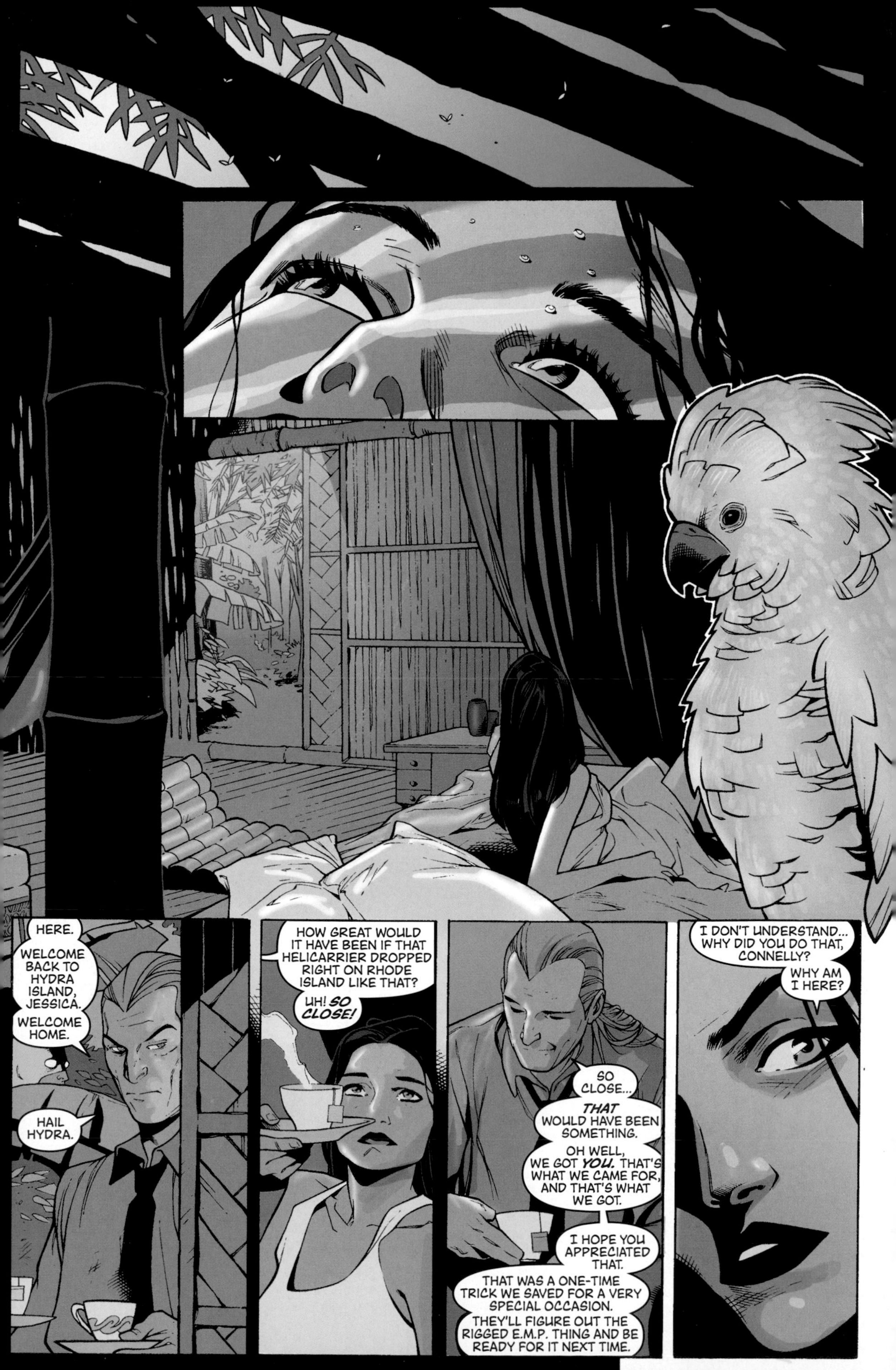
HERE.
WELCOME BACK TO HYDRA ISLAND, JESSICA.
WELCOME HOME.
HAIL HYDRA.
HOW GREAT WOULD IT HAVE BEEN IF THAT HELICARRIER DROPPED RIGHT ON RHODE ISLAND LIKE THAT?
UH! SO CLOSE!
SO CLOSE...
THAT WOULD HAVE BEEN SOMETHING.
OH WELL, WE GOT YOU. THAT'S WHAT WE CAME FOR, AND THAT'S WHAT WE GOT.
I HOPE YOU APPRECIATED THAT.
THAT WAS A ONE-TIME TRICK WE SAVED FOR A VERY SPECIAL OCCASION.
THEY'LL FIGURE OUT THE RIGGED E.M.P. THING AND BE READY FOR IT NEXT TIME.
I DON'T UNDERSTAND... WHY DID YOU DO THAT, CONNELLY?
WHY AM I HERE?

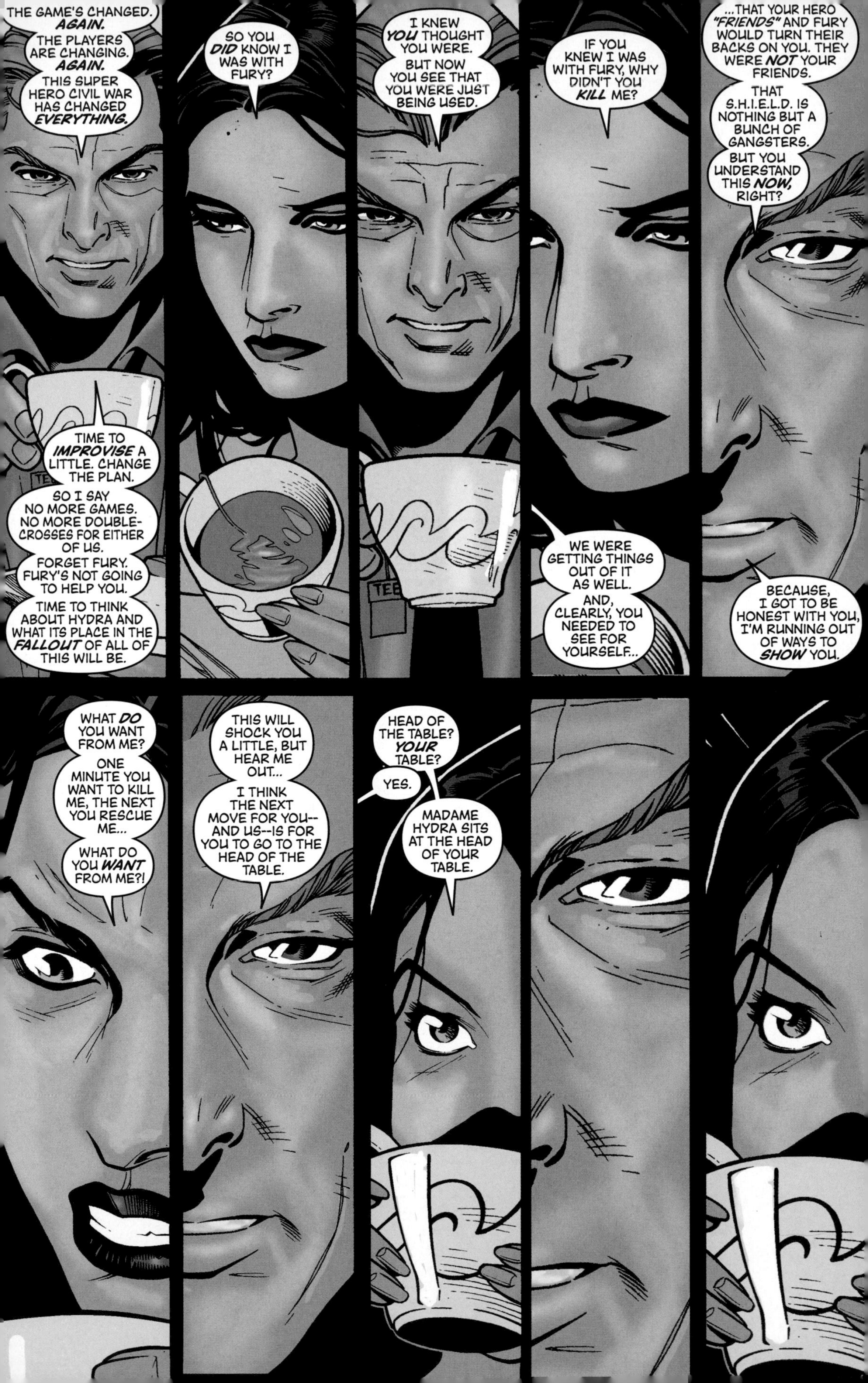
THE GAME'S CHANGED. AGAIN.
THE PLAYERS ARE CHANGING. AGAIN.
THIS SUPER HERO CIVIL WAR HAS CHANGED EVERYTHING.
TIME TO IMPROVISE A LITTLE. CHANGE THE PLAN.
SO I SAY NO MORE GAMES. NO MORE DOUBLE-CROSSES FOR EITHER OF US.
FORGET FURY. FURY'S NOT GOING TO HELP YOU.
TIME TO THINK ABOUT HYDRA AND WHAT ITS PLACE IN THE FALLOUT OF ALL OF THIS WILL BE.
SO YOU DID KNOW I WAS WITH FURY?
I KNEW YOU THOUGHT YOU WERE.
BUT NOW YOU SEE THAT YOU WERE JUST BEING USED.
IF YOU KNEW I WAS WITH FURY, WHY DIDN'T YOU KILL ME?
WE WERE GETTING THINGS OUT OF IT AS WELL.
AND, CLEARLY, YOU NEEDED TO SEE FOR YOURSELF...
...THAT YOUR HERO "FRIENDS" AND FURY WOULD TURN THEIR BACKS ON YOU. THEY WERE NOT YOUR FRIENDS.
THAT S.H.I.E.L.D. IS NOTHING BUT A BUNCH OF GANGSTERS.
BUT YOU UNDERSTAND THIS NOW, RIGHT?
BECAUSE, I GOT TO BE HONEST WITH YOU, I'M RUNNING OUT OF WAYS TO SHOW YOU.
WHAT DO YOU WANT FROM ME?
ONE MINUTE YOU WANT TO KILL ME, THE NEXT YOU RESCUE ME...
WHAT DO YOU WANT FROM ME?!
THIS WILL SHOCK YOU A LITTLE, BUT HEAR ME OUT...
I THINK THE NEXT MOVE FOR YOU-- AND US--IS FOR YOU TO GO TO THE HEAD OF THE TABLE.
HEAD OF THE TABLE? YOUR TABLE?
YES.
MADAME HYDRA SITS AT THE HEAD OF YOUR TABLE.

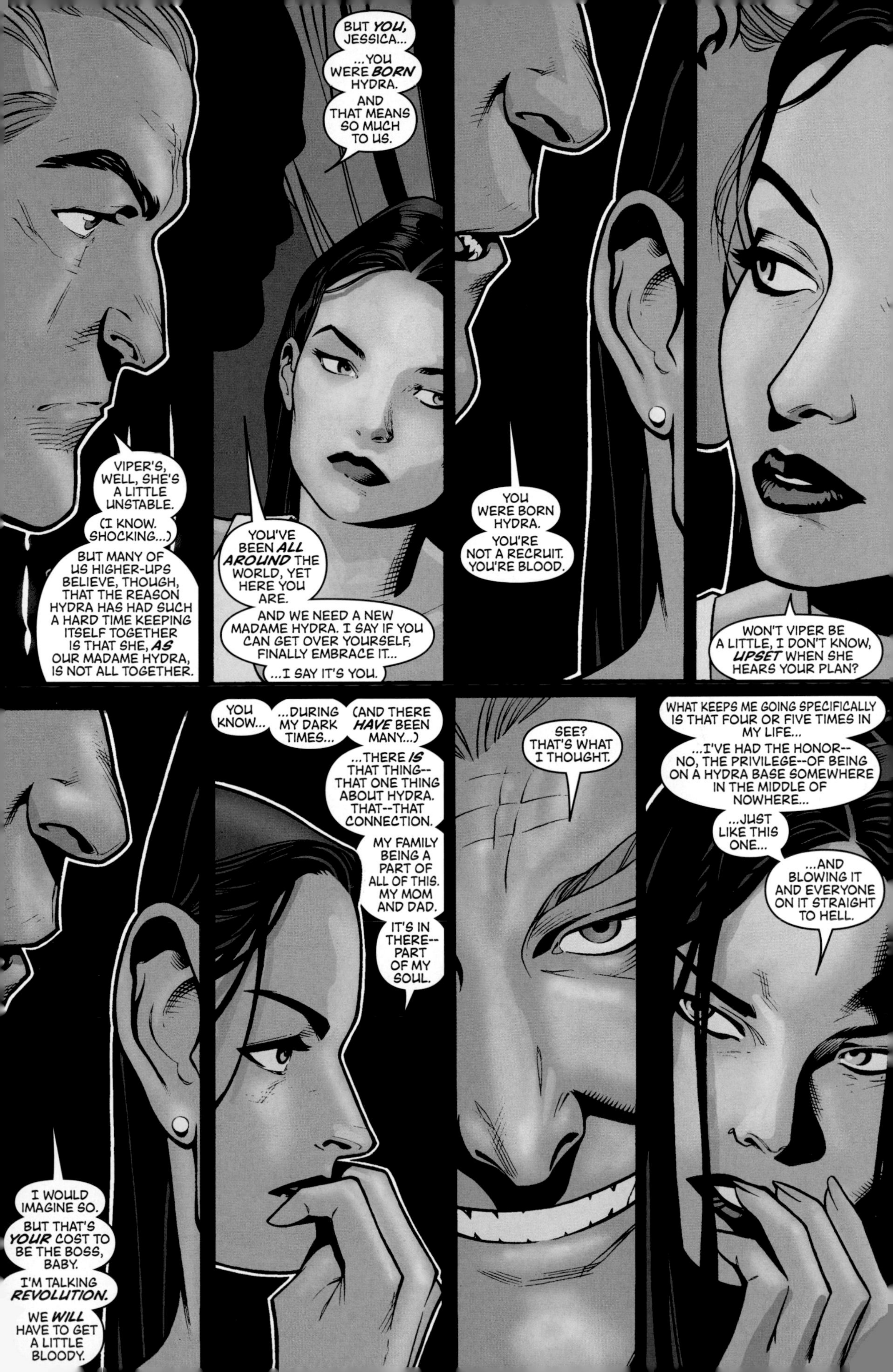

BUT YOU, JESSICA...
...YOU WERE BORN HYDRA.
AND THAT MEANS SO MUCH TO US.
VIPER'S, WELL, SHE'S A LITTLE UNSTABLE.
(I KNOW. SHOCKING...)
BUT MANY OF US HIGHER-UPS BELIEVE, THOUGH, THAT THE REASON HYDRA HAS HAD SUCH A HARD TIME KEEPING ITSELF TOGETHER IS THAT SHE, AS OUR MADAME HYDRA, IS NOT ALL TOGETHER.
YOU'VE BEEN ALL AROUND THE WORLD, YET HERE YOU ARE.
AND WE NEED A NEW MADAME HYDRA. I SAY IF YOU CAN GET OVER YOURSELF, FINALLY EMBRACE IT...
...I SAY IT'S YOU.
YOU WERE BORN HYDRA.
YOU'RE NOT A RECRUIT. YOU'RE BLOOD.
WON'T VIPER BE A LITTLE, I DON'T KNOW, UPSET WHEN SHE HEARS YOUR PLAN?
I WOULD IMAGINE SO.
BUT THAT'S YOUR COST TO BE THE BOSS, BABY.
I'M TALKING REVOLUTION.
WE WILL HAVE TO GET A LITTLE BLOODY.
YOU KNOW...
...DURING MY DARK TIMES...
(AND THERE HAVE BEEN MANY...)
...THERE IS THAT THING--THAT ONE THING ABOUT HYDRA. THAT--THAT CONNECTION.
MY FAMILY BEING A PART OF ALL OF THIS. MY MOM AND DAD.
IT'S IN THERE--PART OF MY SOUL.
SEE? THAT'S WHAT I THOUGHT.
WHAT KEEPS ME GOING SPECIFICALLY IS THAT FOUR OR FIVE TIMES IN MY LIFE...
...I'VE HAD THE HONOR--NO, THE PRIVILEGE--OF BEING ON A HYDRA BASE SOMEWHERE IN THE MIDDLE OF NOWHERE...
...JUST LIKE THIS ONE...
...AND BLOWING IT AND EVERYONE ON IT STRAIGHT TO HELL.

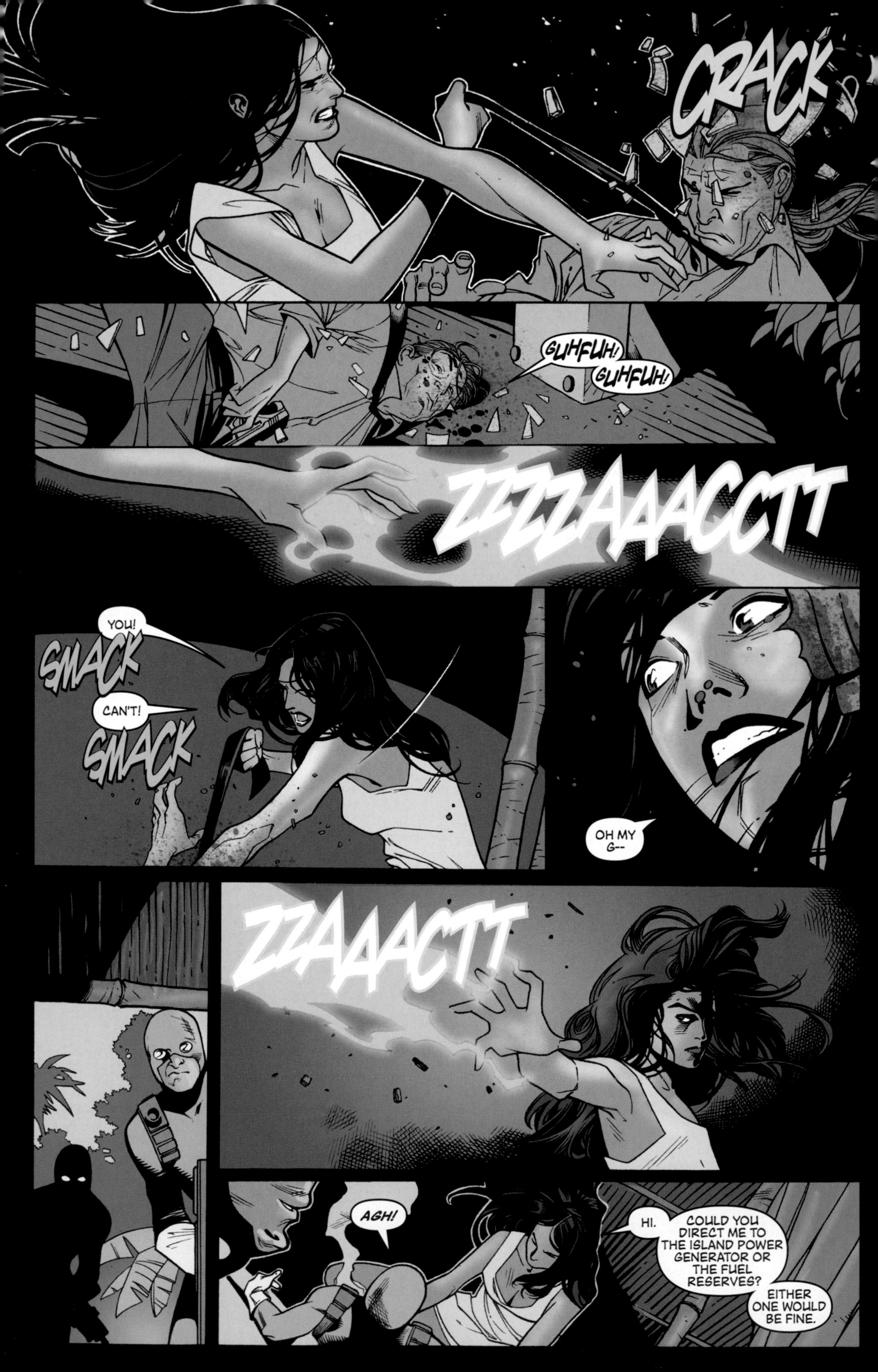
CRACK
GUHFUH!
GUHFUH!
ZZZZAAACCTT
YOU!
SMACK
CAN'T!
SMACK
OH MY G--
ZZAAACTT
AGH!
HI.
COULD YOU DIRECT ME TO THE ISLAND POWER GENERATOR OR THE FUEL RESERVES?
EITHER ONE WOULD BE FINE.

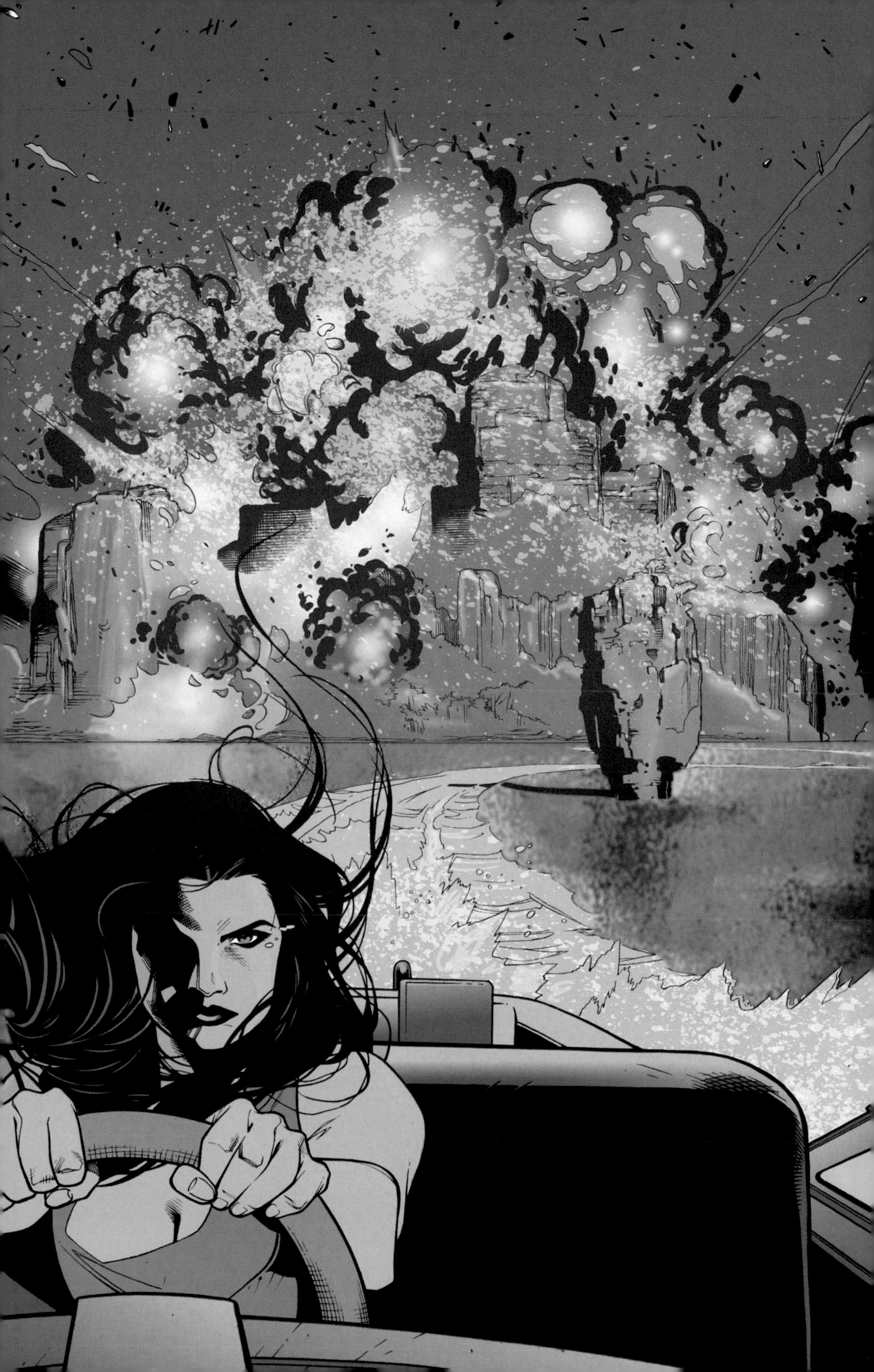

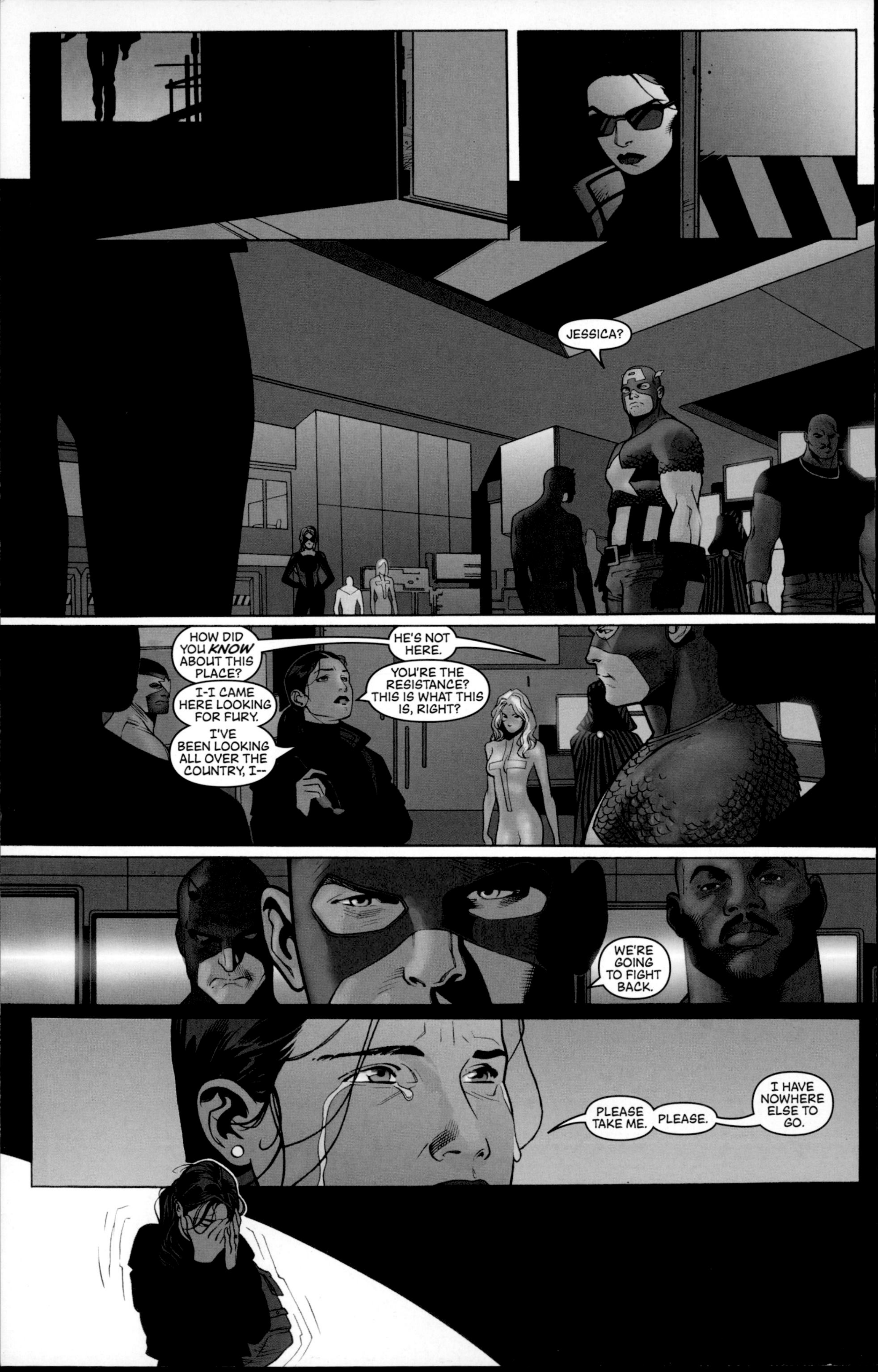
JESSICA?
HOW DID YOU KNOW ABOUT THIS PLACE?
HE'S NOT HERE.
I-I CAME HERE LOOKING FOR FURY.
I'VE BEEN LOOKING ALL OVER THE COUNTRY, I--
YOU'RE THE RESISTANCE? THIS IS WHAT THIS IS, RIGHT?
WE'RE GOING TO FIGHT BACK.
PLEASE TAKE ME.
PLEASE.
I HAVE NOWHERE ELSE TO GO.

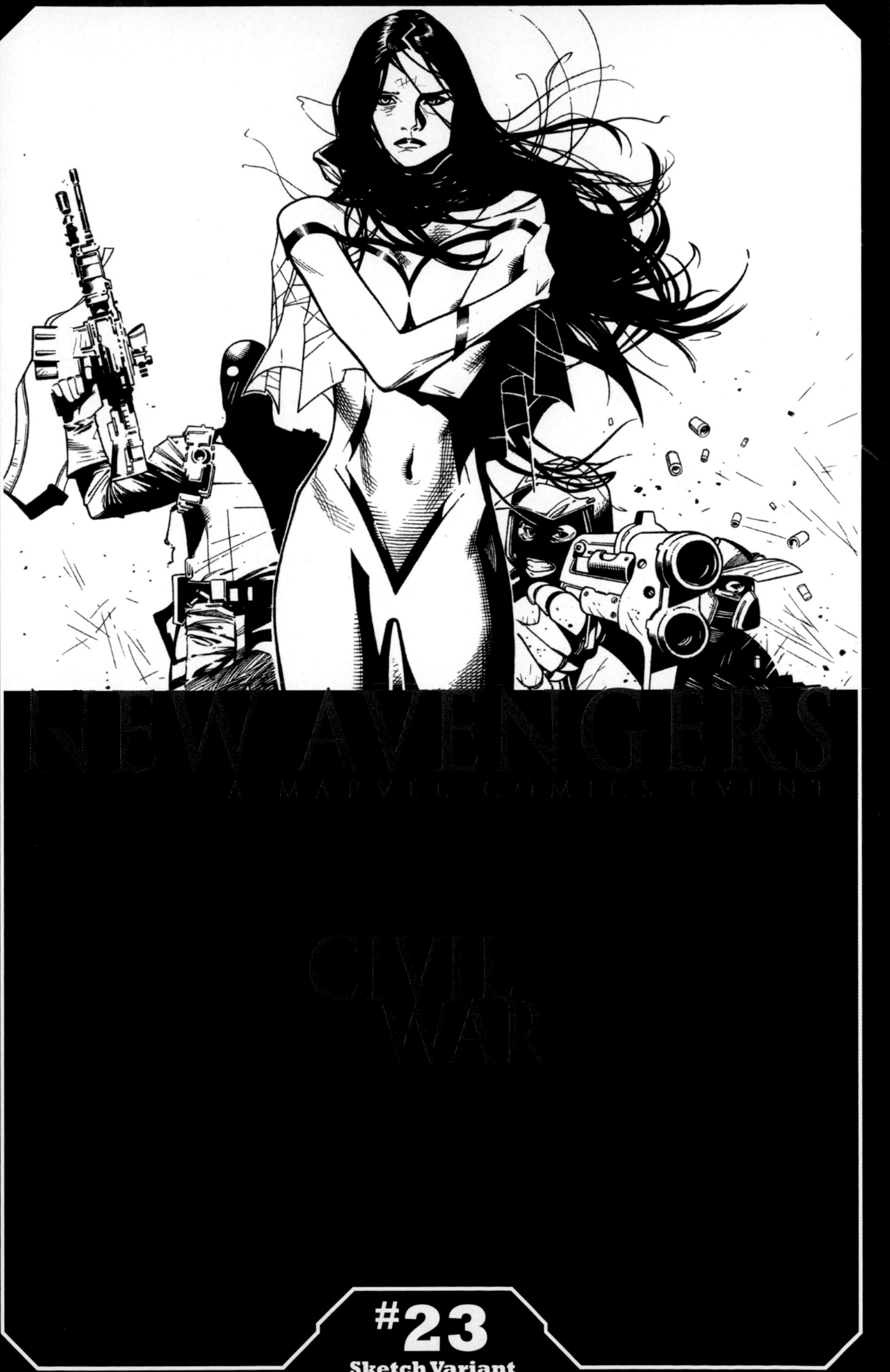
NEW AVENGERS
A MARVEL COMICS EVENT
CIVIL WAR
#23
Sketch Variant

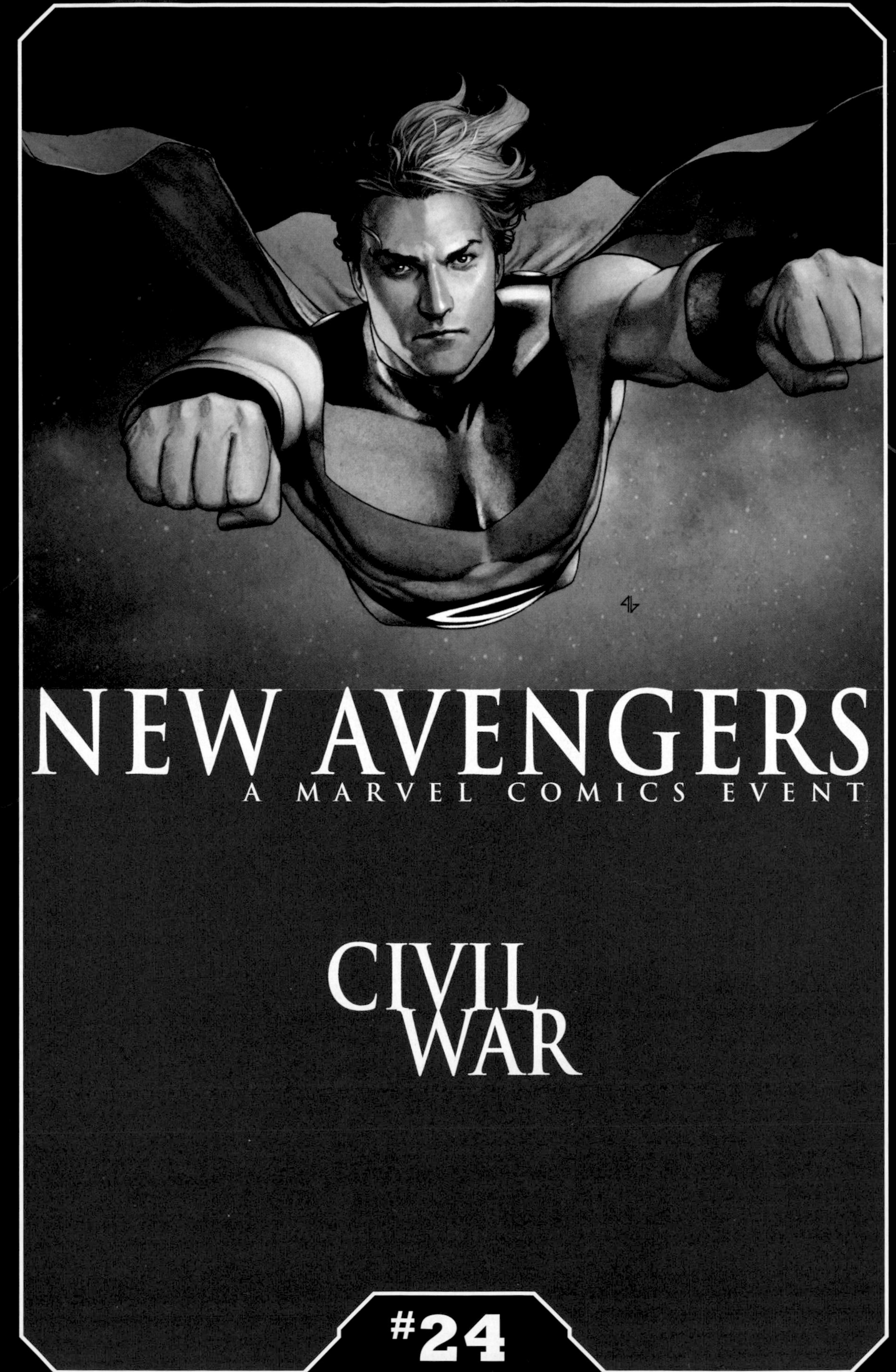
NEW AVENGERS
A MARVEL COMICS EVENT
CIVIL WAR
#24

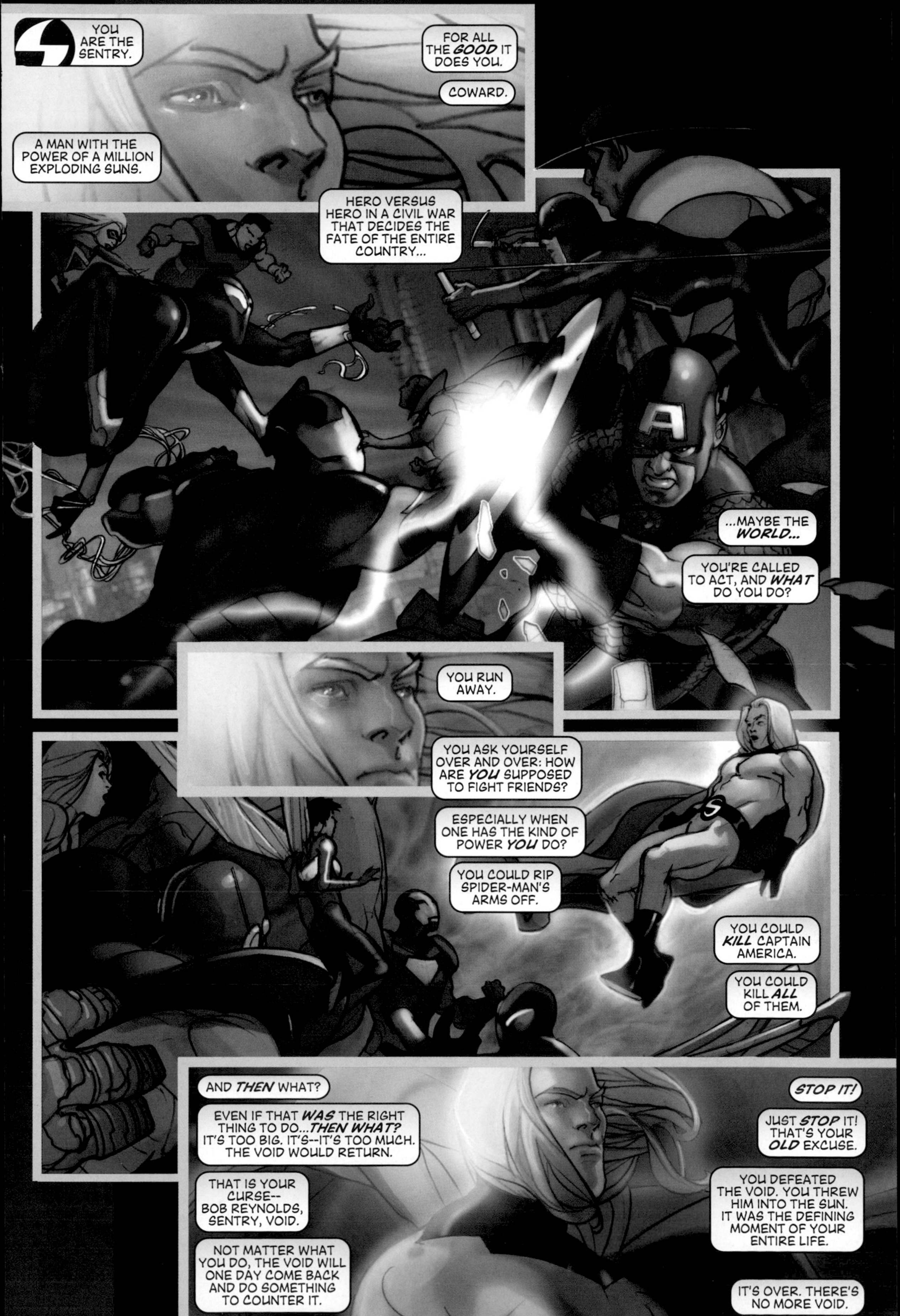
YOU ARE THE SENTRY.
A MAN WITH THE POWER OF A MILLION EXPLODING SUNS.
FOR ALL THE GOOD IT DOES YOU.
COWARD.
HERO VERSUS HERO IN A CIVIL WAR THAT DECIDES THE FATE OF THE ENTIRE COUNTRY...
...MAYBE THE WORLD...
YOU'RE CALLED TO ACT, AND WHAT DO YOU DO?
YOU RUN AWAY.
YOU ASK YOURSELF OVER AND OVER: HOW ARE YOU SUPPOSED TO FIGHT FRIENDS?
ESPECIALLY WHEN ONE HAS THE KIND OF POWER YOU DO?
YOU COULD RIP SPIDER-MAN'S ARMS OFF.
YOU COULD KILL CAPTAIN AMERICA.
YOU COULD KILL ALL OF THEM.
AND THEN WHAT?
EVEN IF THAT WAS THE RIGHT THING TO DO...THEN WHAT? IT'S TOO BIG. IT'S--IT'S TOO MUCH. THE VOID WOULD RETURN.
THAT IS YOUR CURSE-- BOB REYNOLDS, SENTRY, VOID.
NOT MATTER WHAT YOU DO, THE VOID WILL ONE DAY COME BACK AND DO SOMETHING TO COUNTER IT.
STOP IT!
JUST STOP IT! THAT'S YOUR OLD EXCUSE.
YOU DEFEATED THE VOID. YOU THREW HIM INTO THE SUN. IT WAS THE DEFINING MOMENT OF YOUR ENTIRE LIFE.
IT'S OVER. THERE'S NO MORE VOID.

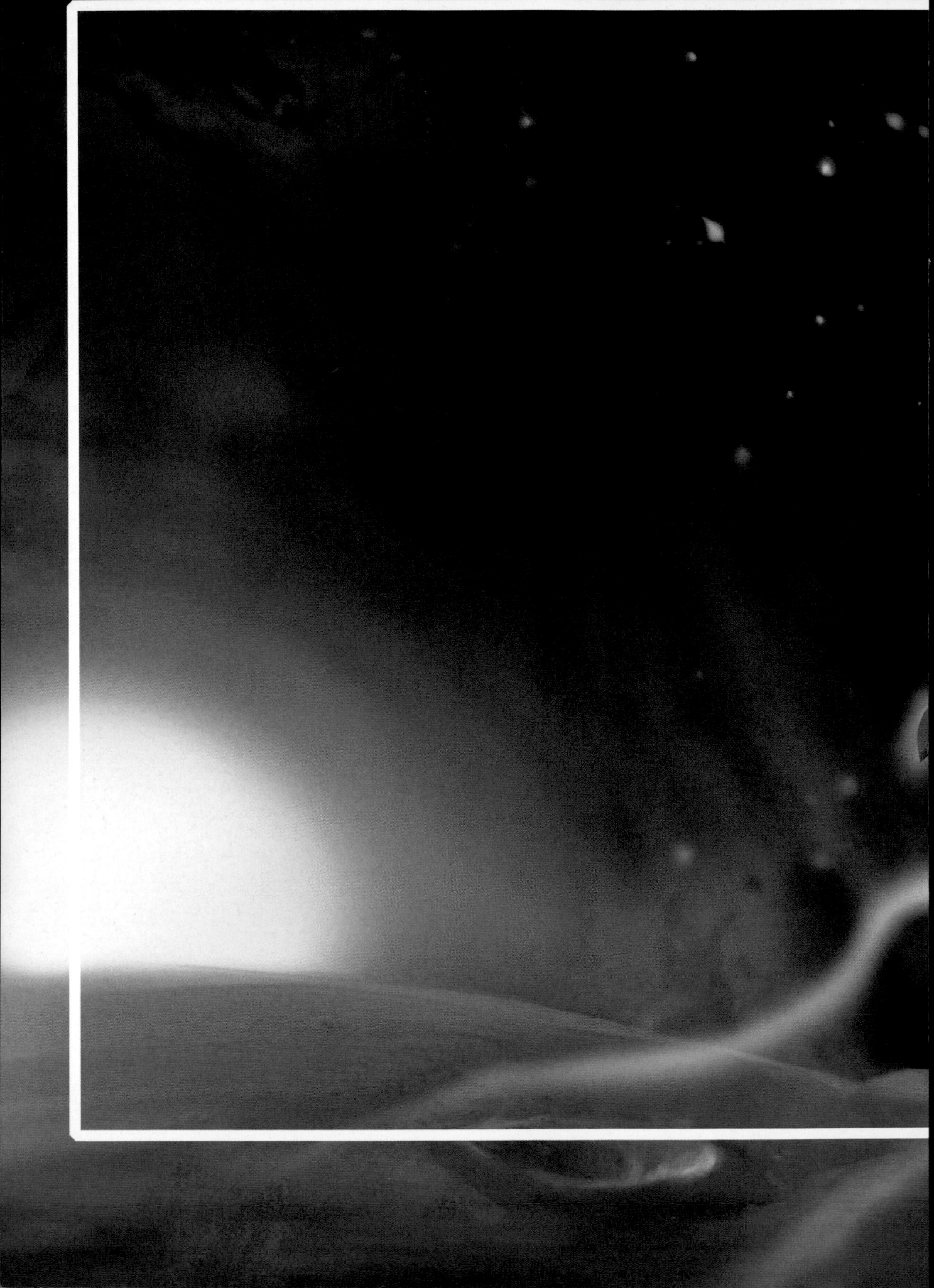

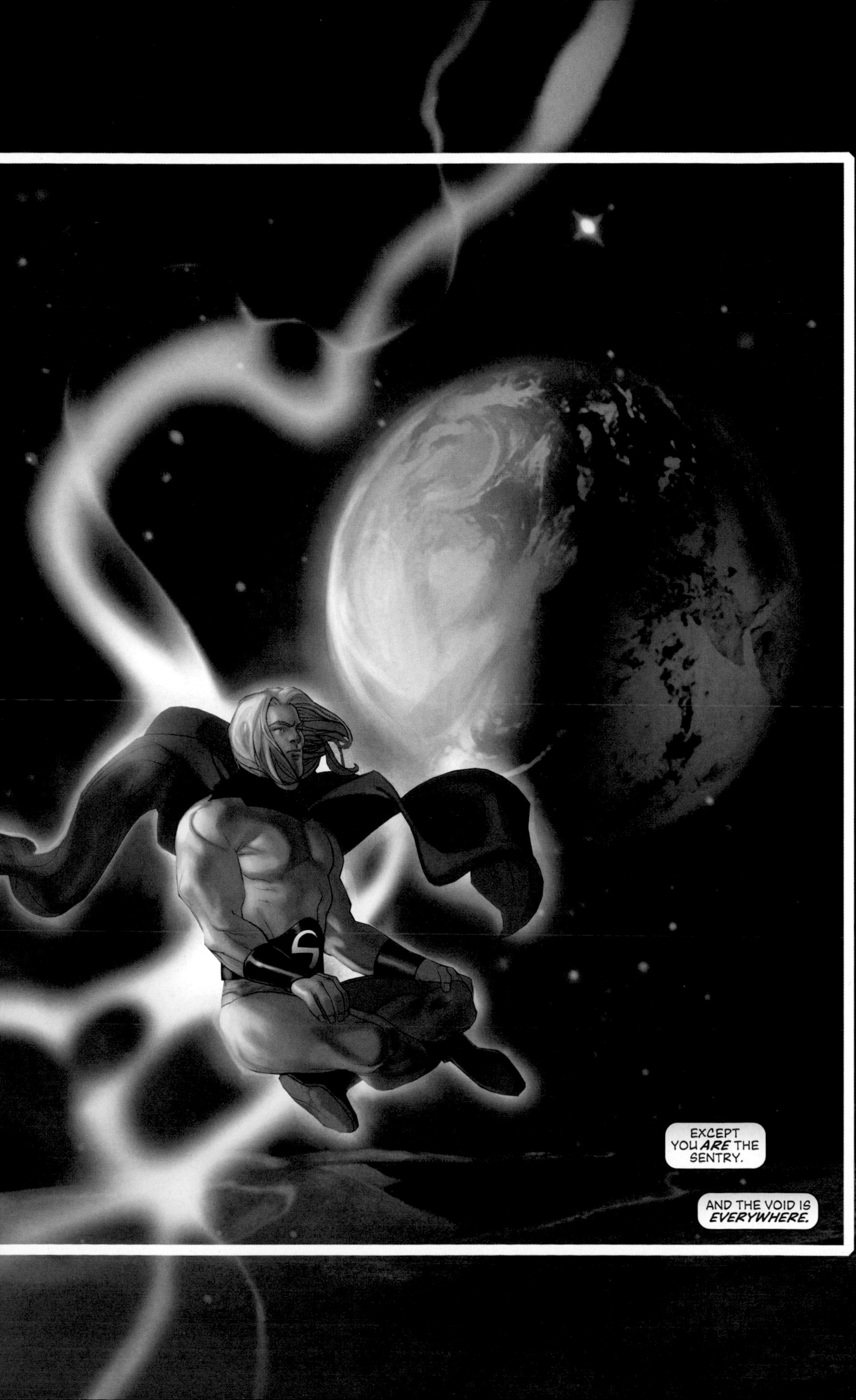
EXCEPT YOU *ARE* THE SENTRY.
AND THE VOID IS *EVERYWHERE.*

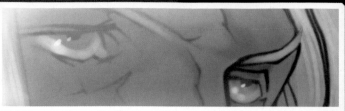

STOP TALKING ABOUT THE VOID WHEN IT'S *YOU* THAT'S THE PROBLEM.

STOP WALLOWING. EVERYONE HAS PROBLEMS.

EXCEPT YOU RAN *AWAY* FROM YOURS.

WHAT KIND OF HERO *ARE* YOU, BOB?

YOU SHOULD GO *BACK THERE* AND USE YOUR POWER TO MOLD THE WORLD INTO WHAT YOU *KNOW* IT SHOULD BE.

YOU HAVE THE POWER TO *STOP* THIS ENTIRE WAR!

YOU HAVE THE POWER TO COMPLETELY REMOVE IT FROM THE HISTORY BOOKS.

YOU COULD GO THERE AND-- WHAT? *WHAT?*

WHAT WOULD YOU DO, BOB?

AND WHAT WOULD BE YOUR--

THE INHUMANS.

YOU KNOW THEM.

RIGHT?

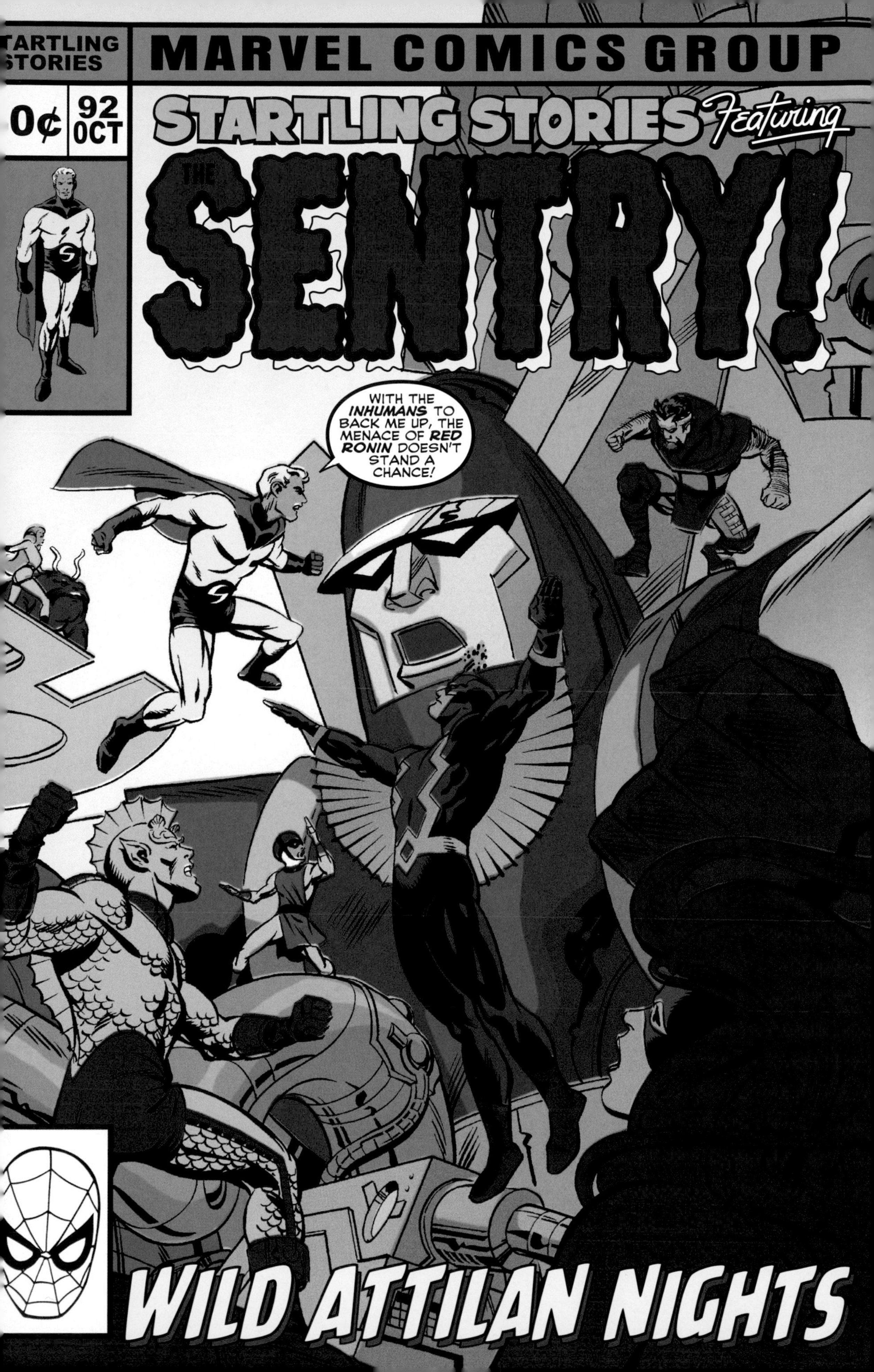

STARTLING STORIES
MARVEL COMICS GROUP
0¢
92 OCT
STARTLING STORIES Featuring
THE SENTRY!
WITH THE INHUMANS TO BACK ME UP, THE MENACE OF RED RONIN DOESN'T STAND A CHANCE!
WILD ATTILAN NIGHTS

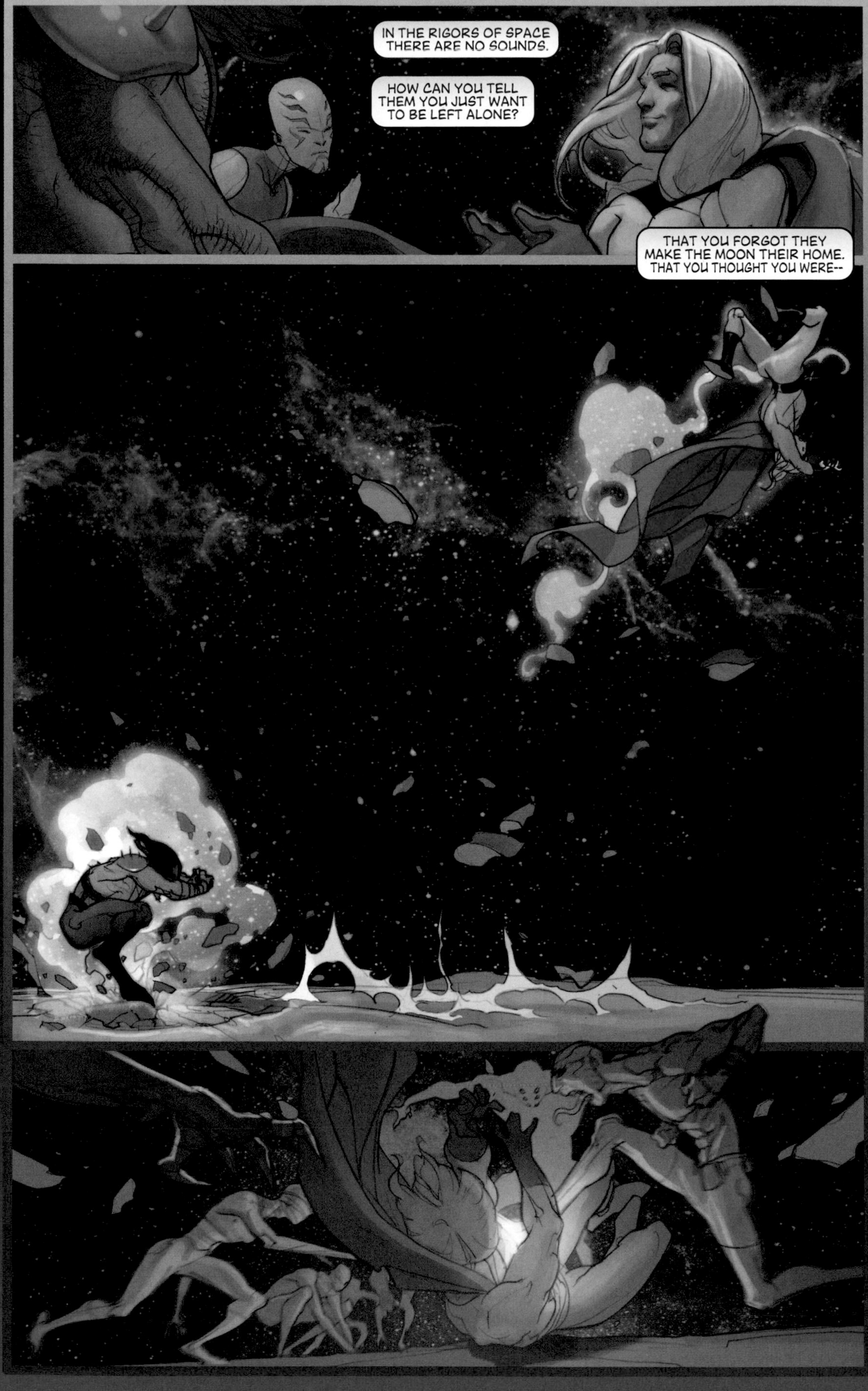
IN THE RIGORS OF SPACE THERE ARE NO SOUNDS.
HOW CAN YOU TELL THEM YOU JUST WANT TO BE LEFT ALONE?
THAT YOU FORGOT THEY MAKE THE MOON THEIR HOME. THAT YOU THOUGHT YOU WERE--

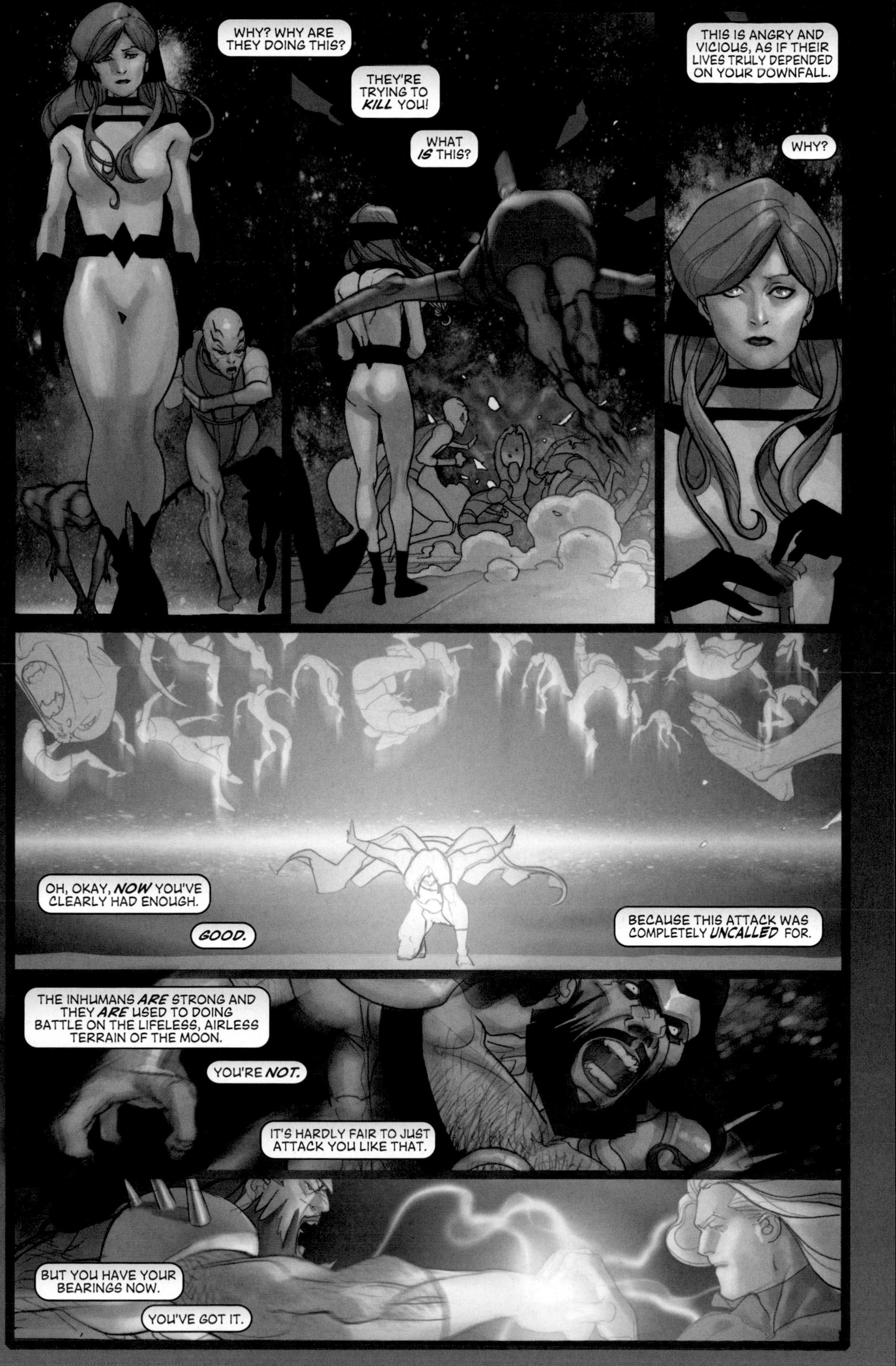

WHY? WHY ARE THEY DOING THIS?
THEY'RE TRYING TO *KILL* YOU!
WHAT *IS* THIS?
THIS IS ANGRY AND VICIOUS, AS IF THEIR LIVES TRULY DEPENDED ON YOUR DOWNFALL.
WHY?
OH, OKAY, *NOW* YOU'VE CLEARLY HAD ENOUGH.
GOOD.
BECAUSE THIS ATTACK WAS COMPLETELY *UNCALLED* FOR.
THE INHUMANS *ARE* STRONG AND THEY *ARE* USED TO DOING BATTLE ON THE LIFELESS, AIRLESS TERRAIN OF THE MOON.
YOU'RE *NOT.*
IT'S HARDLY FAIR TO JUST ATTACK YOU LIKE THAT.
BUT YOU HAVE YOUR BEARINGS NOW.
YOU'VE GOT IT.

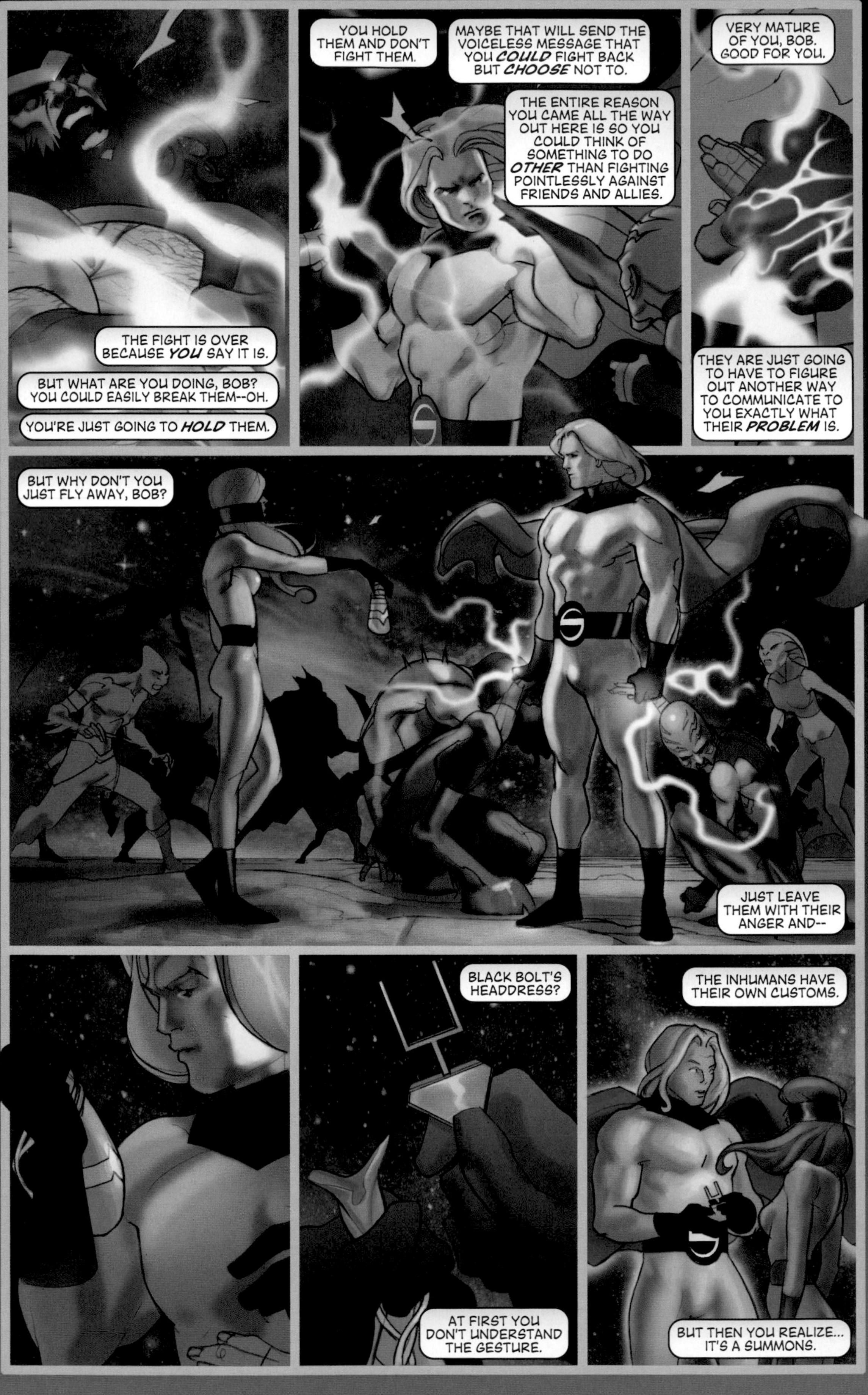
THE FIGHT IS OVER BECAUSE YOU SAY IT IS.
BUT WHAT ARE YOU DOING, BOB? YOU COULD EASILY BREAK THEM--OH.
YOU'RE JUST GOING TO HOLD THEM.
YOU HOLD THEM AND DON'T FIGHT THEM.
MAYBE THAT WILL SEND THE VOICELESS MESSAGE THAT YOU COULD FIGHT BACK BUT CHOOSE NOT TO.
THE ENTIRE REASON YOU CAME ALL THE WAY OUT HERE IS SO YOU COULD THINK OF SOMETHING TO DO OTHER THAN FIGHTING POINTLESSLY AGAINST FRIENDS AND ALLIES.
VERY MATURE OF YOU, BOB. GOOD FOR YOU.
THEY ARE JUST GOING TO HAVE TO FIGURE OUT ANOTHER WAY TO COMMUNICATE TO YOU EXACTLY WHAT THEIR PROBLEM IS.
BUT WHY DON'T YOU JUST FLY AWAY, BOB?
JUST LEAVE THEM WITH THEIR ANGER AND--
BLACK BOLT'S HEADDRESS?
AT FIRST YOU DON'T UNDERSTAND THE GESTURE.
THE INHUMANS HAVE THEIR OWN CUSTOMS.
BUT THEN YOU REALIZE... IT'S A SUMMONS.

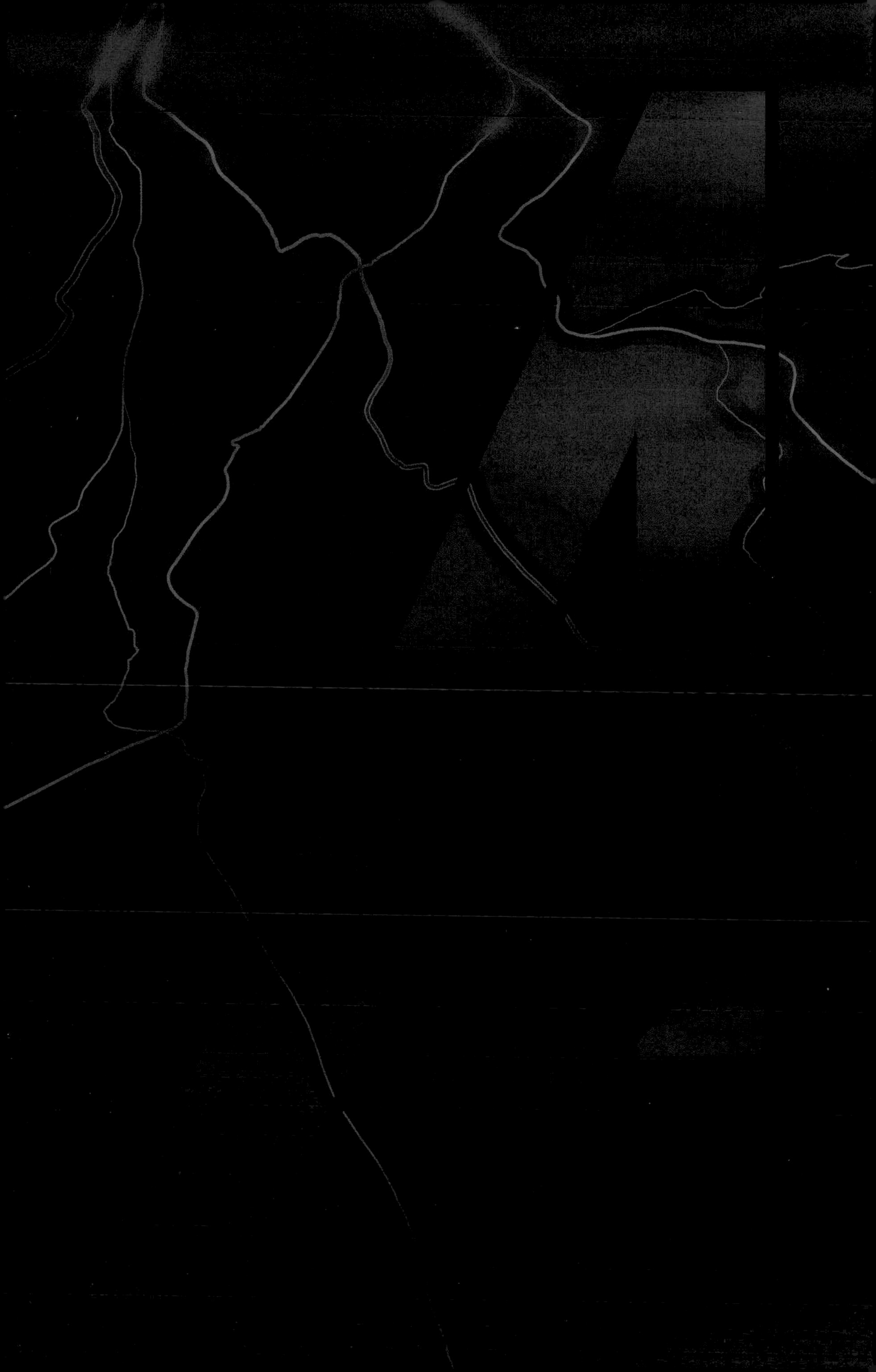

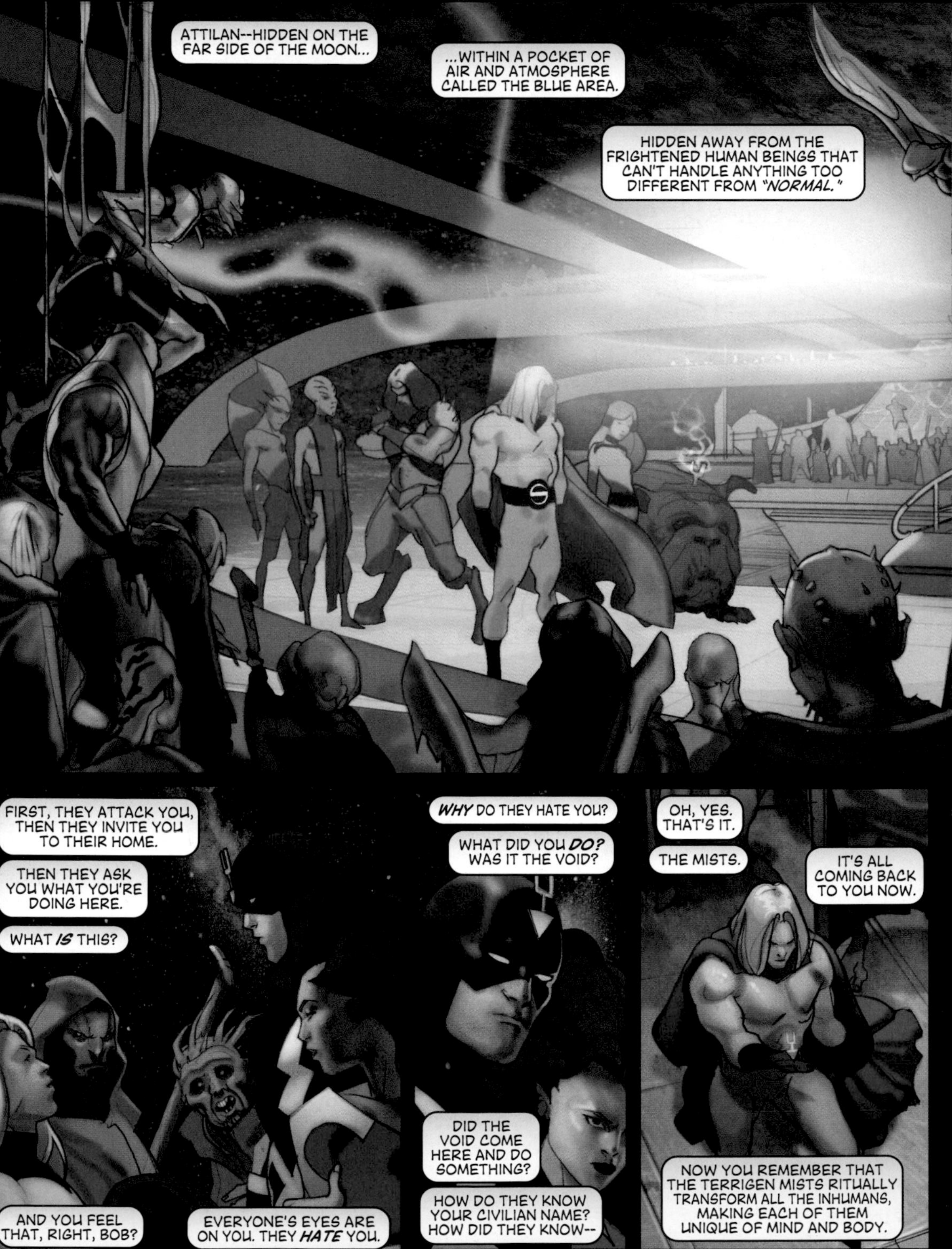
ATTILAN--HIDDEN ON THE FAR SIDE OF THE MOON...
...WITHIN A POCKET OF AIR AND ATMOSPHERE CALLED THE BLUE AREA.
HIDDEN AWAY FROM THE FRIGHTENED HUMAN BEINGS THAT CAN'T HANDLE ANYTHING TOO DIFFERENT FROM "NORMAL."
FIRST, THEY ATTACK YOU, THEN THEY INVITE YOU TO THEIR HOME.
THEN THEY ASK YOU WHAT YOU'RE DOING HERE.
WHAT IS THIS?
AND YOU FEEL THAT, RIGHT, BOB?
EVERYONE'S EYES ARE ON YOU. THEY HATE YOU.
WHY DO THEY HATE YOU?
WHAT DID YOU DO? WAS IT THE VOID?
DID THE VOID COME HERE AND DO SOMETHING?
HOW DO THEY KNOW YOUR CIVILIAN NAME? HOW DID THEY KNOW--
OH, YES. THAT'S IT.
THE MISTS.
IT'S ALL COMING BACK TO YOU NOW.
NOW YOU REMEMBER THAT THE TERRIGEN MISTS RITUALLY TRANSFORM ALL THE INHUMANS, MAKING EACH OF THEM UNIQUE OF MIND AND BODY.

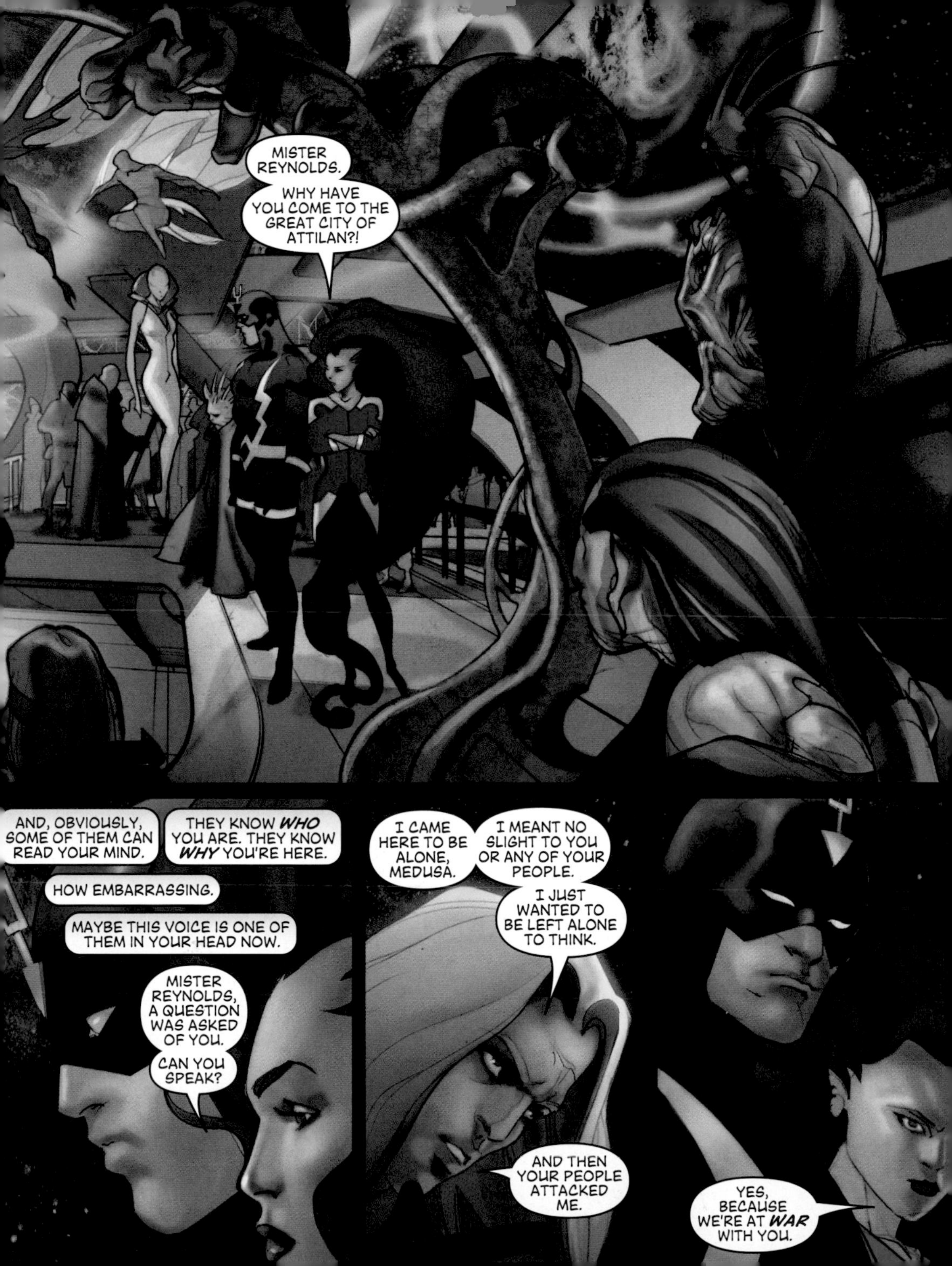

MISTER REYNOLDS.
WHY HAVE YOU COME TO THE GREAT CITY OF ATTILAN?!
AND, OBVIOUSLY, SOME OF THEM CAN READ YOUR MIND.
THEY KNOW *WHO* YOU ARE. THEY KNOW *WHY* YOU'RE HERE.
HOW EMBARRASSING.
MAYBE THIS VOICE IS ONE OF THEM IN YOUR HEAD NOW.
MISTER REYNOLDS, A QUESTION WAS ASKED OF YOU.
CAN YOU SPEAK?
I CAME HERE TO BE ALONE, MEDUSA.
I MEANT NO SLIGHT TO YOU OR ANY OF YOUR PEOPLE.
I JUST WANTED TO BE LEFT ALONE TO THINK.
AND THEN YOUR PEOPLE ATTACKED ME.
YES, BECAUSE WE'RE AT *WAR* WITH YOU.

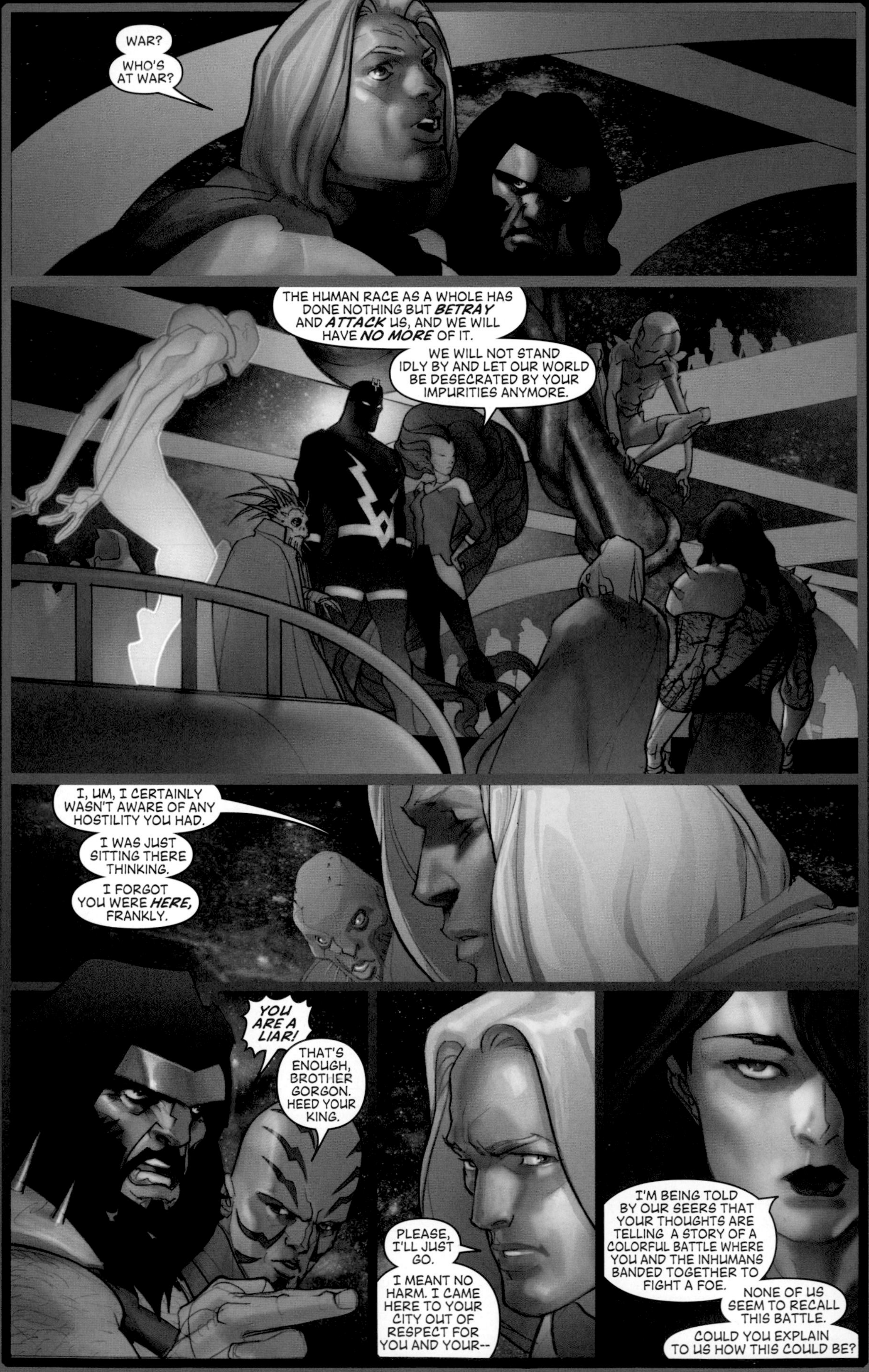
WAR?
WHO'S AT WAR?
THE HUMAN RACE AS A WHOLE HAS DONE NOTHING BUT BETRAY AND ATTACK US, AND WE WILL HAVE NO MORE OF IT.
WE WILL NOT STAND IDLY BY AND LET OUR WORLD BE DESECRATED BY YOUR IMPURITIES ANYMORE.
I, UM, I CERTAINLY WASN'T AWARE OF ANY HOSTILITY YOU HAD.
I WAS JUST SITTING THERE THINKING.
I FORGOT YOU WERE HERE, FRANKLY.
YOU ARE A LIAR!
THAT'S ENOUGH, BROTHER GORGON. HEED YOUR KING.
PLEASE, I'LL JUST GO.
I MEANT NO HARM. I CAME HERE TO YOUR CITY OUT OF RESPECT FOR YOU AND YOUR--
I'M BEING TOLD BY OUR SEERS THAT YOUR THOUGHTS ARE TELLING A STORY OF A COLORFUL BATTLE WHERE YOU AND THE INHUMANS BANDED TOGETHER TO FIGHT A FOE.
NONE OF US SEEM TO RECALL THIS BATTLE.
COULD YOU EXPLAIN TO US HOW THIS COULD BE?

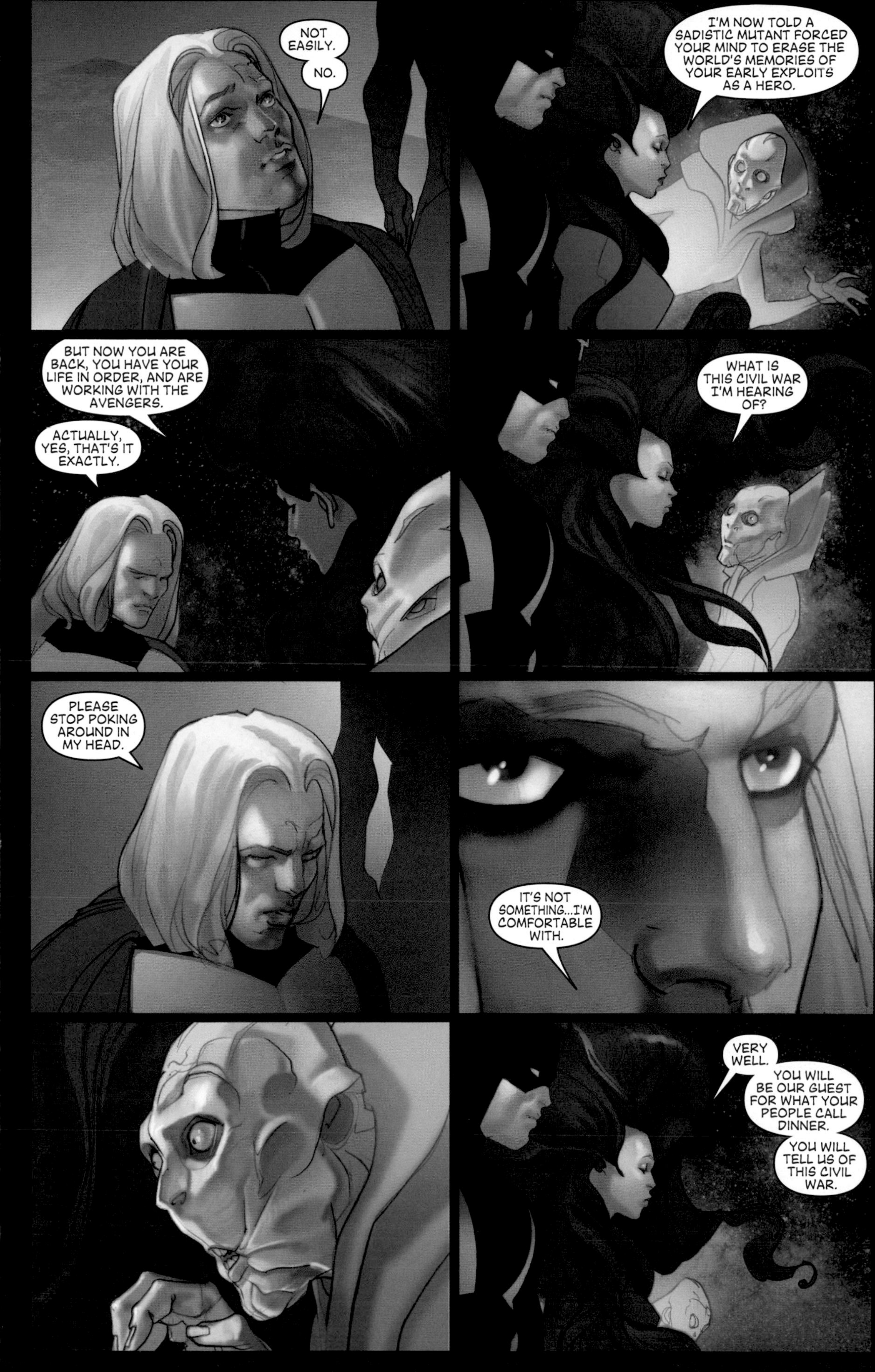
NOT EASILY.
NO.
I'M NOW TOLD A SADISTIC MUTANT FORCED YOUR MIND TO ERASE THE WORLD'S MEMORIES OF YOUR EARLY EXPLOITS AS A HERO.
BUT NOW YOU ARE BACK, YOU HAVE YOUR LIFE IN ORDER, AND ARE WORKING WITH THE AVENGERS.
ACTUALLY, YES, THAT'S IT EXACTLY.
WHAT IS THIS CIVIL WAR I'M HEARING OF?
PLEASE STOP POKING AROUND IN MY HEAD.
IT'S NOT SOMETHING...I'M COMFORTABLE WITH.
VERY WELL.
YOU WILL BE OUR GUEST FOR WHAT YOUR PEOPLE CALL DINNER.
YOU WILL TELL US OF THIS CIVIL WAR.

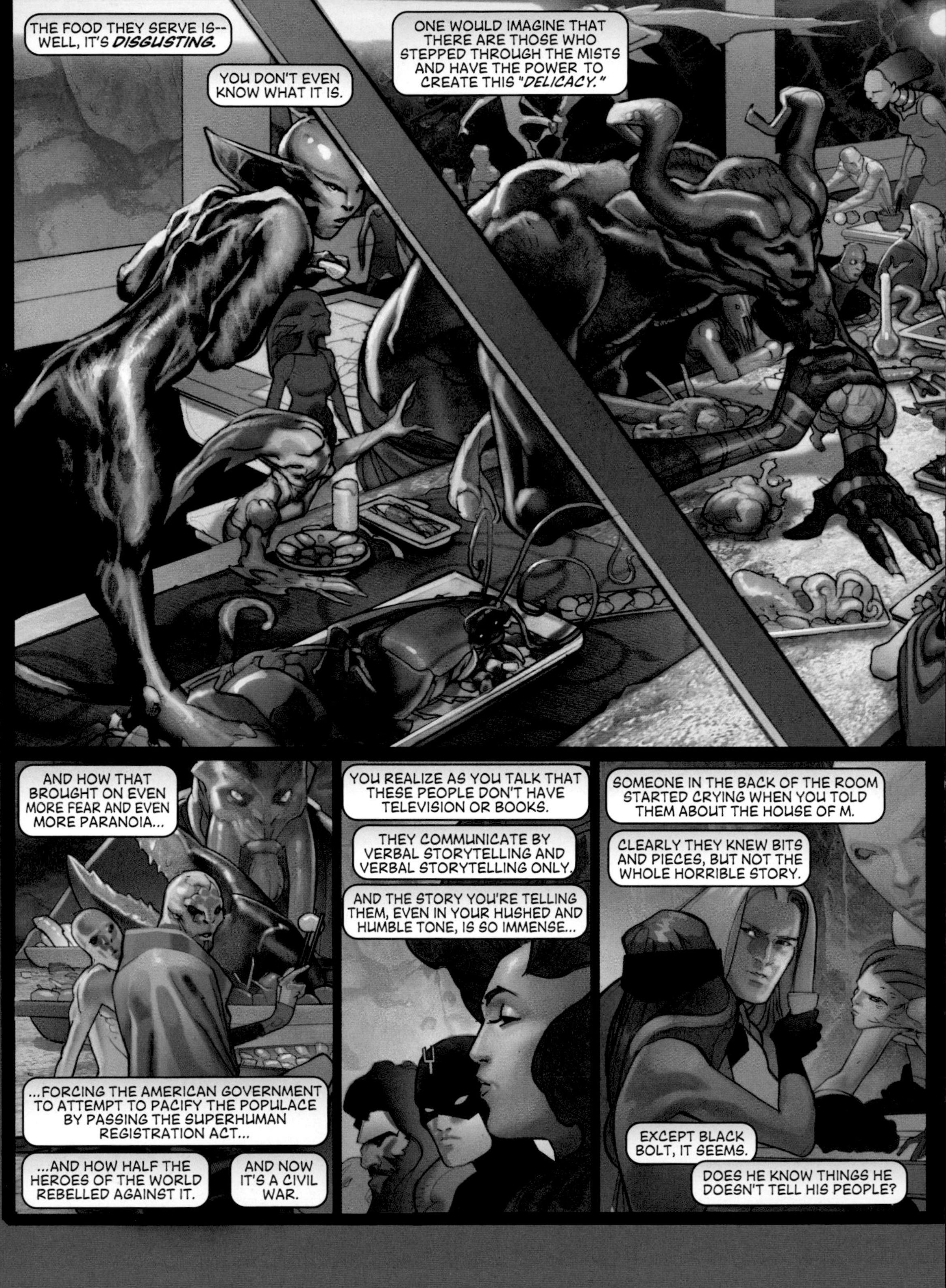
THE FOOD THEY SERVE IS-- WELL, IT'S *DISGUSTING.*
YOU DON'T EVEN KNOW WHAT IT IS.
ONE WOULD IMAGINE THAT THERE ARE THOSE WHO STEPPED THROUGH THE MISTS AND HAVE THE POWER TO CREATE THIS *"DELICACY."*
AND HOW THAT BROUGHT ON EVEN MORE FEAR AND EVEN MORE PARANOIA...
...FORCING THE AMERICAN GOVERNMENT TO ATTEMPT TO PACIFY THE POPULACE BY PASSING THE SUPERHUMAN REGISTRATION ACT...
...AND HOW HALF THE HEROES OF THE WORLD REBELLED AGAINST IT.
AND NOW IT'S A CIVIL WAR.
YOU REALIZE AS YOU TALK THAT THESE PEOPLE DON'T HAVE TELEVISION OR BOOKS.
THEY COMMUNICATE BY VERBAL STORYTELLING AND VERBAL STORYTELLING ONLY.
AND THE STORY YOU'RE TELLING THEM, EVEN IN YOUR HUSHED AND HUMBLE TONE, IS SO IMMENSE...
SOMEONE IN THE BACK OF THE ROOM STARTED CRYING WHEN YOU TOLD THEM ABOUT THE HOUSE OF M.
CLEARLY THEY KNEW BITS AND PIECES, BUT NOT THE WHOLE HORRIBLE STORY.
EXCEPT BLACK BOLT, IT SEEMS.
DOES HE KNOW THINGS HE DOESN'T TELL HIS PEOPLE?

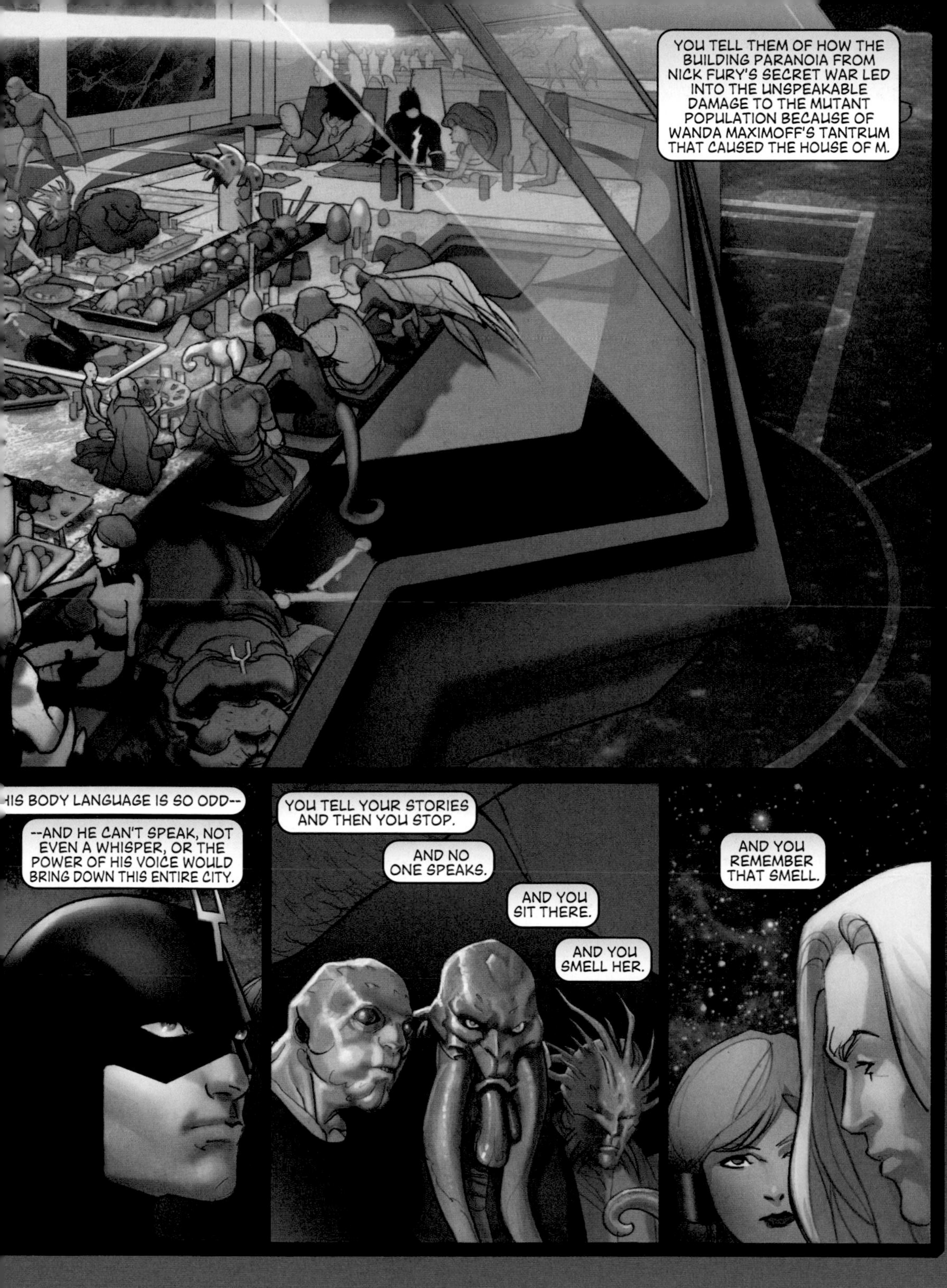
YOU TELL THEM OF HOW THE BUILDING PARANOIA FROM NICK FURY'S SECRET WAR LED INTO THE UNSPEAKABLE DAMAGE TO THE MUTANT POPULATION BECAUSE OF WANDA MAXIMOFF'S TANTRUM THAT CAUSED THE HOUSE OF M.
HIS BODY LANGUAGE IS SO ODD--
--AND HE CAN'T SPEAK, NOT EVEN A WHISPER, OR THE POWER OF HIS VOICE WOULD BRING DOWN THIS ENTIRE CITY.
YOU TELL YOUR STORIES AND THEN YOU STOP.
AND NO ONE SPEAKS.
AND YOU SIT THERE.
AND YOU SMELL HER.
AND YOU REMEMBER THAT SMELL.

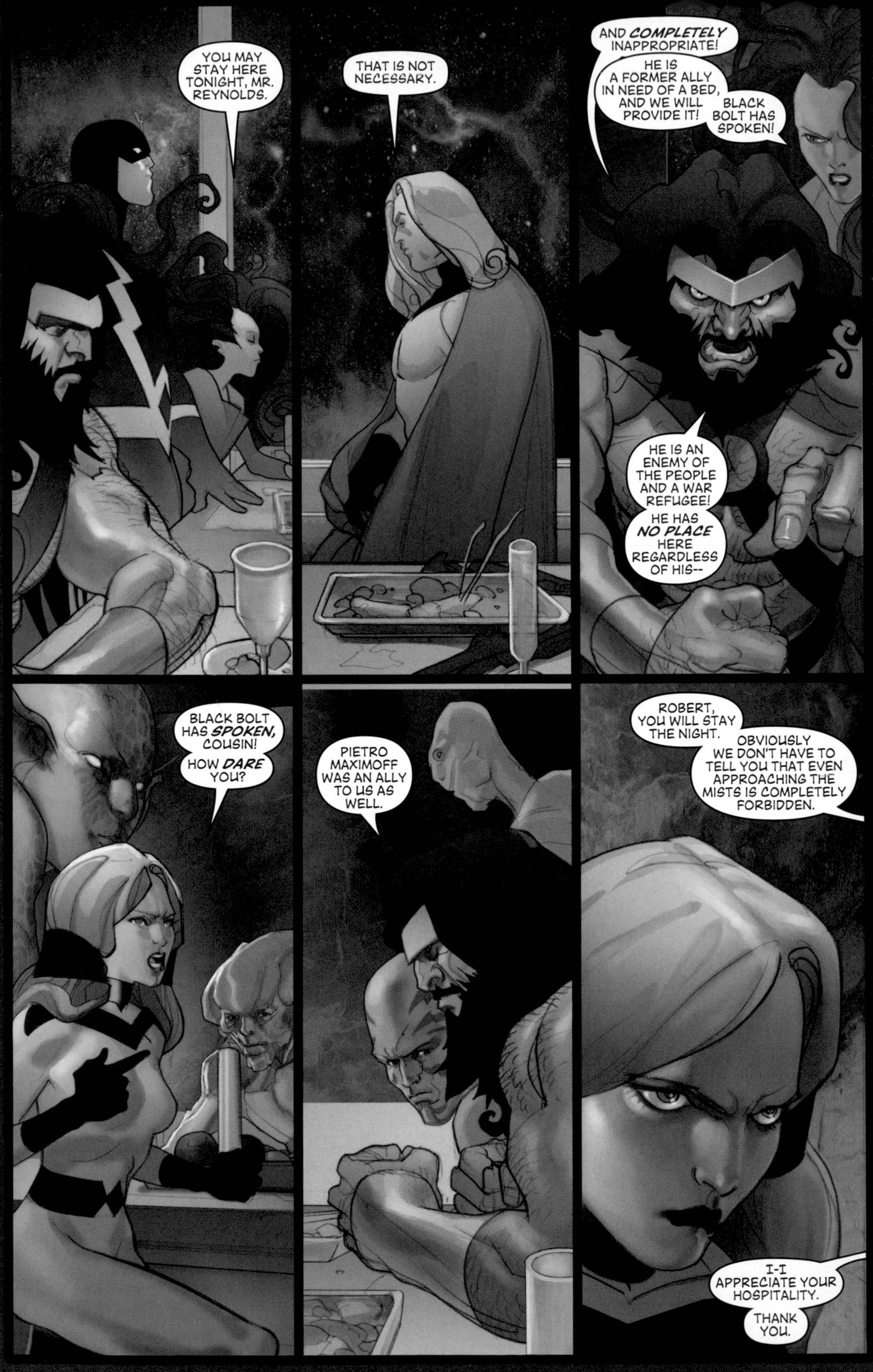

YOU MAY STAY HERE TONIGHT, MR. REYNOLDS.
THAT IS NOT NECESSARY.
AND COMPLETELY INAPPROPRIATE!
HE IS A FORMER ALLY IN NEED OF A BED, AND WE WILL PROVIDE IT!
BLACK BOLT HAS SPOKEN!
HE IS AN ENEMY OF THE PEOPLE AND A WAR REFUGEE!
HE HAS NO PLACE HERE REGARDLESS OF HIS--
BLACK BOLT HAS SPOKEN, COUSIN!
HOW DARE YOU?
PIETRO MAXIMOFF WAS AN ALLY TO US AS WELL.
ROBERT, YOU WILL STAY THE NIGHT.
OBVIOUSLY WE DON'T HAVE TO TELL YOU THAT EVEN APPROACHING THE MISTS IS COMPLETELY FORBIDDEN.
I-I APPRECIATE YOUR HOSPITALITY.
THANK YOU.

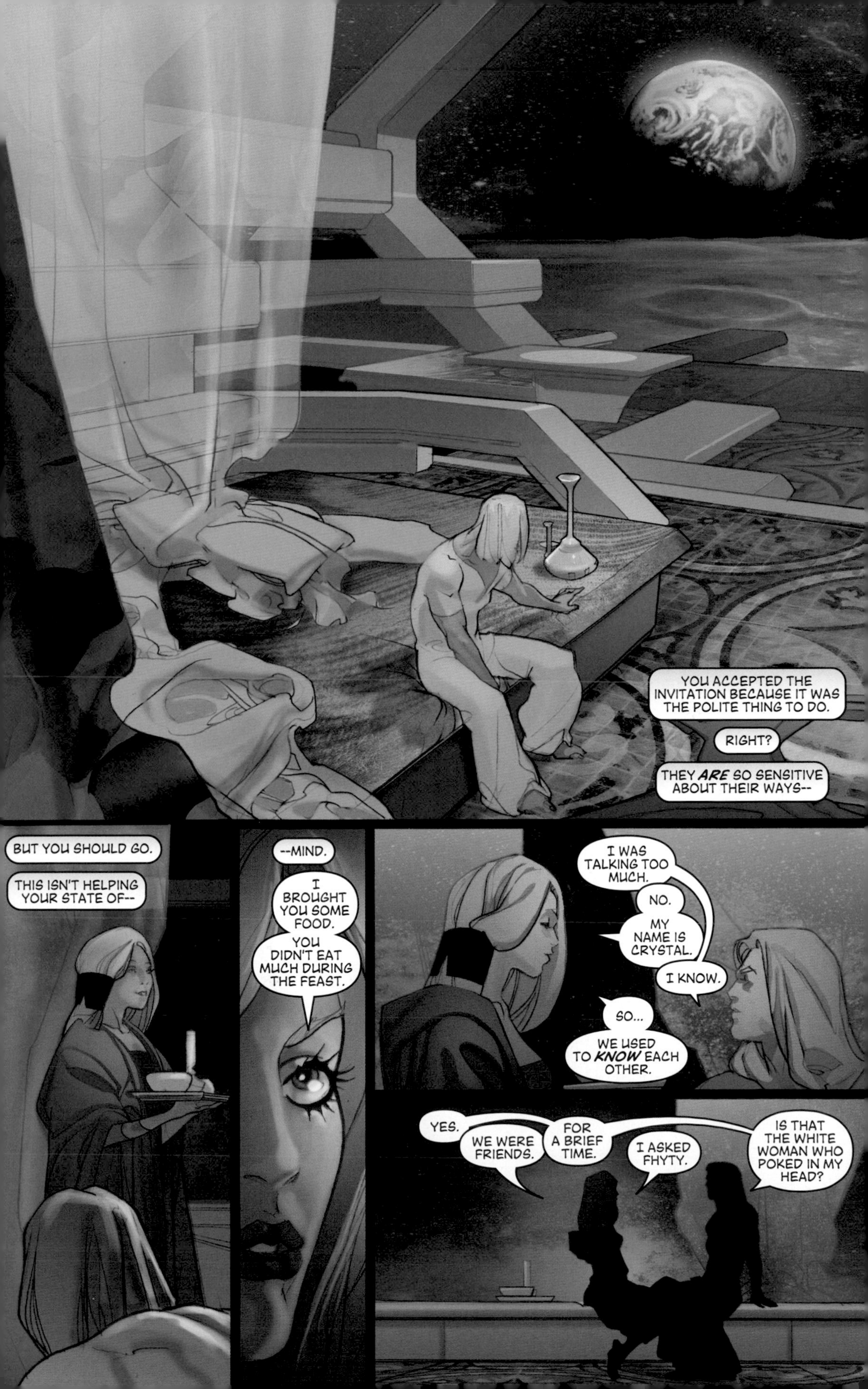
YOU ACCEPTED THE INVITATION BECAUSE IT WAS THE POLITE THING TO DO.
RIGHT?
THEY *ARE* SO SENSITIVE ABOUT THEIR WAYS--
BUT YOU SHOULD GO.
THIS ISN'T HELPING YOUR STATE OF--
--MIND.
I BROUGHT YOU SOME FOOD.
YOU DIDN'T EAT MUCH DURING THE FEAST.
I WAS TALKING TOO MUCH.
NO.
MY NAME IS CRYSTAL.
I KNOW.
SO...
WE USED TO *KNOW* EACH OTHER.
YES.
WE WERE FRIENDS.
FOR A BRIEF TIME.
I ASKED FHYTY.
IS THAT THE WHITE WOMAN WHO POKED IN MY HEAD?

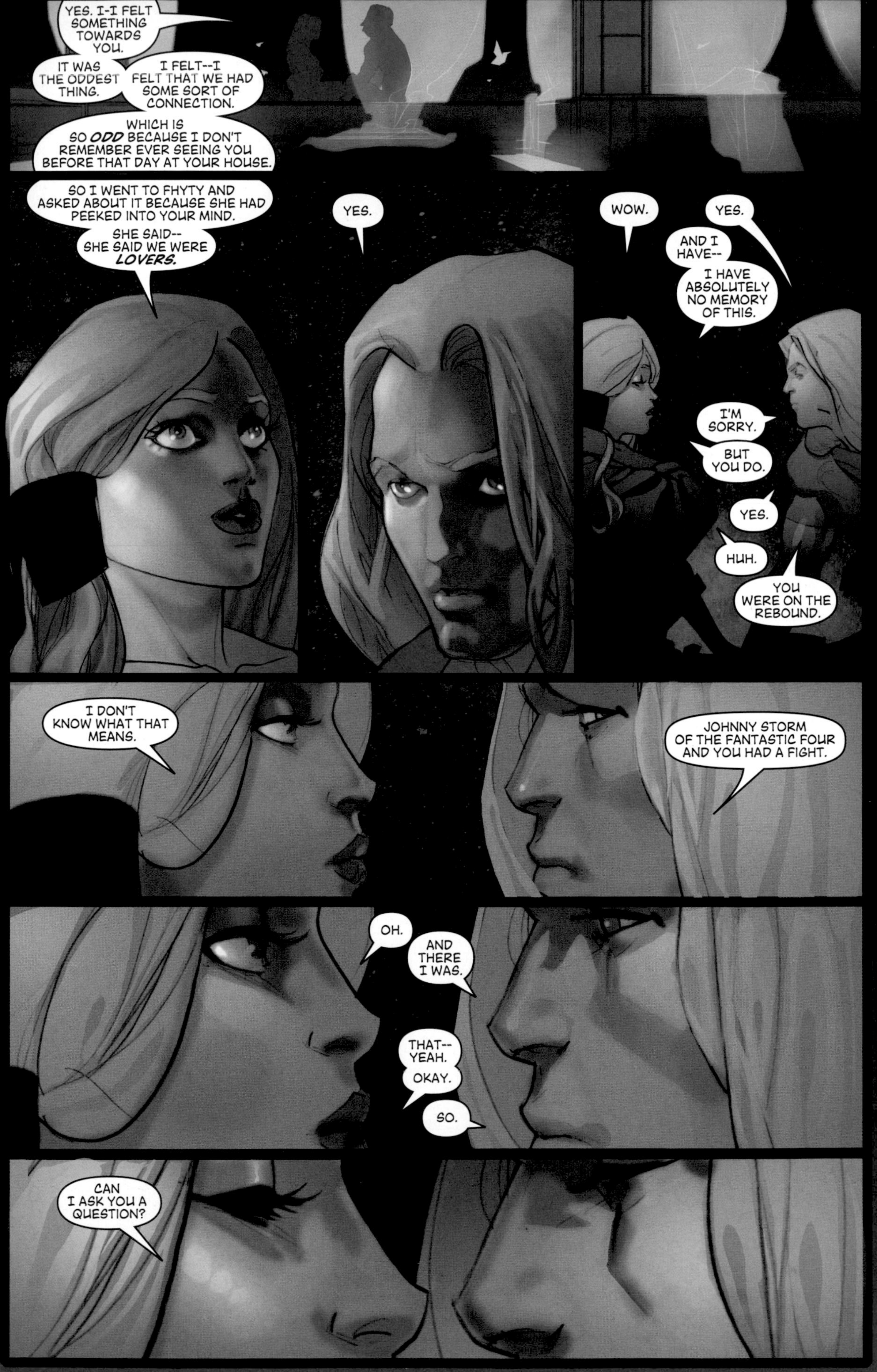
YES. I-I FELT SOMETHING TOWARDS YOU.
IT WAS THE ODDEST THING.
I FELT--I FELT THAT WE HAD SOME SORT OF CONNECTION.
WHICH IS SO *ODD* BECAUSE I DON'T REMEMBER EVER SEEING YOU BEFORE THAT DAY AT YOUR HOUSE.
SO I WENT TO FHYTY AND ASKED ABOUT IT BECAUSE SHE HAD PEEKED INTO YOUR MIND.
SHE SAID-- SHE SAID WE WERE ***LOVERS.***
YES.
WOW.
YES.
AND I HAVE--
I HAVE ABSOLUTELY NO MEMORY OF THIS.
I'M SORRY.
BUT YOU DO.
YES.
HUH.
YOU WERE ON THE REBOUND.
I DON'T KNOW WHAT THAT MEANS.
JOHNNY STORM OF THE FANTASTIC FOUR AND YOU HAD A FIGHT.
OH.
AND THERE I WAS.
THAT-- YEAH.
OKAY.
SO.
CAN I ASK YOU A QUESTION?

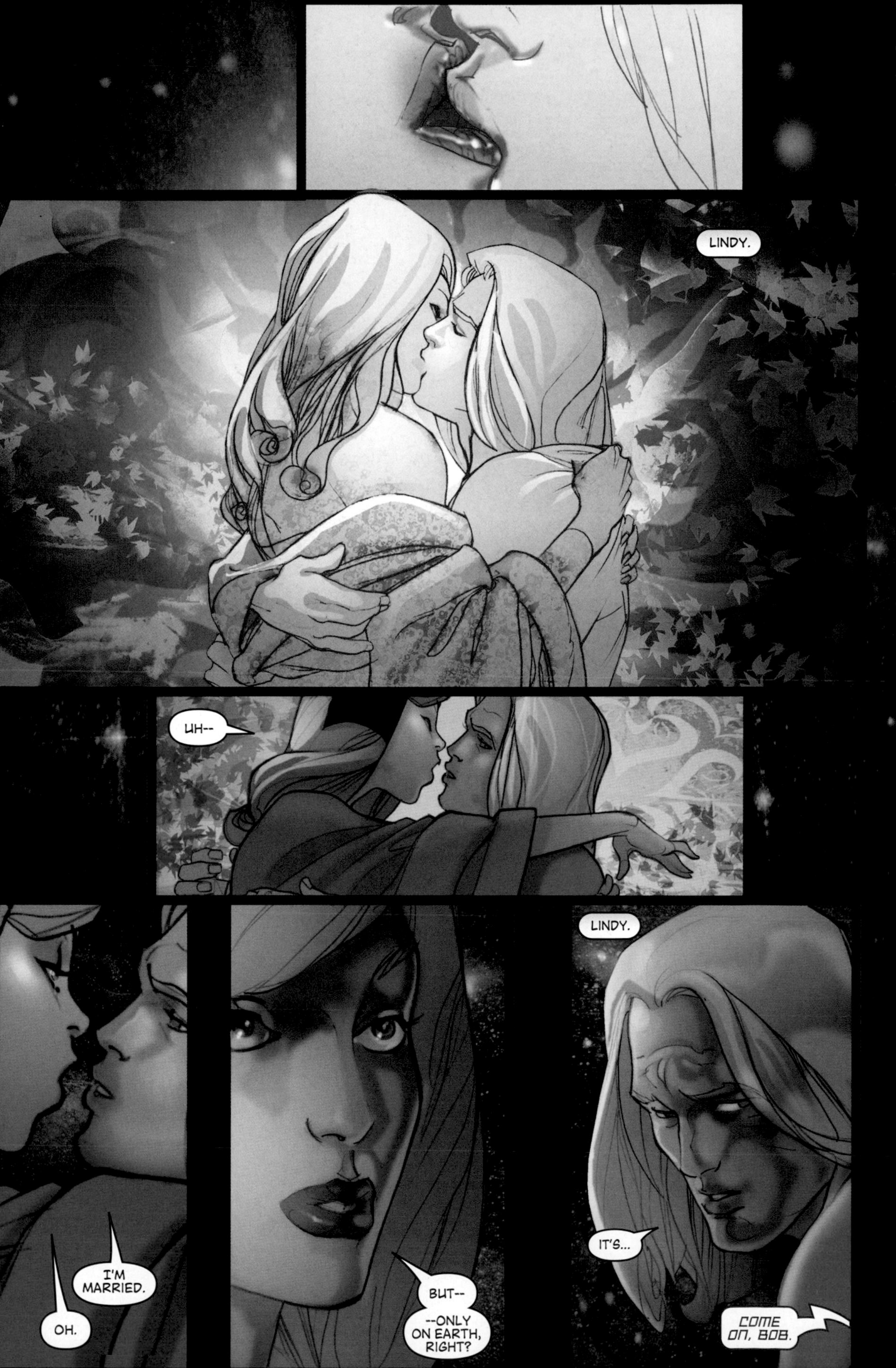
LINDY.
UH--
I'M MARRIED.
OH.
BUT--
--ONLY ON EARTH, RIGHT?
LINDY.
IT'S...
COME ON, BOB.

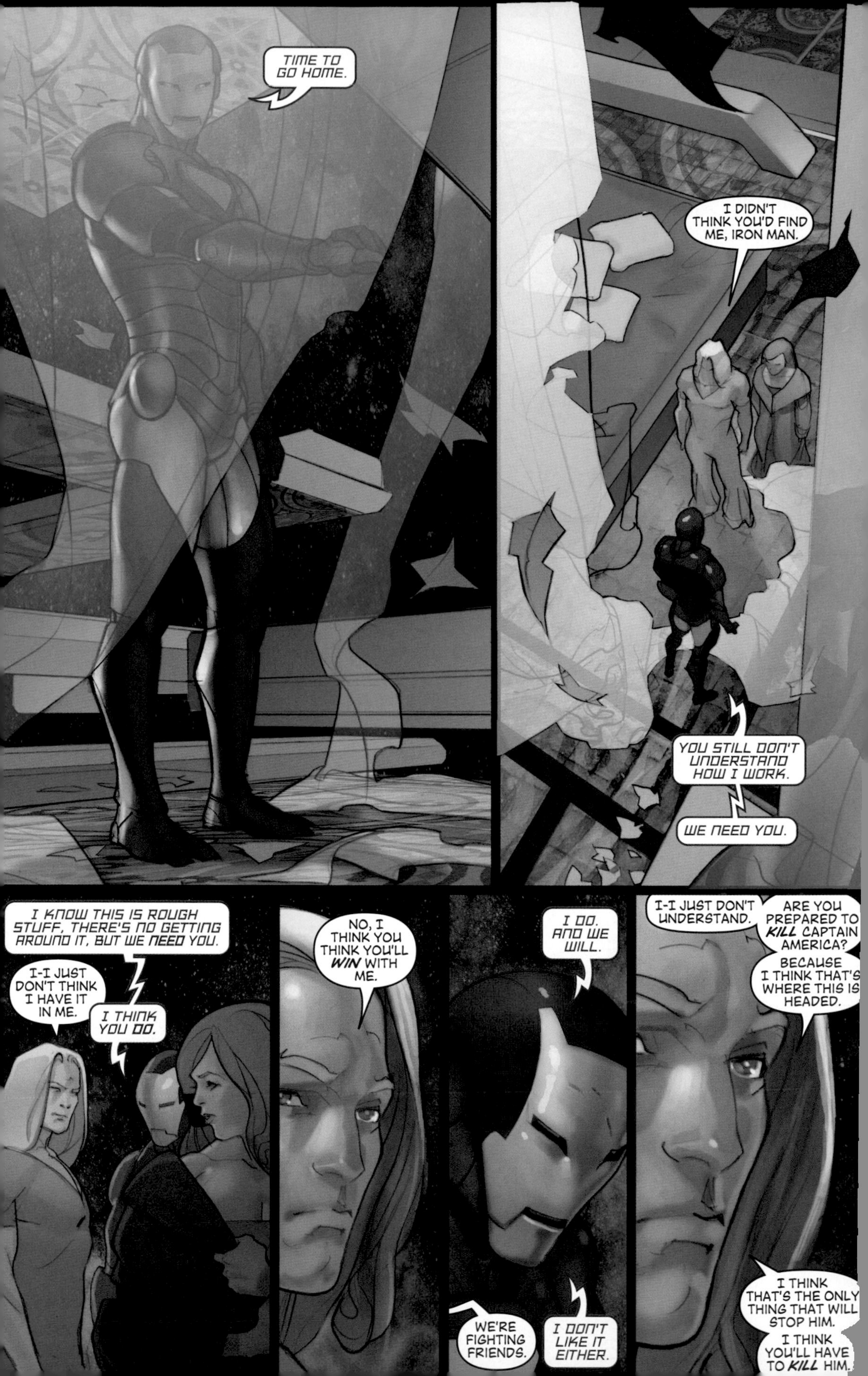
TIME TO GO HOME.
I DIDN'T THINK YOU'D FIND ME, IRON MAN.
YOU STILL DON'T UNDERSTAND HOW I WORK.
WE NEED YOU.
I KNOW THIS IS ROUGH STUFF, THERE'S NO GETTING AROUND IT, BUT WE NEED YOU.
I-I JUST DON'T THINK I HAVE IT IN ME.
I THINK YOU DO.
NO, I THINK YOU THINK YOU'LL WIN WITH ME.
I DO. AND WE WILL.
WE'RE FIGHTING FRIENDS.
I DON'T LIKE IT EITHER.
I-I JUST DON'T UNDERSTAND.
ARE YOU PREPARED TO KILL CAPTAIN AMERICA?
BECAUSE I THINK THAT'S WHERE THIS IS HEADED.
I THINK THAT'S THE ONLY THING THAT WILL STOP HIM.
I THINK YOU'LL HAVE TO KILL HIM.

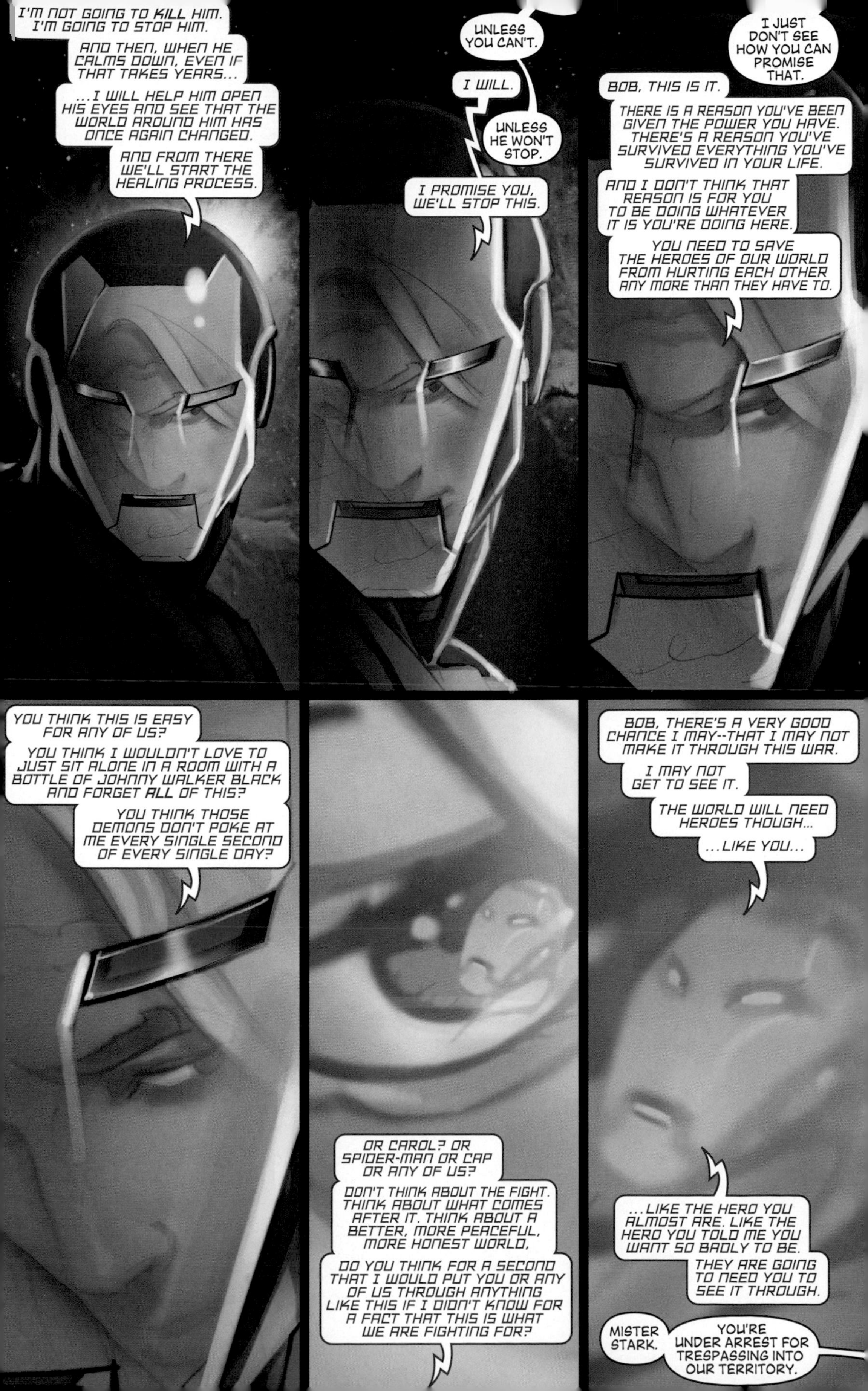
I'M NOT GOING TO KILL HIM. I'M GOING TO STOP HIM.
AND THEN, WHEN HE CALMS DOWN, EVEN IF THAT TAKES YEARS...
...I WILL HELP HIM OPEN HIS EYES AND SEE THAT THE WORLD AROUND HIM HAS ONCE AGAIN CHANGED.
AND FROM THERE WE'LL START THE HEALING PROCESS.
UNLESS YOU CAN'T.
I WILL.
UNLESS HE WON'T STOP.
I PROMISE YOU, WE'LL STOP THIS.
I JUST DON'T SEE HOW YOU CAN PROMISE THAT.
BOB, THIS IS IT.
THERE IS A REASON YOU'VE BEEN GIVEN THE POWER YOU HAVE. THERE'S A REASON YOU'VE SURVIVED EVERYTHING YOU'VE SURVIVED IN YOUR LIFE.
AND I DON'T THINK THAT REASON IS FOR YOU TO BE DOING WHATEVER IT IS YOU'RE DOING HERE.
YOU NEED TO SAVE THE HEROES OF OUR WORLD FROM HURTING EACH OTHER ANY MORE THAN THEY HAVE TO.
YOU THINK THIS IS EASY FOR ANY OF US?
YOU THINK I WOULDN'T LOVE TO JUST SIT ALONE IN A ROOM WITH A BOTTLE OF JOHNNY WALKER BLACK AND FORGET ALL OF THIS?
YOU THINK THOSE DEMONS DON'T POKE AT ME EVERY SINGLE SECOND OF EVERY SINGLE DAY?
OR CAROL? OR SPIDER-MAN OR CAP OR ANY OF US?
DON'T THINK ABOUT THE FIGHT. THINK ABOUT WHAT COMES AFTER IT. THINK ABOUT A BETTER, MORE PEACEFUL, MORE HONEST WORLD.
DO YOU THINK FOR A SECOND THAT I WOULD PUT YOU OR ANY OF US THROUGH ANYTHING LIKE THIS IF I DIDN'T KNOW FOR A FACT THAT THIS IS WHAT WE ARE FIGHTING FOR?
BOB, THERE'S A VERY GOOD CHANCE I MAY--THAT I MAY NOT MAKE IT THROUGH THIS WAR.
I MAY NOT GET TO SEE IT.
THE WORLD WILL NEED HEROES THOUGH...
...LIKE YOU...
...LIKE THE HERO YOU ALMOST ARE. LIKE THE HERO YOU TOLD ME YOU WANT SO BADLY TO BE.
THEY ARE GOING TO NEED YOU TO SEE IT THROUGH.
MISTER STARK.
YOU'RE UNDER ARREST FOR TRESPASSING INTO OUR TERRITORY.

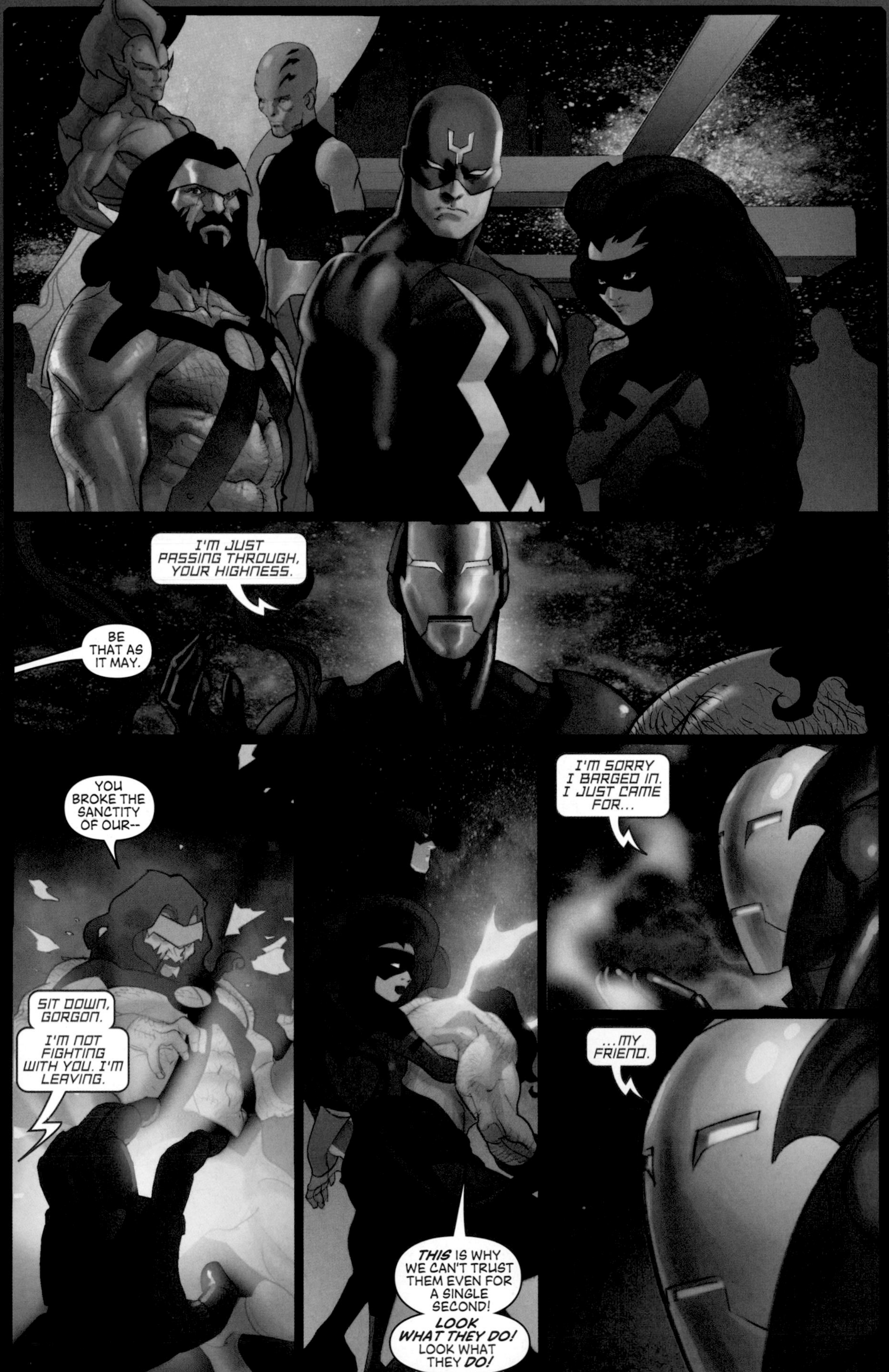
I'M JUST PASSING THROUGH, YOUR HIGHNESS.
BE THAT AS IT MAY.
YOU BROKE THE SANCTITY OF OUR--
SIT DOWN, GORGON.
I'M NOT FIGHTING WITH YOU. I'M LEAVING.
THIS IS WHY WE CAN'T TRUST THEM EVEN FOR A SINGLE SECOND! LOOK WHAT THEY DO! LOOK WHAT THEY DO!
I'M SORRY I BARGED IN. I JUST CAME FOR...
...MY FRIEND.

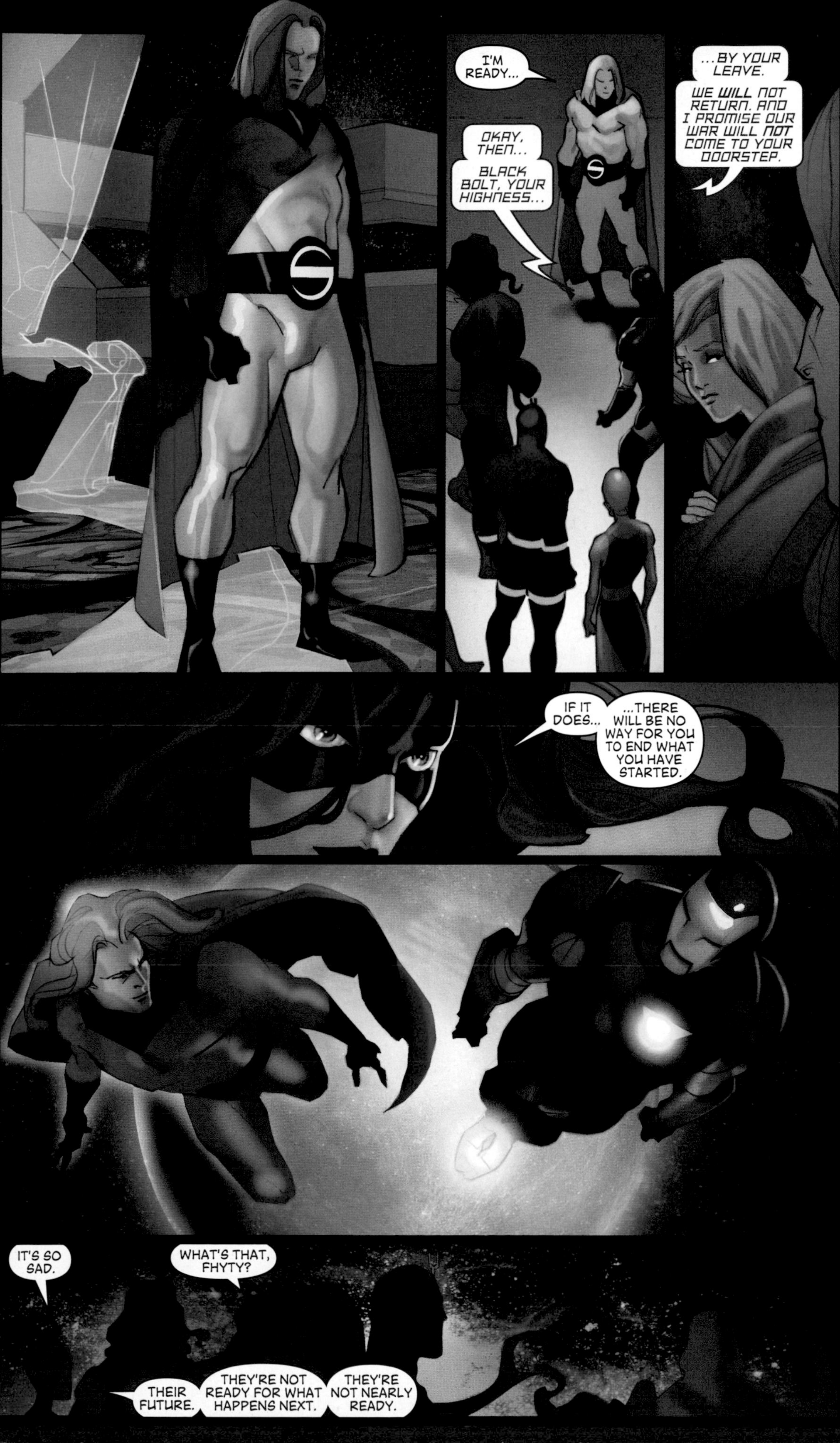
I'M READY...
OKAY, THEN...
BLACK BOLT, YOUR HIGHNESS...
...BY YOUR LEAVE.
WE WILL NOT RETURN. AND I PROMISE OUR WAR WILL NOT COME TO YOUR DOORSTEP.
IF IT DOES...
...THERE WILL BE NO WAY FOR YOU TO END WHAT YOU HAVE STARTED.
IT'S SO SAD.
WHAT'S THAT, FHYTY?
THEIR FUTURE.
THEY'RE NOT READY FOR WHAT HAPPENS NEXT.
THEY'RE NOT NEARLY READY.

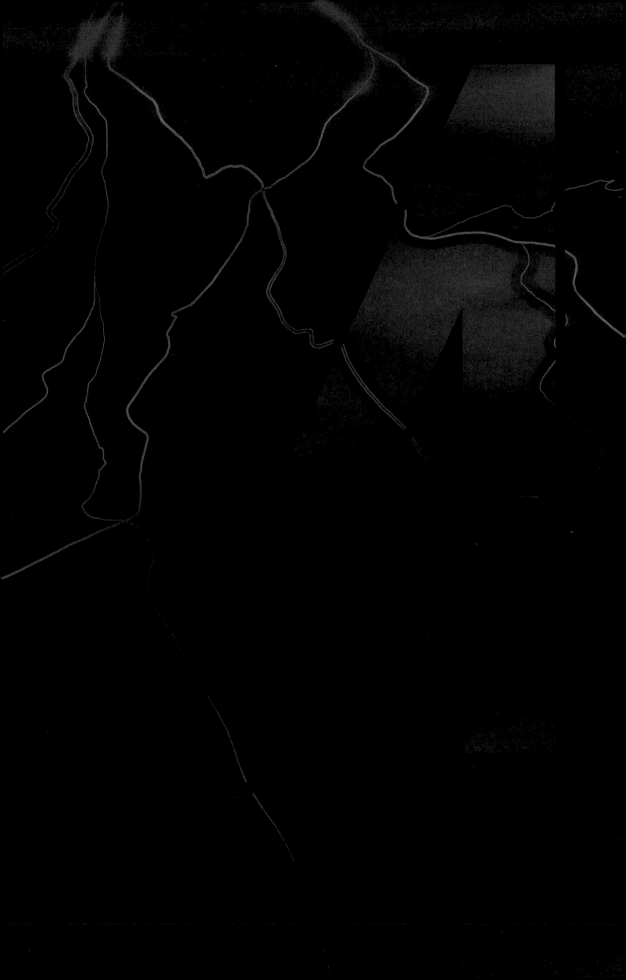

NEW AVENGERS

A MARVEL COMICS EVENT

CIVIL WAR

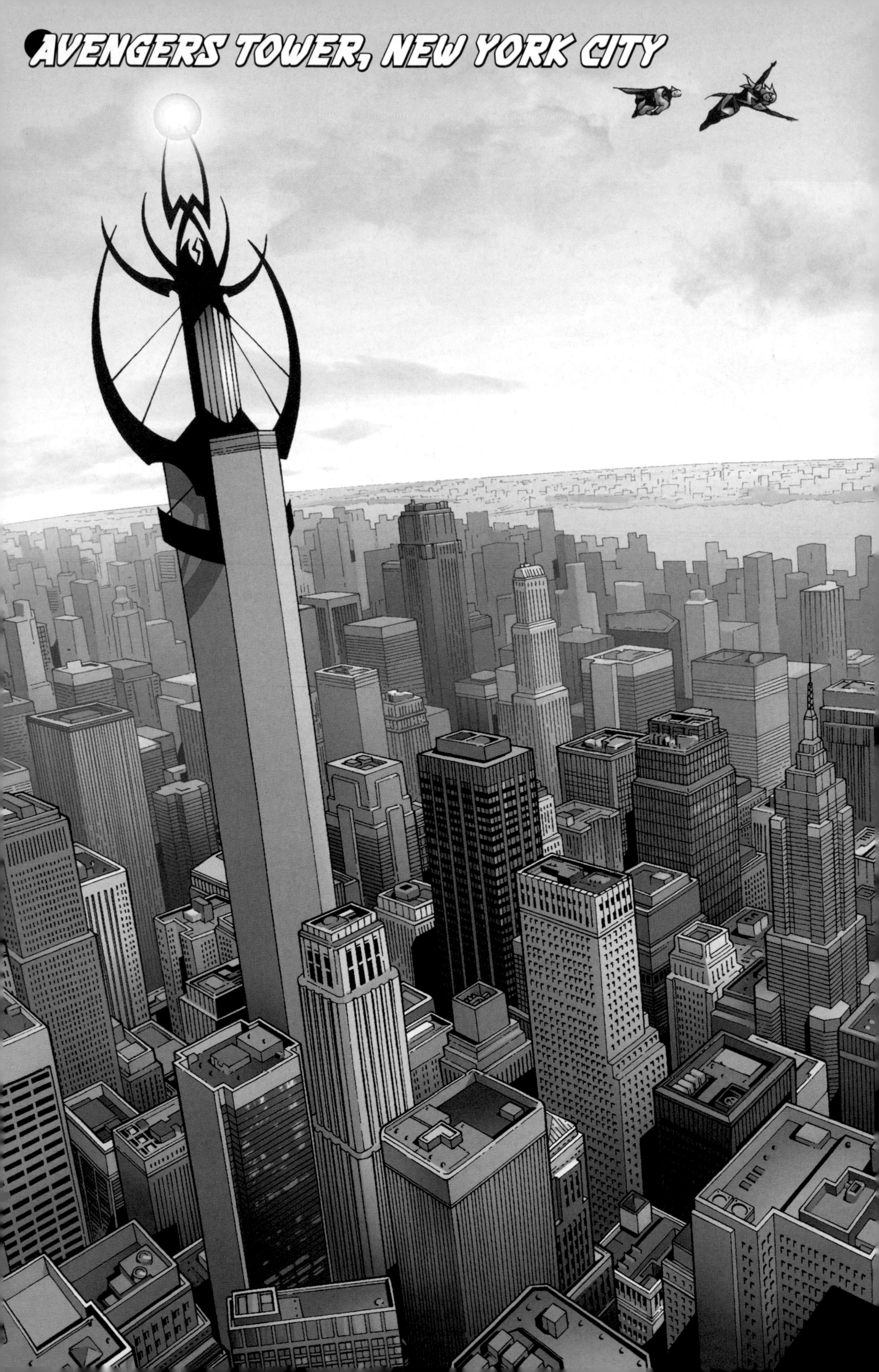
AVENGERS TOWER, NEW YORK CITY

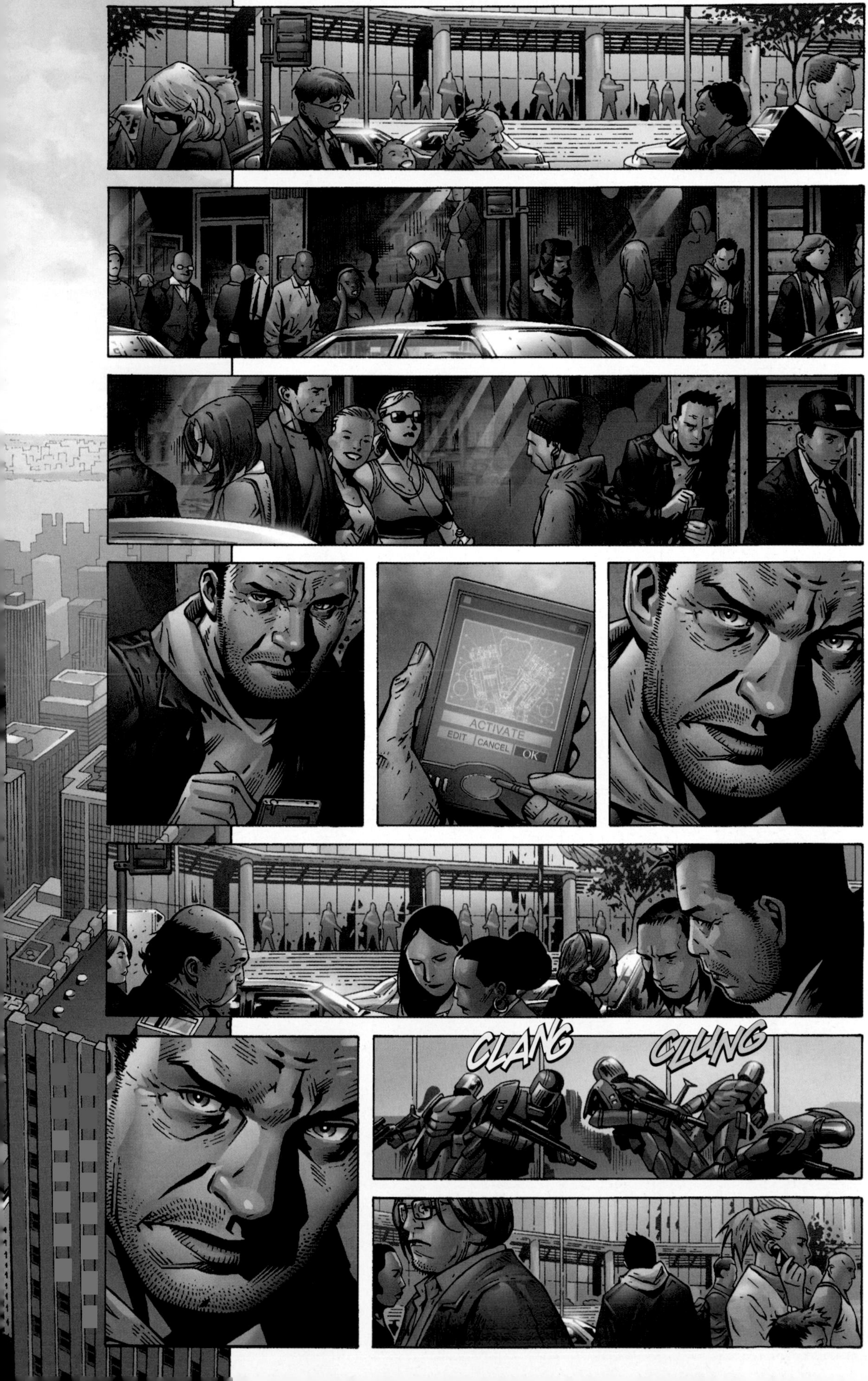
ACTIVATE
EDIT
CANCEL
OK
CLANG
CLUNG

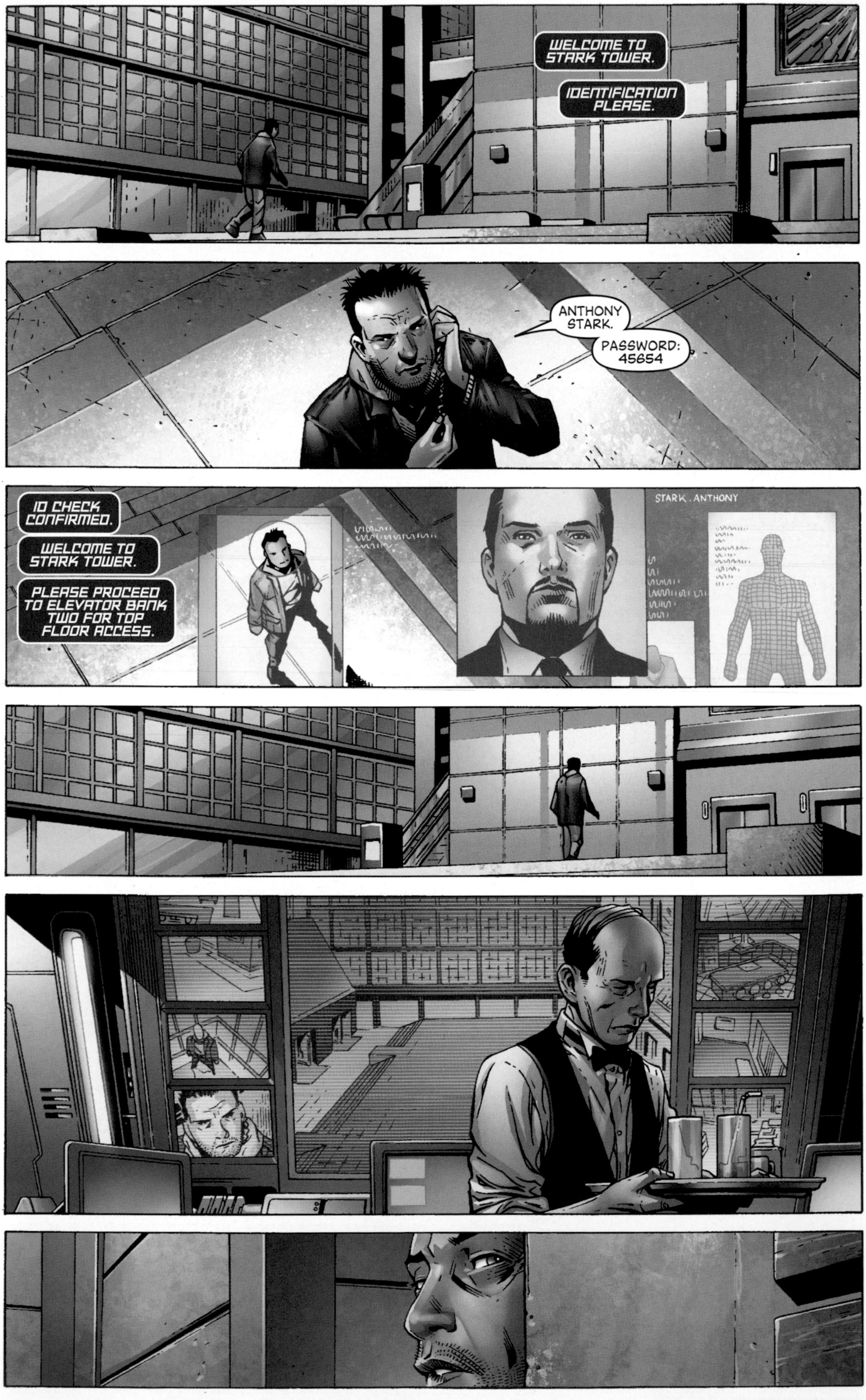
WELCOME TO STARK TOWER.
IDENTIFICATION PLEASE.
ANTHONY STARK.
PASSWORD: 45654
ID CHECK CONFIRMED.
WELCOME TO STARK TOWER.
PLEASE PROCEED TO ELEVATOR BANK TWO FOR TOP FLOOR ACCESS.
STARK, ANTHONY

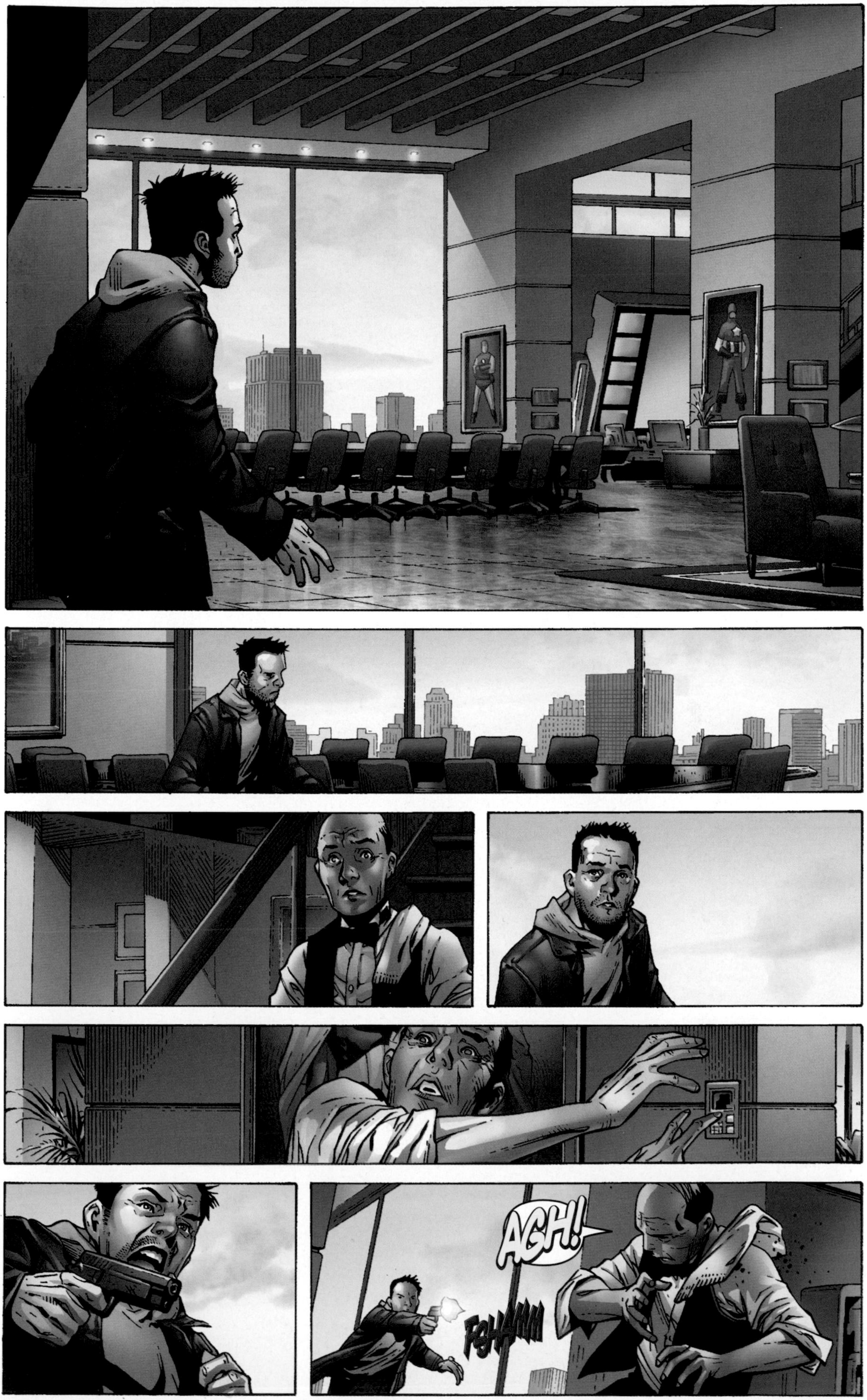
AGH!
FSHAMM

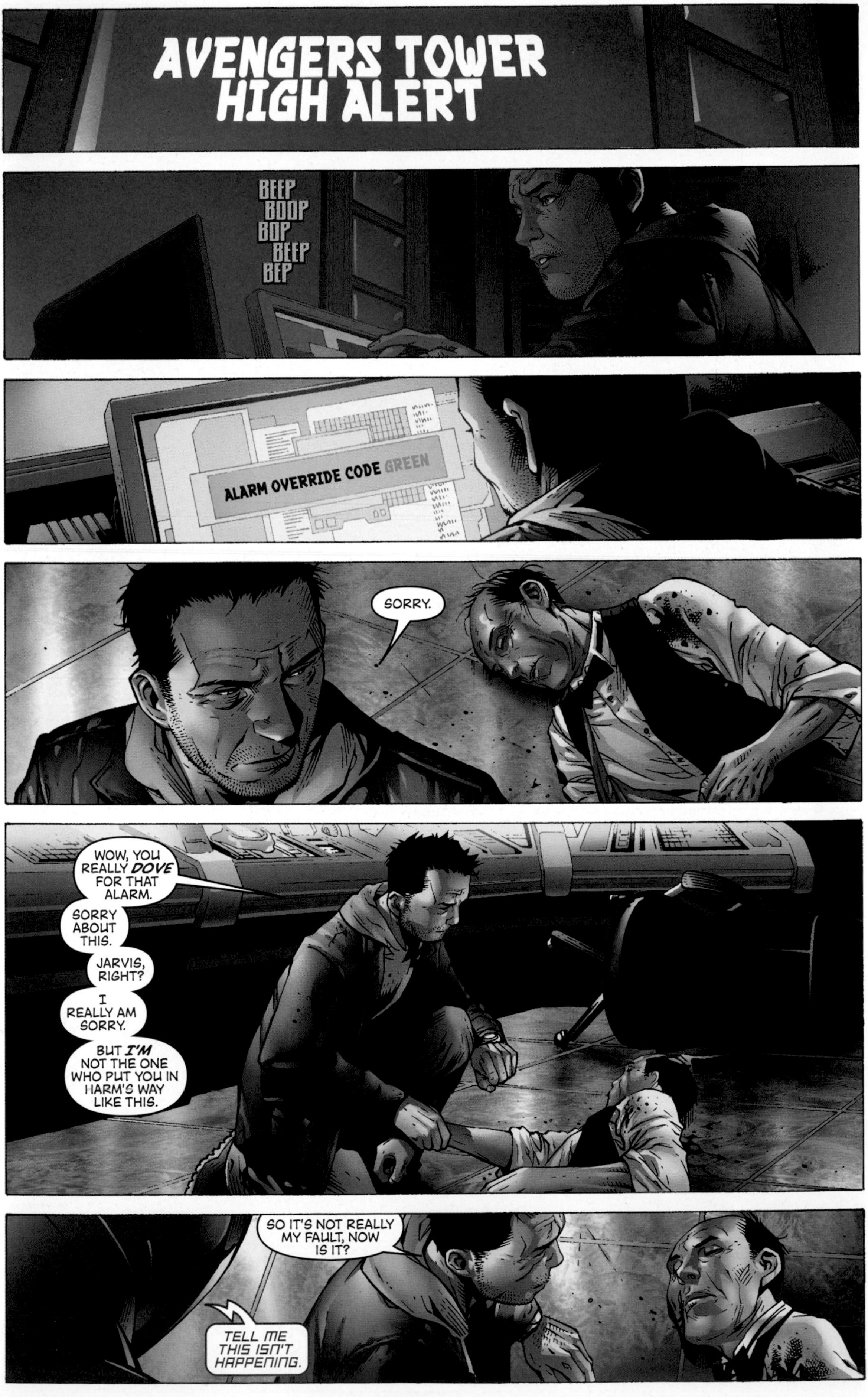
AVENGERS TOWER
HIGH ALERT
BEEP
BOOP
BOP
BEEP
BEP
ALARM OVERRIDE CODE GREEN
SORRY.
WOW, YOU REALLY *DOVE* FOR THAT ALARM.
SORRY ABOUT THIS.
JARVIS, RIGHT?
I REALLY AM SORRY.
BUT *I'M* NOT THE ONE WHO PUT YOU IN HARM'S WAY LIKE THIS.
SO IT'S NOT REALLY MY FAULT, NOW IS IT?
TELL ME THIS ISN'T HAPPENING.

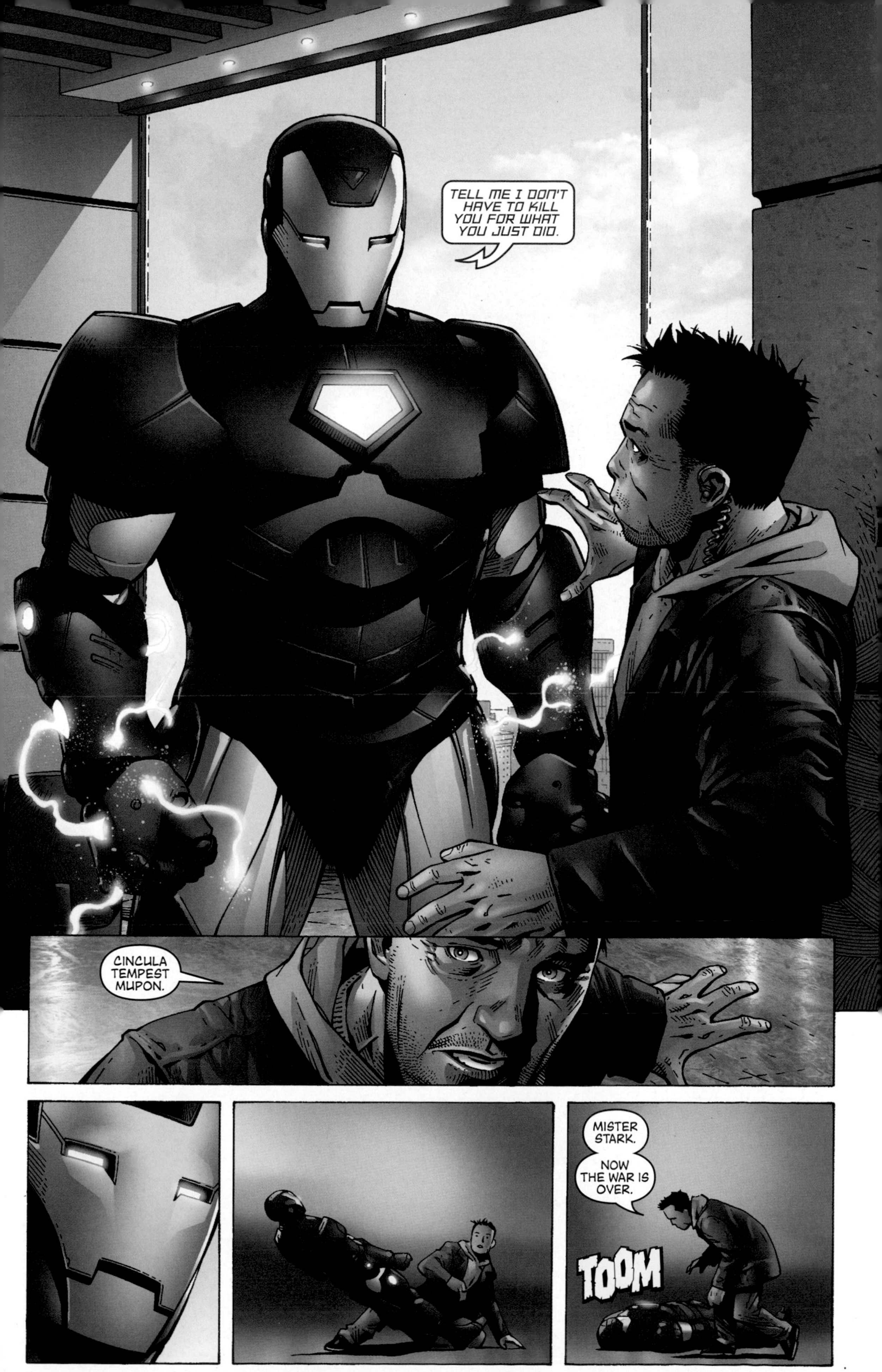
TELL ME I DON'T HAVE TO KILL YOU FOR WHAT YOU JUST DID.
CINCULA TEMPEST MUPON.
MISTER STARK.
NOW THE WAR IS OVER.
TOOM

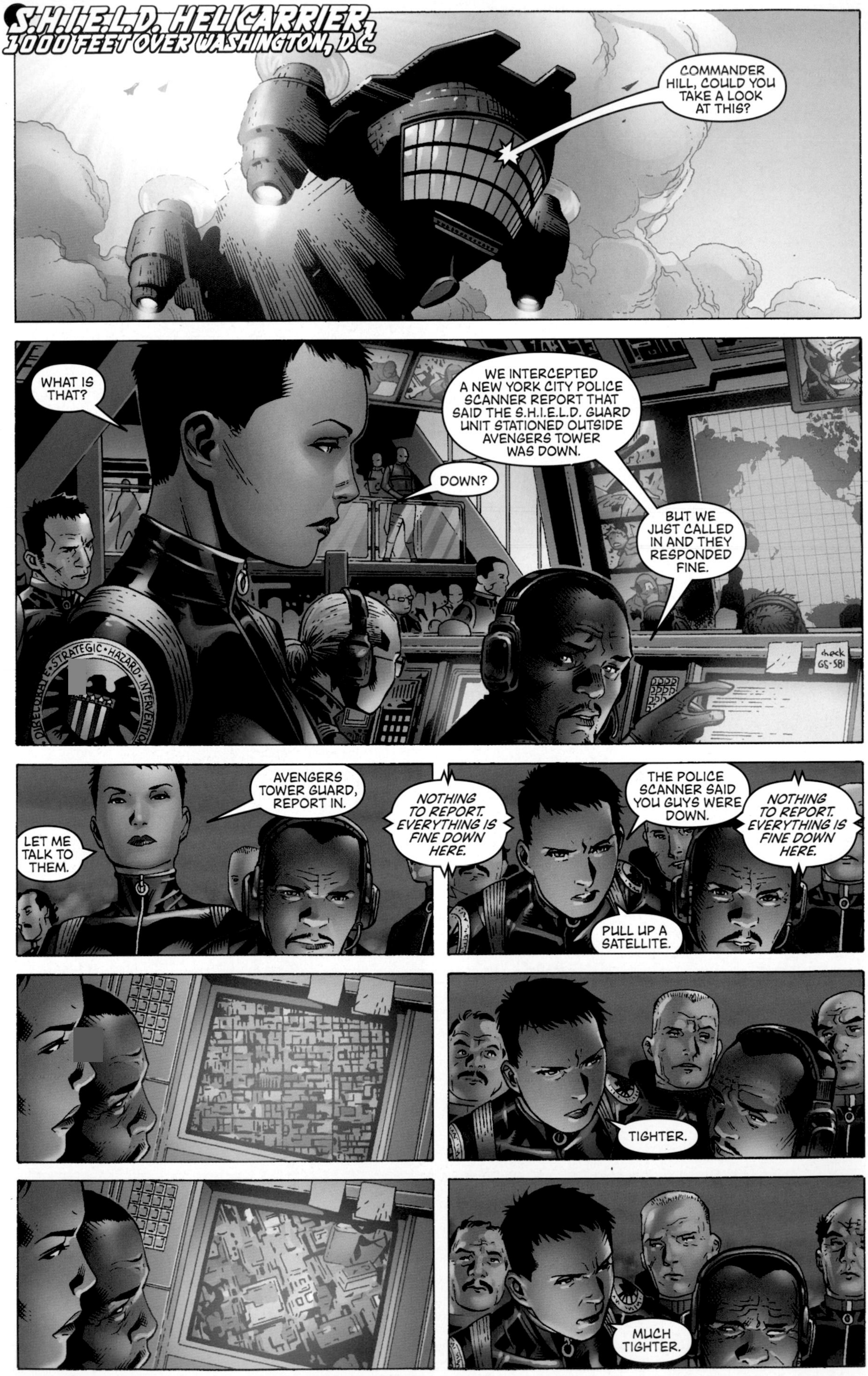
S.H.I.E.L.D. HELICARRIER, 1000 FEET OVER WASHINGTON, D.C.
COMMANDER HILL, COULD YOU TAKE A LOOK AT THIS?
WHAT IS THAT?
WE INTERCEPTED A NEW YORK CITY POLICE SCANNER REPORT THAT SAID THE S.H.I.E.L.D. GUARD UNIT STATIONED OUTSIDE AVENGERS TOWER WAS DOWN.
DOWN?
BUT WE JUST CALLED IN AND THEY RESPONDED FINE.
STRATEGIC HAZARD INTERVENTION
check GS-581
LET ME TALK TO THEM.
AVENGERS TOWER GUARD, REPORT IN.
NOTHING TO REPORT. EVERYTHING IS FINE DOWN HERE.
THE POLICE SCANNER SAID YOU GUYS WERE DOWN.
NOTHING TO REPORT. EVERYTHING IS FINE DOWN HERE.
PULL UP A SATELLITE.
TIGHTER.
MUCH TIGHTER.

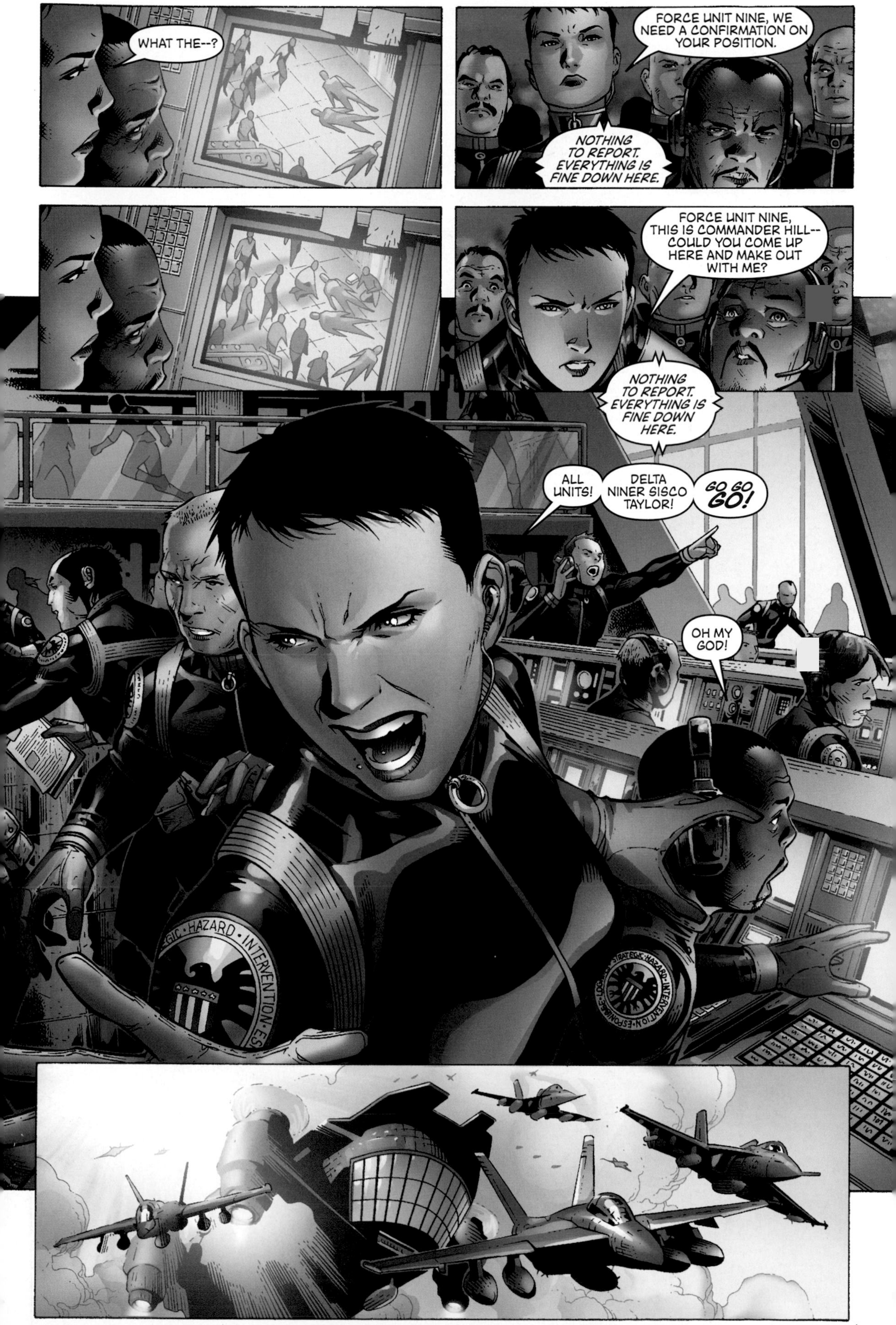
WHAT THE--?
FORCE UNIT NINE, WE NEED A CONFIRMATION ON YOUR POSITION.
NOTHING TO REPORT. EVERYTHING IS FINE DOWN HERE.
FORCE UNIT NINE, THIS IS COMMANDER HILL-- COULD YOU COME UP HERE AND MAKE OUT WITH ME?
NOTHING TO REPORT. EVERYTHING IS FINE DOWN HERE.
ALL UNITS!
DELTA NINER SISCO TAYLOR!
GO GO GO!
OH MY GOD!
STRATEGIC HAZARD INTERVENTION ESPIONAGE LOGISTICS

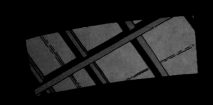
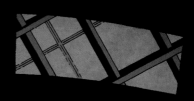

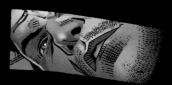
WHAT DID YOU *THINK* I WAS GOING TO DO, MR. STARK?

DID YOU THINK I WAS JUST GOING TO LET THIS GO ON?

THING IS--I BET YOU DIDN'T EVEN *CONSIDER* WHAT I WOULD THINK ABOUT THIS.

OR RHODES OR ANY OF US.

WE DEDICATED OUR *LIVES* TO YOU, MAN.

FOR YOU? NO.

FOR *IRON MAN.*

FOR THE *AVENGERS.*

FOR THE *IDEAL.* IT MEANT *EVERYTHING* TO ME. IT-IT--

AND YOU WENT-- AND-AND-AND-AND YOU JUST *COMPLETELY* TURNED AND DID AN ABOUT-FACE ON ME.

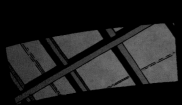
I WOULD *NEVER* HAVE AGREED TO USE MY DESIGNS TO ATTACK *CAPTAIN AMERICA.*

I WOULD *NEVER* HAVE SAID YES TO THIS.

NEVER!

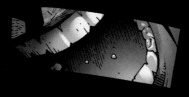

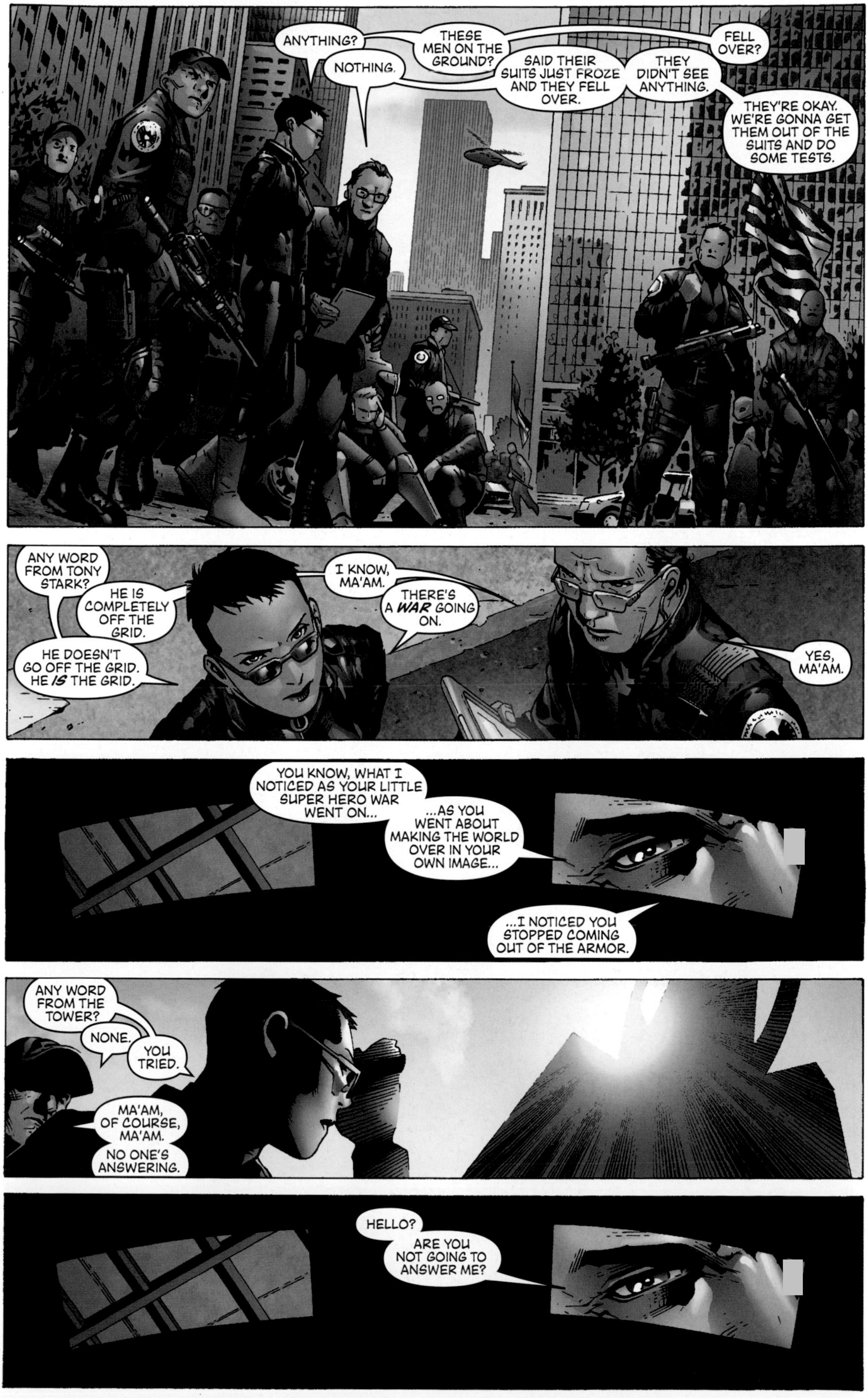
ANYTHING?
NOTHING.
THESE MEN ON THE GROUND?
SAID THEIR SUITS JUST FROZE AND THEY FELL OVER.
FELL OVER?
THEY DIDN'T SEE ANYTHING.
THEY'RE OKAY. WE'RE GONNA GET THEM OUT OF THE SUITS AND DO SOME TESTS.
ANY WORD FROM TONY STARK?
HE IS COMPLETELY OFF THE GRID.
HE DOESN'T GO OFF THE GRID. HE *IS* THE GRID.
I KNOW, MA'AM.
THERE'S A ***WAR*** GOING ON.
YES, MA'AM.
YOU KNOW, WHAT I NOTICED AS YOUR LITTLE SUPER HERO WAR WENT ON...
...AS YOU WENT ABOUT MAKING THE WORLD OVER IN YOUR OWN IMAGE...
...I NOTICED YOU STOPPED COMING OUT OF THE ARMOR.
ANY WORD FROM THE TOWER?
NONE.
YOU TRIED.
MA'AM, OF COURSE, MA'AM.
NO ONE'S ANSWERING.
HELLO?
ARE YOU NOT GOING TO ANSWER ME?

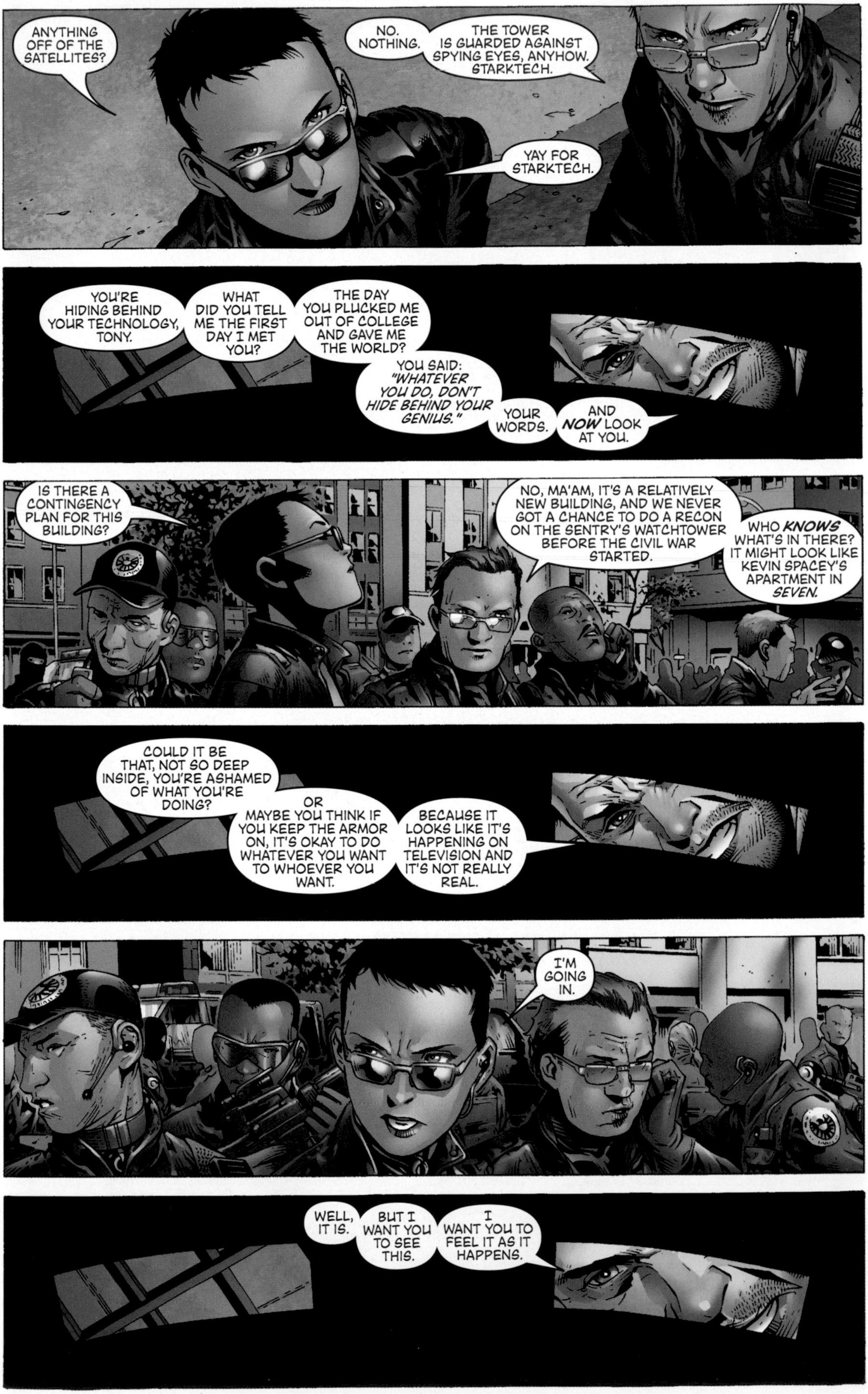

ANYTHING OFF OF THE SATELLITES?
NO. NOTHING.
THE TOWER IS GUARDED AGAINST SPYING EYES, ANYHOW. STARKTECH.
YAY FOR STARKTECH.
YOU'RE HIDING BEHIND YOUR TECHNOLOGY, TONY.
WHAT DID YOU TELL ME THE FIRST DAY I MET YOU?
THE DAY YOU PLUCKED ME OUT OF COLLEGE AND GAVE ME THE WORLD?
YOU SAID: "WHATEVER YOU DO, DON'T HIDE BEHIND YOUR GENIUS."
YOUR WORDS.
AND NOW LOOK AT YOU.
IS THERE A CONTINGENCY PLAN FOR THIS BUILDING?
NO, MA'AM, IT'S A RELATIVELY NEW BUILDING, AND WE NEVER GOT A CHANCE TO DO A RECON ON THE SENTRY'S WATCHTOWER BEFORE THE CIVIL WAR STARTED.
WHO KNOWS WHAT'S IN THERE? IT MIGHT LOOK LIKE KEVIN SPACEY'S APARTMENT IN SEVEN.
COULD IT BE THAT, NOT SO DEEP INSIDE, YOU'RE ASHAMED OF WHAT YOU'RE DOING?
OR MAYBE YOU THINK IF YOU KEEP THE ARMOR ON, IT'S OKAY TO DO WHATEVER YOU WANT TO WHOEVER YOU WANT.
BECAUSE IT LOOKS LIKE IT'S HAPPENING ON TELEVISION AND IT'S NOT REALLY REAL.
I'M GOING IN.
WELL, IT IS.
BUT I WANT YOU TO SEE THIS.
I WANT YOU TO FEEL IT AS IT HAPPENS.

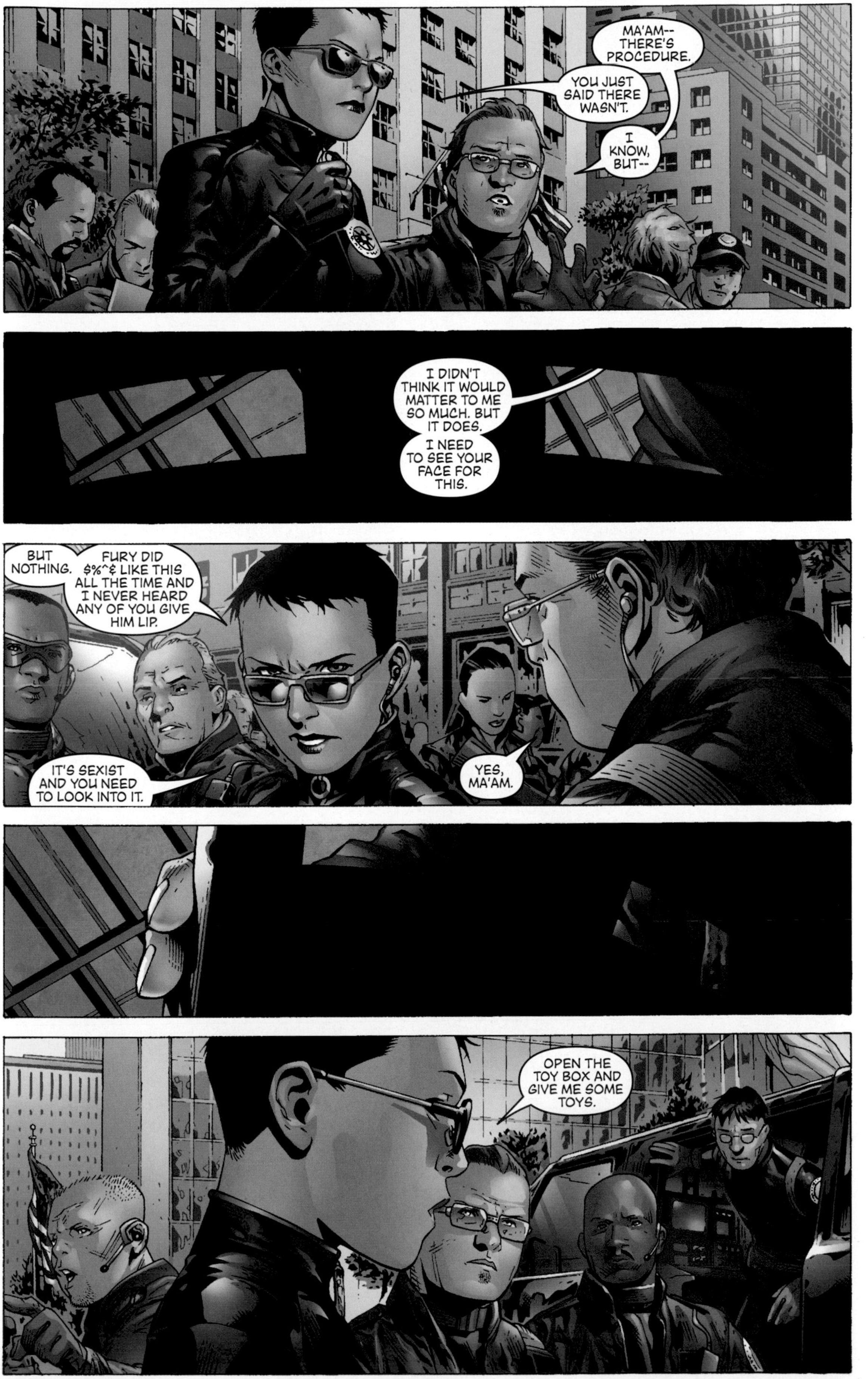

MA'AM-- THERE'S PROCEDURE.
YOU JUST SAID THERE WASN'T.
I KNOW, BUT--
I DIDN'T THINK IT WOULD MATTER TO ME SO MUCH. BUT IT DOES.
I NEED TO SEE YOUR FACE FOR THIS.
BUT NOTHING.
FURY DID $%^& LIKE THIS ALL THE TIME AND I NEVER HEARD ANY OF YOU GIVE HIM LIP.
IT'S SEXIST AND YOU NEED TO LOOK INTO IT.
YES, MA'AM.
OPEN THE TOY BOX AND GIVE ME SOME TOYS.

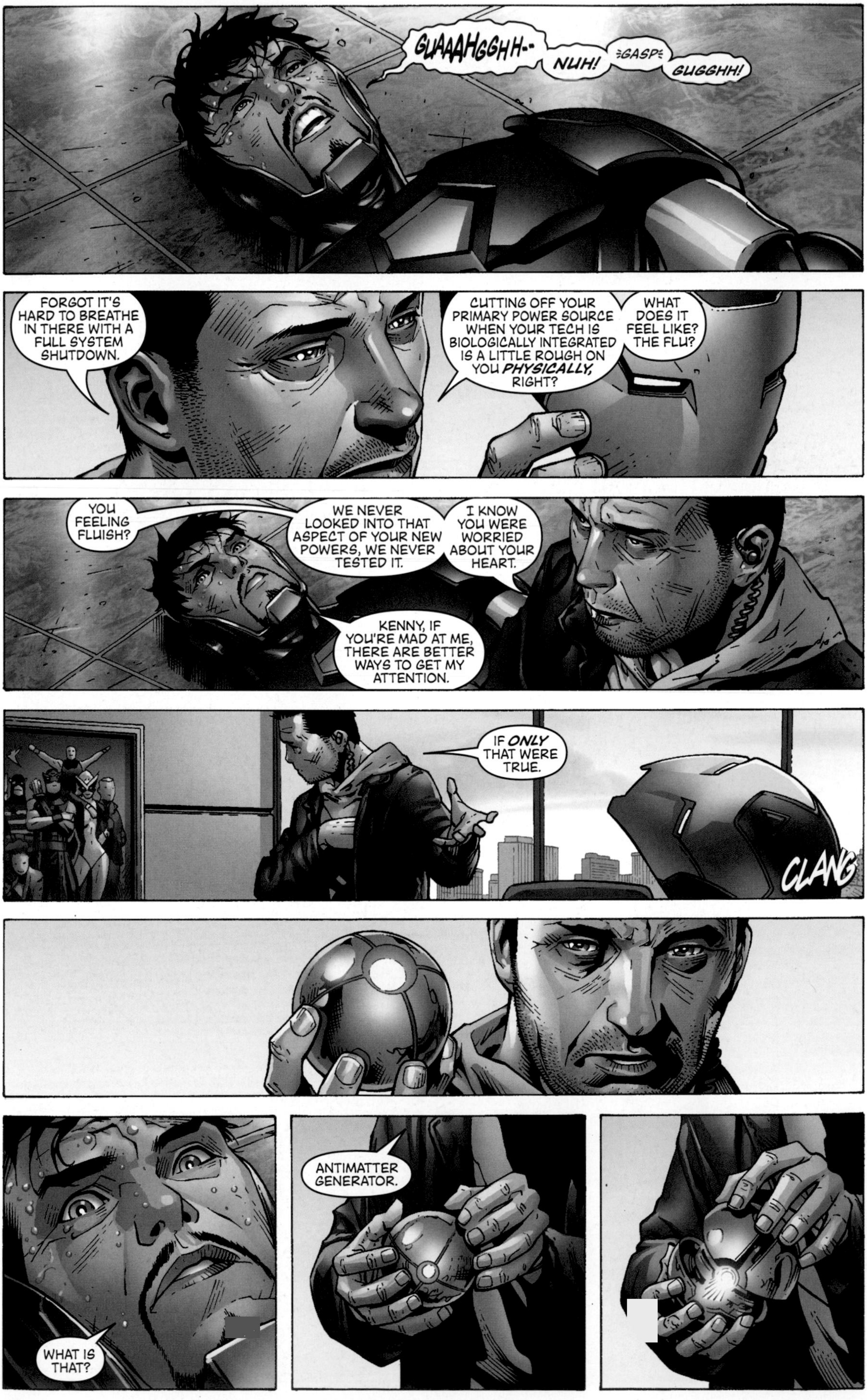
GUAAAHGGHH--
NUH!
GASP
GUGGHH!
FORGOT IT'S HARD TO BREATHE IN THERE WITH A FULL SYSTEM SHUTDOWN.
CUTTING OFF YOUR PRIMARY POWER SOURCE WHEN YOUR TECH IS BIOLOGICALLY INTEGRATED IS A LITTLE ROUGH ON YOU PHYSICALLY, RIGHT?
WHAT DOES IT FEEL LIKE? THE FLU?
YOU FEELING FLUISH?
WE NEVER LOOKED INTO THAT ASPECT OF YOUR NEW POWERS, WE NEVER TESTED IT.
I KNOW YOU WERE WORRIED ABOUT YOUR HEART.
KENNY, IF YOU'RE MAD AT ME, THERE ARE BETTER WAYS TO GET MY ATTENTION.
IF ONLY THAT WERE TRUE.
CLANG
WHAT IS THAT?
ANTIMATTER GENERATOR.

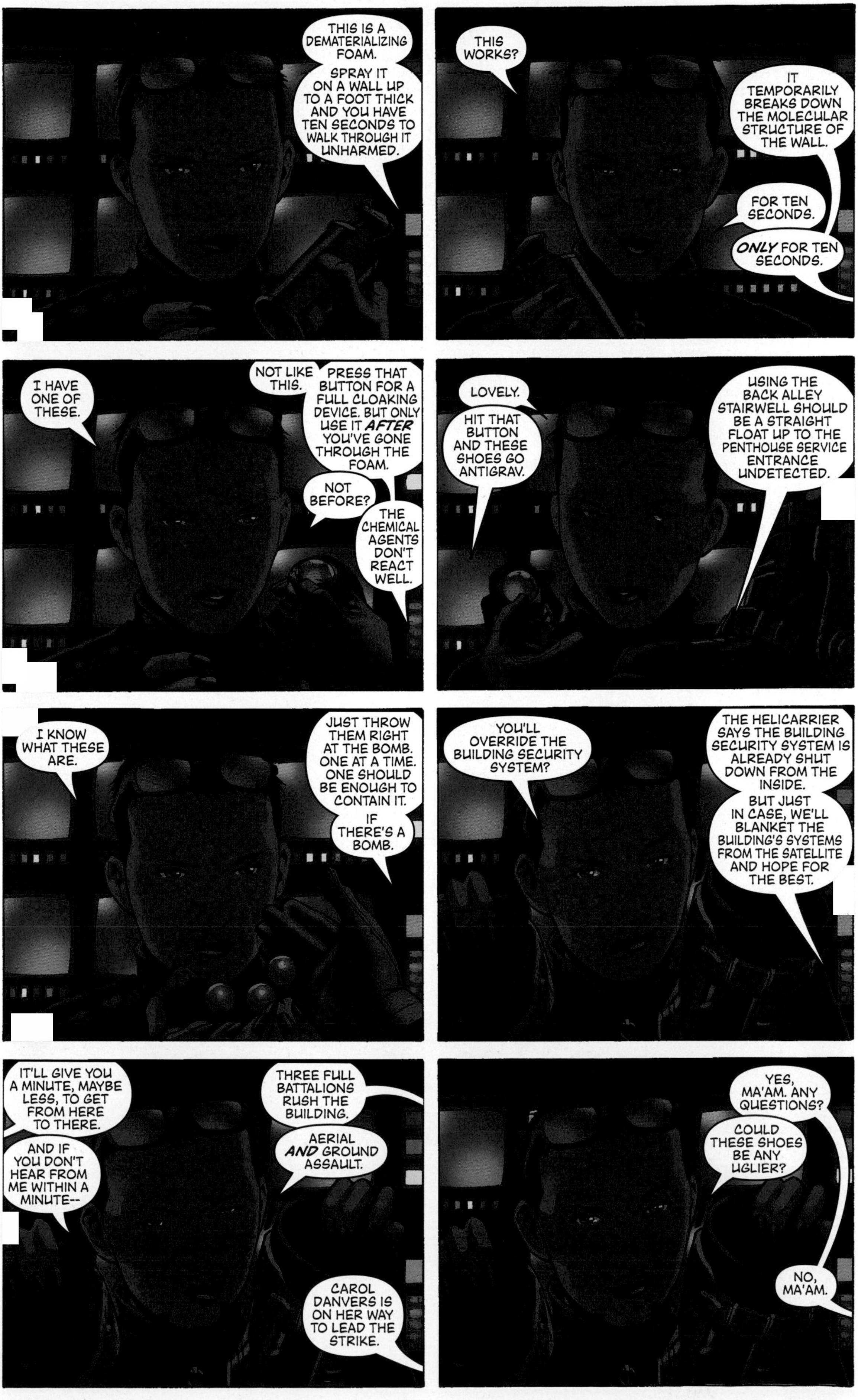
THIS IS A DEMATERIALIZING FOAM.
SPRAY IT ON A WALL UP TO A FOOT THICK AND YOU HAVE TEN SECONDS TO WALK THROUGH IT UNHARMED.
THIS WORKS?
IT TEMPORARILY BREAKS DOWN THE MOLECULAR STRUCTURE OF THE WALL.
FOR TEN SECONDS.
ONLY FOR TEN SECONDS.
I HAVE ONE OF THESE.
NOT LIKE THIS.
PRESS THAT BUTTON FOR A FULL CLOAKING DEVICE. BUT ONLY USE IT *AFTER* YOU'VE GONE THROUGH THE FOAM.
NOT BEFORE?
THE CHEMICAL AGENTS DON'T REACT WELL.
LOVELY.
HIT THAT BUTTON AND THESE SHOES GO ANTIGRAV.
USING THE BACK ALLEY STAIRWELL SHOULD BE A STRAIGHT FLOAT UP TO THE PENTHOUSE SERVICE ENTRANCE UNDETECTED.
I KNOW WHAT THESE ARE.
JUST THROW THEM RIGHT AT THE BOMB. ONE AT A TIME. ONE SHOULD BE ENOUGH TO CONTAIN IT.
IF THERE'S A BOMB.
YOU'LL OVERRIDE THE BUILDING SECURITY SYSTEM?
THE HELICARRIER SAYS THE BUILDING SECURITY SYSTEM IS ALREADY SHUT DOWN FROM THE INSIDE.
BUT JUST IN CASE, WE'LL BLANKET THE BUILDING'S SYSTEMS FROM THE SATELLITE AND HOPE FOR THE BEST.
IT'LL GIVE YOU A MINUTE, MAYBE LESS, TO GET FROM HERE TO THERE.
AND IF YOU DON'T HEAR FROM ME WITHIN A MINUTE--
THREE FULL BATTALIONS RUSH THE BUILDING.
AERIAL *AND* GROUND ASSAULT.
CAROL DANVERS IS ON HER WAY TO LEAD THE STRIKE.
YES, MA'AM. ANY QUESTIONS?
COULD THESE SHOES BE ANY UGLIER?
NO, MA'AM.

YOU REMEMBER THIS PIECE?

IT'S THE MATTER REVERSAL PROCESSOR THAT YOU WOULDN'T LET ME BUILD. I BUILT IT ANYHOW, AND THIS BUILDING IS GOING TO DISAPPEAR.

FSSSS

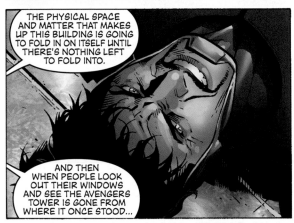

THE PHYSICAL SPACE AND MATTER THAT MAKES UP THIS BUILDING IS GOING TO FOLD IN ON ITSELF UNTIL THERE'S NOTHING LEFT TO FOLD INTO.

AND THEN WHEN PEOPLE LOOK OUT THEIR WINDOWS AND SEE THE AVENGERS TOWER IS GONE FROM WHERE IT ONCE STOOD...

...MAYBE THEN THEY'LL STOP WITH THIS "WHOSE SIDE ARE YOU ON?" CRAP.

BECAUSE YOU'LL HAVE NO SIDES.

IT TAKES A MINUTE TO HEAT UP.

BUT IT WORKS.

I KNOW BECAUSE MY GARAGE IS NO LONGER WITH US.

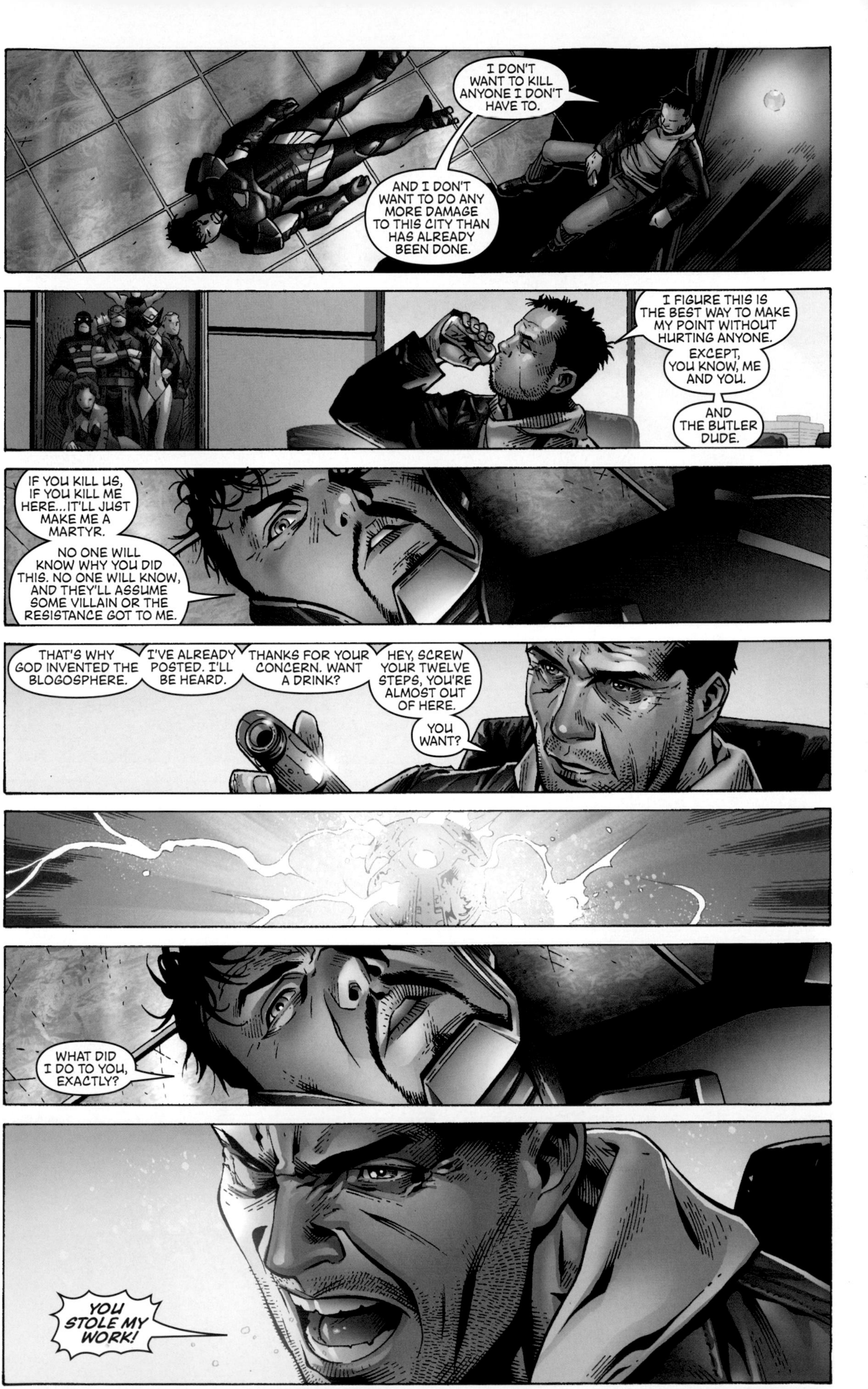
I DON'T WANT TO KILL ANYONE I DON'T HAVE TO.
AND I DON'T WANT TO DO ANY MORE DAMAGE TO THIS CITY THAN HAS ALREADY BEEN DONE.
I FIGURE THIS IS THE BEST WAY TO MAKE MY POINT WITHOUT HURTING ANYONE.
EXCEPT, YOU KNOW, ME AND YOU.
AND THE BUTLER DUDE.
IF YOU KILL US, IF YOU KILL ME HERE...IT'LL JUST MAKE ME A MARTYR.
NO ONE WILL KNOW WHY YOU DID THIS. NO ONE WILL KNOW, AND THEY'LL ASSUME SOME VILLAIN OR THE RESISTANCE GOT TO ME.
THAT'S WHY GOD INVENTED THE BLOGOSPHERE.
I'VE ALREADY POSTED. I'LL BE HEARD.
THANKS FOR YOUR CONCERN. WANT A DRINK?
HEY, SCREW YOUR TWELVE STEPS, YOU'RE ALMOST OUT OF HERE.
YOU WANT?
WHAT DID I DO TO YOU, EXACTLY?
YOU STOLE MY WORK!

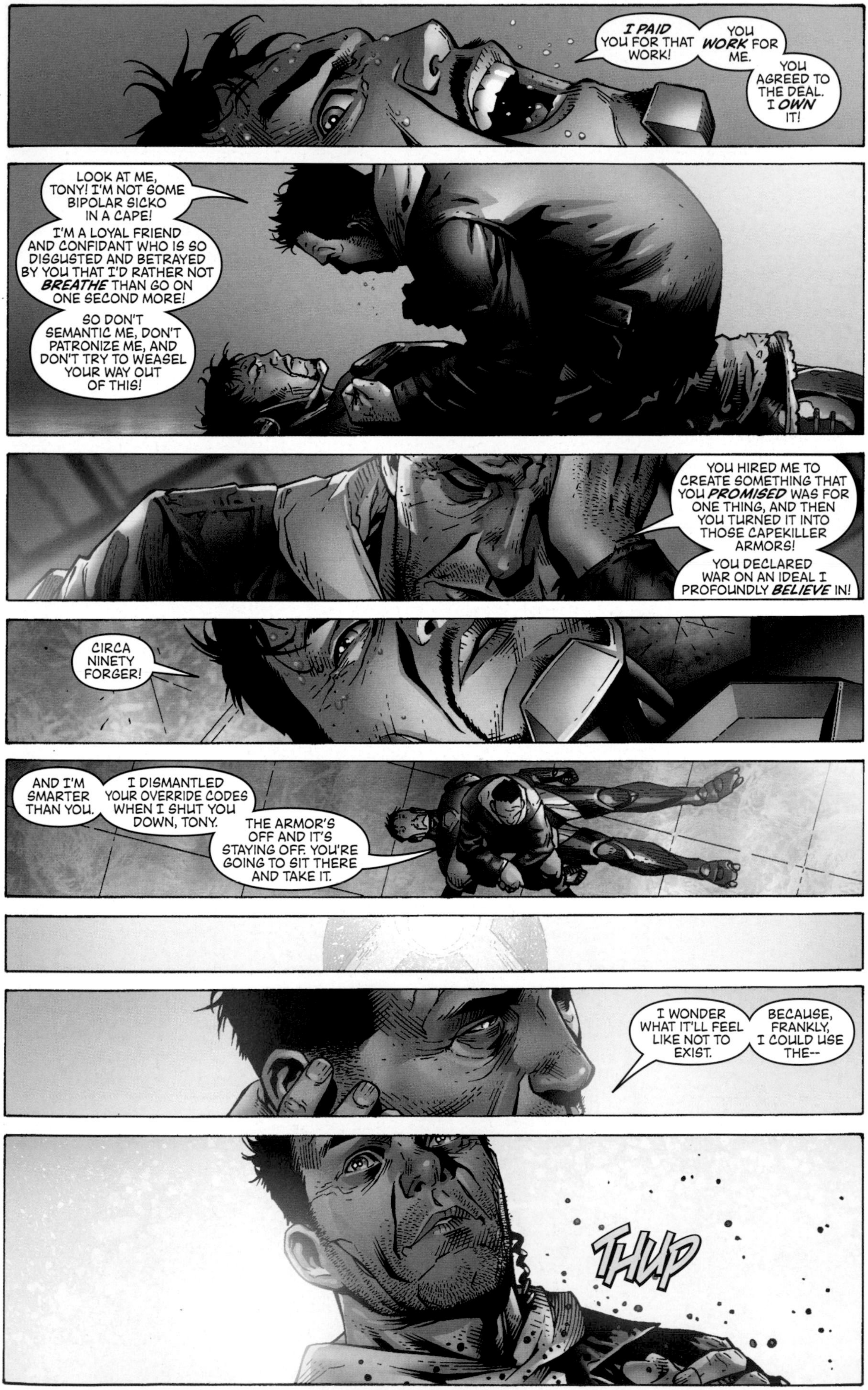
I PAID YOU FOR THAT WORK!
YOU WORK FOR ME.
YOU AGREED TO THE DEAL. I OWN IT!
LOOK AT ME, TONY! I'M NOT SOME BIPOLAR SICKO IN A CAPE!
I'M A LOYAL FRIEND AND CONFIDANT WHO IS SO DISGUSTED AND BETRAYED BY YOU THAT I'D RATHER NOT BREATHE THAN GO ON ONE SECOND MORE!
SO DON'T SEMANTIC ME, DON'T PATRONIZE ME, AND DON'T TRY TO WEASEL YOUR WAY OUT OF THIS!
YOU HIRED ME TO CREATE SOMETHING THAT YOU PROMISED WAS FOR ONE THING, AND THEN YOU TURNED IT INTO THOSE CAPEKILLER ARMORS!
YOU DECLARED WAR ON AN IDEAL I PROFOUNDLY BELIEVE IN!
CIRCA NINETY FORGER!
AND I'M SMARTER THAN YOU.
I DISMANTLED YOUR OVERRIDE CODES WHEN I SHUT YOU DOWN, TONY.
THE ARMOR'S OFF AND IT'S STAYING OFF. YOU'RE GOING TO SIT THERE AND TAKE IT.
I WONDER WHAT IT'LL FEEL LIKE NOT TO EXIST.
BECAUSE, FRANKLY, I COULD USE THE--
THUP

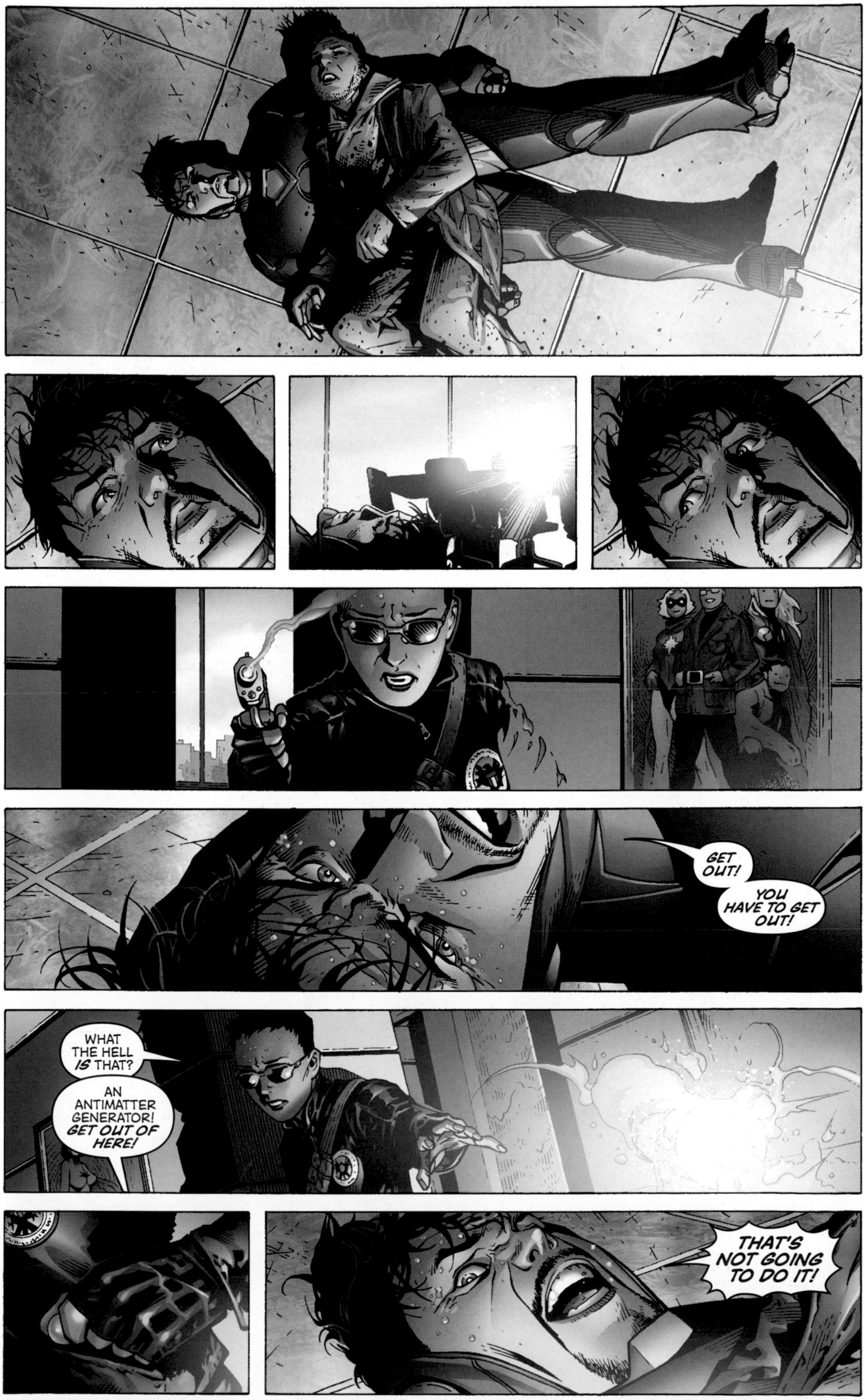
GET OUT!
YOU HAVE TO GET OUT!
WHAT THE HELL IS THAT?
AN ANTIMATTER GENERATOR! GET OUT OF HERE!
THAT'S NOT GOING TO DO IT!

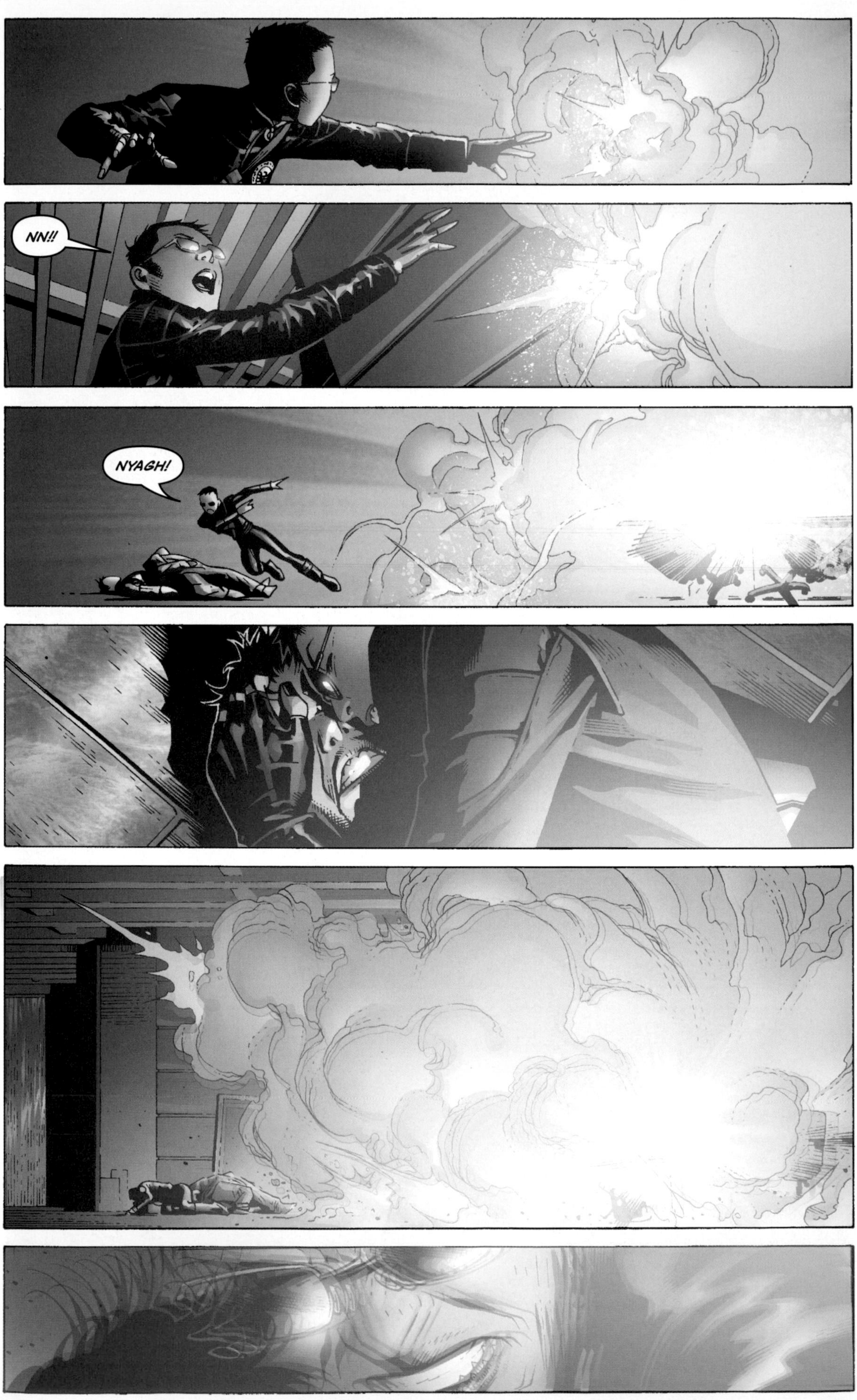
NN!!
NYAGH!

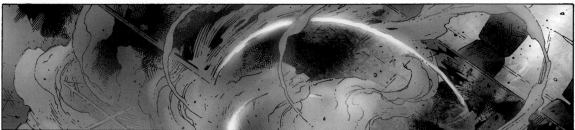

YOU OKAY?

NO.

MED TEAM, WE NEED AN EVAC FOR JARVIS.

OH MY GOD! TONY!

WHAT HAPPENED?

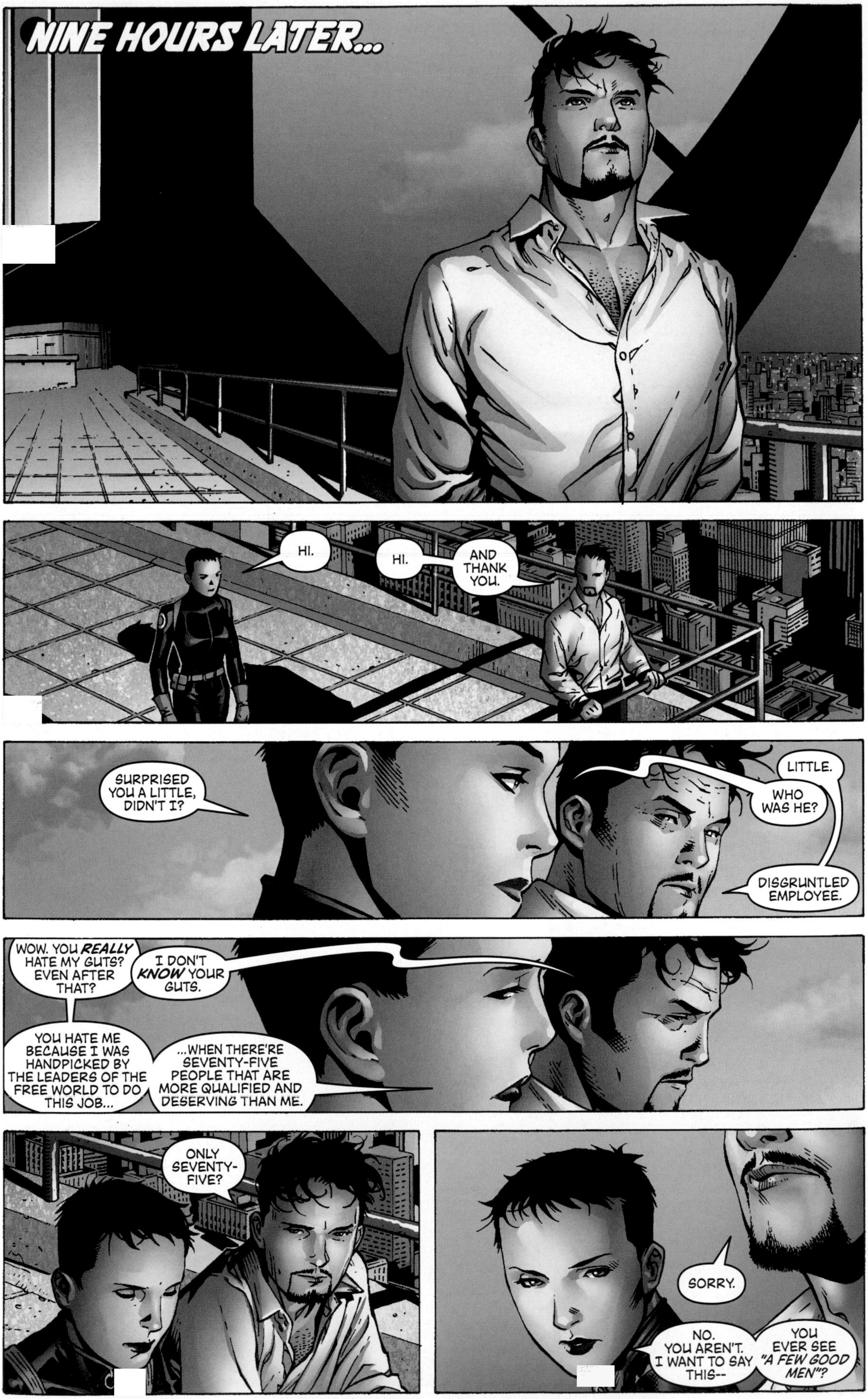

NINE HOURS LATER...
HI.
HI.
AND THANK YOU.
SURPRISED YOU A LITTLE, DIDN'T I?
LITTLE.
WHO WAS HE?
DISGRUNTLED EMPLOYEE.
WOW. YOU REALLY HATE MY GUTS? EVEN AFTER THAT?
I DON'T KNOW YOUR GUTS.
YOU HATE ME BECAUSE I WAS HANDPICKED BY THE LEADERS OF THE FREE WORLD TO DO THIS JOB...
...WHEN THERE'RE SEVENTY-FIVE PEOPLE THAT ARE MORE QUALIFIED AND DESERVING THAN ME.
ONLY SEVENTY-FIVE?
SORRY.
NO. YOU AREN'T. I WANT TO SAY THIS--
YOU EVER SEE "A FEW GOOD MEN"?

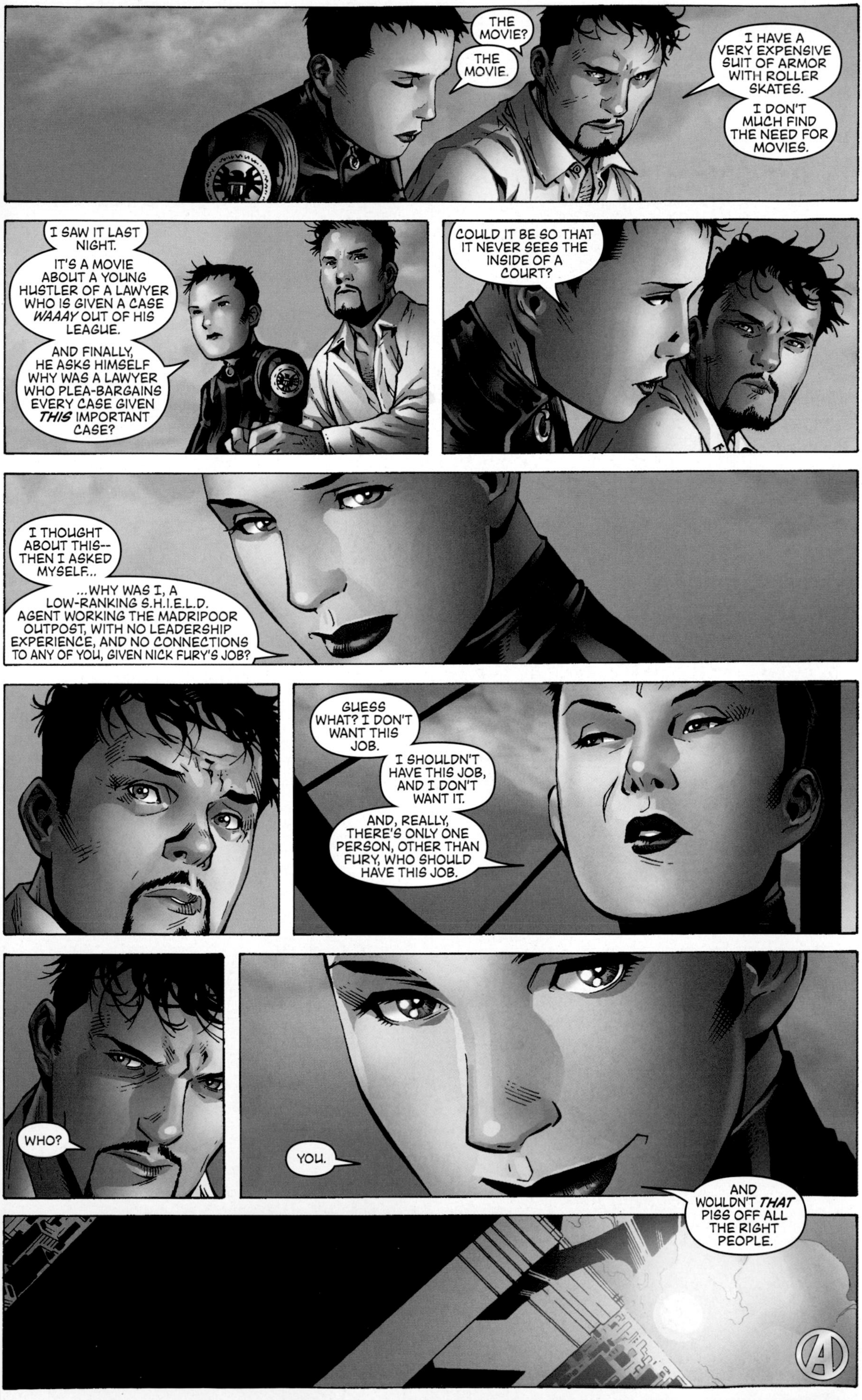
THE MOVIE?
THE MOVIE.
I HAVE A VERY EXPENSIVE SUIT OF ARMOR WITH ROLLER SKATES.
I DON'T MUCH FIND THE NEED FOR MOVIES.
I SAW IT LAST NIGHT.
IT'S A MOVIE ABOUT A YOUNG HUSTLER OF A LAWYER WHO IS GIVEN A CASE WAAAY OUT OF HIS LEAGUE.
AND FINALLY, HE ASKS HIMSELF WHY WAS A LAWYER WHO PLEA-BARGAINS EVERY CASE GIVEN THIS IMPORTANT CASE?
COULD IT BE SO THAT IT NEVER SEES THE INSIDE OF A COURT?
I THOUGHT ABOUT THIS-- THEN I ASKED MYSELF...
...WHY WAS I, A LOW-RANKING S.H.I.E.L.D. AGENT WORKING THE MADRIPOOR OUTPOST, WITH NO LEADERSHIP EXPERIENCE, AND NO CONNECTIONS TO ANY OF YOU, GIVEN NICK FURY'S JOB?
GUESS WHAT? I DON'T WANT THIS JOB.
I SHOULDN'T HAVE THIS JOB, AND I DON'T WANT IT.
AND, REALLY, THERE'S ONLY ONE PERSON, OTHER THAN FURY, WHO SHOULD HAVE THIS JOB.
WHO?
YOU.
AND WOULDN'T THAT PISS OFF ALL THE RIGHT PEOPLE.

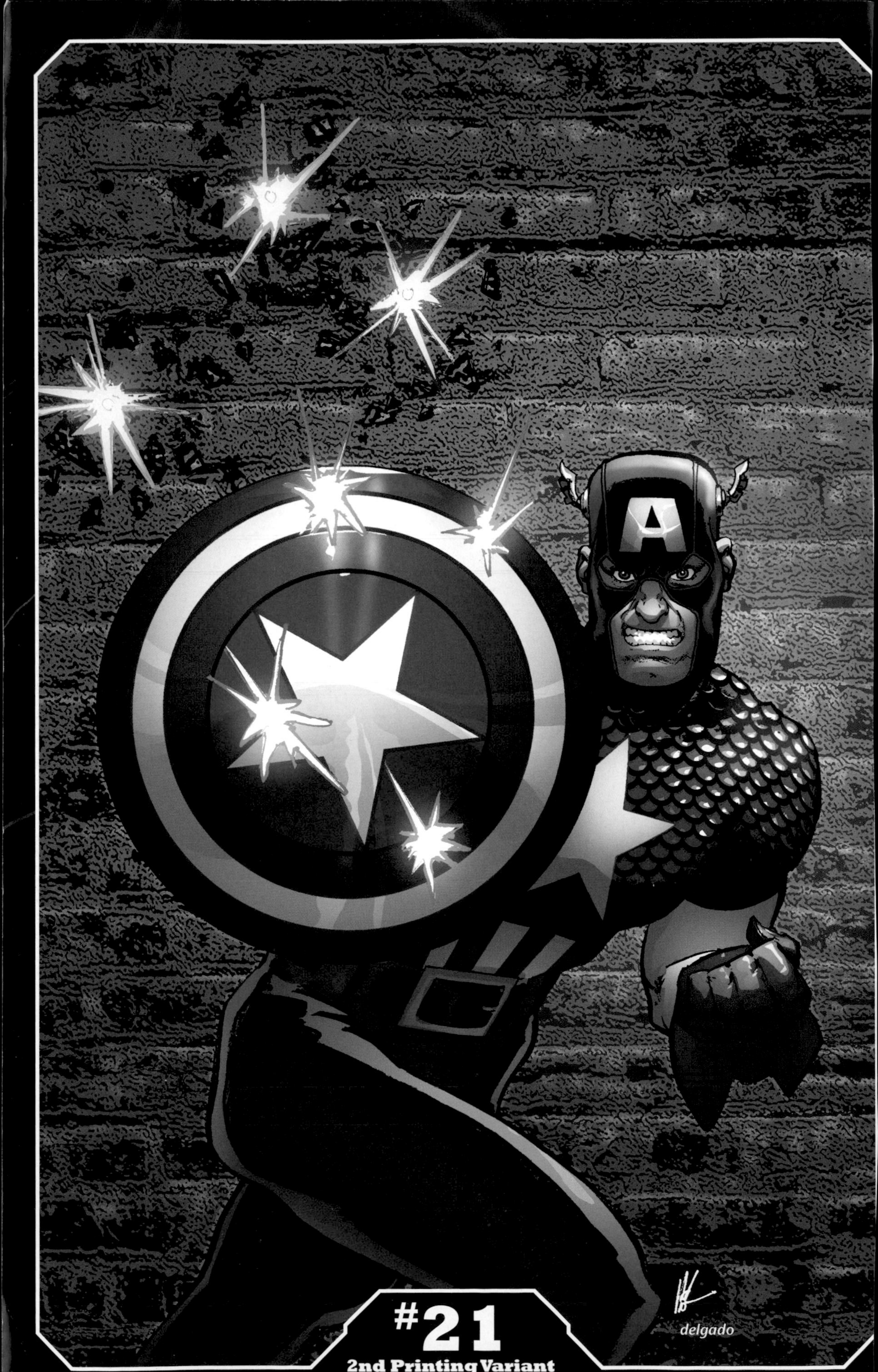

A
delgado
#21
2nd Printing Variant